THE JUDGE BOOK OF SPORTS ANSWERS

Hundreds of sporting arguments settled

Compiled by Norman Giller
Edited by Michael Giller

As featured in

AN nMg PUBLICATION

First published in 2002 by NMG Publishing
PO Box 3386, Ferndown, Dorset BH22 8XT

10 9 8 7 6 5 4 3 2 1

A CIP catalogue for this title is available from the British Library
ISBN 0-9543243-0-7

Printed and bound in the United Kingdom by Antony Rowe Limited
Bumper's Farm, Chippenham, Wiltshire SN14 6LH

PREVIOUS BOOKS BY NORMAN GILLER

Banks of England (with Gordon Banks)
The Glory and the Grief (with George Graham)
The Seventies Revisited (with Kevin Keegan)
The Final Score (with Brian Moore) **ABC of Soccer Sense** (Tommy Docherty)
The Rat Race (with Tommy Docherty) **Denis Compton** (The Untold Stories)
The Book of Rugby Lists (with Gareth Edwards)
The Book of Tennis Lists (with John Newcombe)
The Book of Golf Lists **TV Quiz Trivia** **Sports Quiz Trivia**
Fighting for Peace (Barry McGuigan biography, with Peter Batt)
Know What I Mean (with Frank Bruno) **Eye of the Tiger** (with Frank Bruno)
From Zero to Hero (with Frank Bruno)
Mike Tyson: Iron Mike (Biography, with Reg Gutteridge)
Mike Tyson, the Release of Power (with Reg Gutteridge)
World's Greatest Cricket Matches **World's Greatest Football Matches**
Golden Heroes (with Dennis Signy) **The Judge Book i** (1,001 arguments settled)
Crown of Thorns, the World Heavyweight Championship (with Neil Duncanson)
The Marathon Kings **The Golden Milers** (with Sir Roger Bannister)
Olympic Heroes (Brendan Foster)
Olympics Handbook 1980 **Olympics Handbook 1984**
Book of Cricket Lists (Tom Graveney) **Top Ten Cricket Book** (Tom Graveney)
Cricket Heroes (Eric Morecambe) **Big Fight Quiz Book** **TVIQ Puzzle Book**
Lucky the Fox (with Barbara Wright) **Gloria Hunniford's TV Challenge**
Watt's My Name (with Jim Watt) **Billy Wright** (A Hero for All Seasons)
My Most Memorable Fights (with Henry Cooper)
How to Box (with Henry Cooper) **Henry Cooper's 100 Greatest Boxers**
Comedy novels: **Carry On Doctor Carry On England Carry On Loving**
Carry On Up the Khyber Carry On Abroad Carry On Henry
A Stolen Life (novel) **Mike Baldwin: Mr Heartbreak** (novel) **Hitlergate** (novel)

PLUS books in collaboration with **JIMMY GREAVES**:
This One's On Me The Final (novel) **The Ball Game** (novel)
The Boss (novel) **The Second Half** (novel)
World Cup History GOALS! Stop the Game, I Want to Get On
The Book of Football Lists Taking Sides
Sports Quiz Challenge Sports Quiz Challenge 2
It's A Funny Old Life Saint & Greavsie's World Cup Special
The Sixties Revisited Don't Shoot the Manager

Acknowledgements

THE JUDGE wishes to thank *The Sun* for giving me a home in their exceptional sports section for eight years. I also thank, most sincerely, all those *Sun* readers who have sent in thousands of questions. Without them I would be redundant. I have the space in my column only to answer one in twenty of the questions I receive, and I hope this book goes some way to satisfy the thirst for sports knowledge.

This is a sequel to my first book which answered 1,001 questions. There are hundreds more answered here, many of which have not been published in my column before.

My thanks to Peter Elliott, Jonathan Bullen, Mark Durham and the staff at Antony Rowe for their expert printing and binding work; also to Michael Giller for his Apple-a-day computer skill, and artist David Edwards for his graphic support.

The Judge would not be nearly as knowing without a plethora of record books into which to dip, and he recommends in particular the six bibles of their sport: *Rothmans Football Yearbook, Wisden Cricketers' Almanack, The Ring Record Book, World of Tennis, The Complete Book of the Olympics, Golfer's Handbook,* and any number of *Guinness* sporting record books – particularly those that bear the all-knowing touch of statistical wizard Peter Matthews.

For cricket I have turned to the many works of my old colleague Bill 'The Bearded Wonder' Frindall for extra facts and figures, and the football output from Jack Rollin and his soccer-wise daughter, Glenda, has been a constant source of information. Albert Sewell, a Press box colleague from way back in the early 1960s, has also been a source of inspiration with his statistical work for the BBC and his *News of the World Annual* input. My old sparring partners Reg Gutteridge and Ron Olver have kept me informed on the boxing front, and my old employer *Boxing News* has, as always, been must reading. Barry Hugman's *Football League Players' Records* is another book that has proved invaluable, as have the *Sports Yearbook* annuals edited by the omniscient Peter Nichols.

Finally, a sincere thanks to YOU for buying the book. What a good judge! I hope you find it both enjoyable and enlightening.

Contents

In loving memory of Ken Giller,
who was not only a good judge
but also a magical brother

Introduction

THE JUDGE's verdict has become final for hundreds of sports fans in pubs, clubs, offices and factories across the land as they turn to him for the dispute-settling answers to their sporting questions.

His weekly column in the sports section of *The Sun* has become the settling ground for many sporting arguments. Hundreds of his answers are featured in this second volume of The Judge Book, including many that have not been published before.

They range from the record book variety to the trivial, and in many instances the stars of sport themselves have come up with the answers. And when even The Judge is stumped he consults the huge computer database set up by sports statisticians Michael Giller and Norman Giller, who have had more than fifty sports-linked books published. They are the creators and compilers of the puzzles Sportsword in the *Daily Express*, Times Square in *The Times* and The Name Game in *The Sun*, and between them have an all-encompassing knowledge of the facts and figures of sport.

This is a book you can *play* as well as read! At the foot of each page there is a challenging question that tests your knowledge of sport. Keep a note of each of your answers to the 250 questions. Then check your answers on pages 222 and 223 and see how you rate in the Sports IQ Table.

You can keep up to date with future publications from The Judge's team of sports specialists by visiting our exclusive website at www.thesportsjudge.co.uk

Now it's on with the judging. Let the sporting arguments begin. Here comes The Judge ...

The Judge

FOOTBALL

WHO has won most consecutive England caps without being dropped, rested or injured?

THE JUDGE: Billy Wright set the record with 70 successive caps from October 1951 to May 1959. He played in 105 of England's first 108 post-war matches. Both Wright and Bobby Moore skippered England 90 times.

WHEN was the English Football League first formed, and which were the founder clubs?

THE JUDGE: Scot William McGregor was the driving force behind the formation of the English Football League in 1888. The original members were: Accrington, Aston Villa, Blackburn Rovers, Bolton Wanderers, Burnley, Derby County, Everton, Notts County, Preston North End, Stoke City, West Bromwich Albion and Wolverhampton.

WHO took the kick when Dave Beasant saved a penalty for Wimbledon in the 1988 FA Cup Final?

THE JUDGE: John Aldridge, for Liverpool. It was the first penalty miss in an FA Cup final at Wembley. Aldridge had converted his previous 11 penalties that season. Beasant became the first goalkeeper to captain an FA Cup-winning team.

DID Pat Jennings play more games for Tottenham or for Arsenal?

THE JUDGE: Jennings played 472 League games for Tottenham (1964-76), 237 for Arsenal (1977-84). He also won a record 119 caps for Northern Ireland.

HAS a player ever been transferred between Manchester United and Liverpool?

THE JUDGE: The last major transaction between the sworn rivals was back in 1964 when United sold England Under-23 international Phil Chisnall to Liverpool for £30,000.

THE '250' QUIZ CHALLENGE

1. Who scored Wimbledon's goal when they beat Liverpool 1-0 in the 1988 FA Cup Final at Wembley?

FOOTBALL

WAS Jimmy Greaves on the substitute's bench in the 1966 World Cup final?

THE JUDGE: Substitutes were not introduced until the 1970 tournament in Mexico. Anatoli Pusatch of the Soviet Union was the first player to come off the bench when he replaced captain Albert Shesterniev at half-time in the opening match against the hosts in the Azteca Stadium in Mexico City on May 31 1970.

WHAT have been the attendances for European Cup finals involving British teams?

THE JUDGE: 1967 Celtic (Lisbon) 56,000; 1968 Man United (Wembley) 100,000; 1970 Celtic (Milan) 50,000; 1975 Leeds (Paris) 50,000; 1977 Liverpool (Rome) 57,000; 1978 Liverpool (Wembley) 92,000; 1979 Forest (Munich) 57,500; 1980 Forest (Madrid) 50,000; 1981 Liverpool (Paris) 48,360); 1982 Aston Villa (Rotterdam) 46,000; 1984 Liverpool (Rome) 69,693; 1985 Liverpool (Brussels) 58,000, 1999 Man United (Barcelona) 90,000. Record attendance for a European Cup final: 1960 at Hampden Park when 135,000 saw Real Madrid beat Eintracht Frankfurt 7-3 in a classic.

AGAINST which country did Michael Owen score his first World Cup finals goal?

THE JUDGE: Michael Owen scored in his second World Cup finals match against Romania in France 98. England were beaten 2-1. He made his World Cup debut as a substitute for Teddy Sheringham against Tunisia in the first Group G match, which England won 2-0.

WHO scored the goals when the Republic of Ireland played England in Italia 90?

THE JUDGE: Kevin Sheedy netted a 72nd minute equaliser for Ireland after Gary Lineker had given England an eighth minute lead. The group F match, played in Cagliari on June 11 1990, finished 1-1.

IN which World Cup were penalties introduced to decide the winner of a drawn match?

THE JUDGE: The first World Cup match to be decided by penalties was the 1982 semi-final between West Germany and France in Seville. Germany won 5-4 on penalties following a 3-3 draw after extra-time.

THE '250' QUIZ CHALLENGE

2. Jimmy Greaves started his Football League playing career in 1957 with which London club?

THE JUDGE

WHO has scored most goals in a single World Cup finals match?

THE JUDGE: Oleg Salenko scored a record five goals for Russia against Cameroon in San Francisco on June 28 1994. Russia won 6-1.

WHICH player scored the first hat-trick in a World Cup finals match?

THE JUDGE: Guillermo Stabile of Argentina. It was against Mexico in the first tournament in Uruguay in 1930. Stabile, making his World Cup debut, scored three goals in a 6-3 victory and in a match in which five penalties were awarded. Stabile finished top scorer with eight goals.

WITH which club was Alan Ball playing when he helped England win the World Cup in 1966?

THE JUDGE: Alan, the 'baby' of the England team at 21, was still on Blackpool's books, but had joined Everton for a then record £110,000 within a month of the triumph over West Germany at Wembley on July 30 1966.

WHAT number shirt did Ossie Ardiles wear for Argentina in the 1978 World Cup finals?

THE JUDGE: Ardiles wore the No 2 shirt. The Argentinians handed out their shirts in alphabetical order, with Ossie's midfield partner Alonso wearing No 1.

IS it right that Peter Beardsley captained England in just one game?

THE JUDGE: Beardsley took over from the absent Bryan Robson as skipper in England's goalless draw against Israel in Tel Aviv in 1988.

WHO was manager at Liverpool when Peter Beardsley was sold to Everton?

THE JUDGE: Graeme Souness was the man in charge at Anfield when Beardsley moved to Everton for £1-million in August 1991.

WHERE and when was the first FA Cup final played?

THE JUDGE: Wanderers beat Royal Engineers 1-0 at the Kennington Oval on March 16 1872 in front of 2,000 spectators.

THE '250' QUIZ CHALLENGE

3. With which club did Alan Ball make his SECOND appearance in an FA Cup final at Wembley?

FOOTBALL

IS it true that in the 1950s Chelsea had to score four goals in their final match to avoid relegation – and managed it?

THE JUDGE: Chelsea beat Bolton 4-0 in the last match of the 1950-51 season to stay up by .044 of a goal at the expense of Sheffield Wednesday, who went down to the Second Division despite beating Everton 6-0 in their final match.

HAS any player scored in all English divisions including the Premiership?

THE JUDGE: Alan Cork scored in all four divisions of the Football League and also in the Premiership during his 18 years of goal hunting with Wimbledon, Sheffield United and Fulham.

WAS David Beckham ever on any club's books other than Manchester United?

THE JUDGE: Becks had made up his mind to join Man United from his schoolboy days. Despite stories to the contrary, he did not even consider signing for either of his locals clubs, West Ham or Orient. Spurs and Arsenal were interested, but he elected to go to Old Trafford. He made his Football League debut while on loan from Man United to Preston, scoring two goals during five first-team appearances in 1995.

HOW long have linesmen been used in football in the style that they have today?

THE JUDGE: The duties of the linesmen were originally performed by two umpires. The current system of a referee and two linesmen was introduced in 1891. They are now officially known as referee's assistants.

HOW many weeks did the Pools Panel sit during the Big Freeze winter of 1962-63?

THE JUDGE: The Big Freeze started on December 22 1962 and it was March 16 the following year before a complete programme of League football could be played. For three successive Saturdays in January the Pools were declared void. Then the Panel (Tom Finney, Ted Drake, Tommy Lawton and George Young under the chairmanship of Lord Brabazon) sat for four successive weeks giving what became known as phantom results.

THE '250' QUIZ CHALLENGE

4. What number shirt did David Beckham wear in the 2002 Korea/Japan World Cup finals?

DID George Graham ever play for Manchester United?

THE JUDGE: Graham joined Man United from Arsenal in 1972 for £120,000 and captained the side relegated in 1974. He played 43 League games for United before moving on to Portsmouth. He also played for Aston Villa, Chelsea and Crystal Palace.

HOW many League goals did Jimmy Hagan score, and was he capped by England?

THE JUDGE: Hagan lost his best years to the war, but managed to score seven goals in 30 matches for Derby County and 116 in 361 League games for Sheffield United. A small, well-balanced inside-forward, he was noted for his clever tactical play and was unlucky to win only one England cap. He later managed Peterborough and West Bromwich Albion before taking charge at Benfica.

AGAINST which team did Trevor Francis score four goals in one of his early matches for Birmingham City?

THE JUDGE: Francis, then a precocious 17-year-old, scored 15 goals in his first 15 games for Brum, including four in a Second Division game against Bolton.

DID Kenny Dalglish score more goals for Liverpool or his original club Celtic?

THE JUDGE: Dalglish scored 167 goals in 324 games for Celtic and 172 goals in 514 matches for Liverpool. He is the only player to have scored a century of goals in both the Scottish and English Leagues.

IS it true that Kenny Dalglish once scored for the away team in an international match at Anfield?

THE JUDGE: Wales elected to play their home World Cup qualifying match against Scotland at Anfield on October 12 1977. Dalglish, newly arrived at Liverpool from Celtic, headed Scotland's second goal in their 2-0 victory that clinched a place in the 1978 finals.

WHO scored the first ever goal in the Premiership?

THE JUDGE: Sheffield United's Brian Deane scored after four minutes to put the Blades on the way to a 2-1 victory against eventual champions Manchester United at Bramall Lane.

THE '250' QUIZ CHALLENGE

5. Against which team did Kenny Dalglish score the only goal of the match in a European Cup final?

DID Man United have a forward playing for them known as Pancho following the Munich air disaster?

THE JUDGE: Yorkshireman Mark Pearson, nicknamed Pancho because of his thick sideburns, played 68 First Division matches for United after the Munich tragedy. Unlucky with injuries, he later played for Sheffield Wednesday, Fulham and Halifax. He was no relation to the other Old Trafford Pearsons, Stan and Stuart.

HOW many of Tottenham's 1967 FA Cup winning team later became League managers?

THE JUDGE: Five went on to manage League clubs: Joe Kinnear, Cyril Knowles, Alan Mullery, Dave Mackay and Terry Venables. Centre-half Mike England became manager of Wales, and El Tel manager of England.

WHEN did Gordon McQueen and Joe Jordan leave Leeds to join Manchester United?

THE JUDGE: Jordan moved from Elland Road to Old Trafford on January 6 1978 for £350,000. McQueen followed him 34 days later for £495,000.

SURELY Bill Perry, who scored Blackpool's winner in the 1953 FA Cup final, was the first black player to appear for England.

THE JUDGE: Perry was a white South African, who won three England caps as a winger. Viv Anderson was the first black player to appear in a full international for England in 1978.

WHO scored the goals in the Norwich-Bayern Munich UEFA Cup tie in 1993-94 and which team eventually knocked Norwich out of the competition?

THE JUDGE: Norwich won the first away leg 2-1 with goals from Jeremy Goss and Mark Bowen. Nerlinger scored for Bayern. Goss and Valencia scored in the 1-1 draw at Carrow Road. Norwich went out to eventual winners Inter Milan in the third round.

WHO was the first monarch to present the FA Cup?

THE JUDGE: King George V presented the trophy to Burnley captain Tom Boyle after they had beaten Liverpool 1-0 at Crystal Palace in 1914.

THE '250' QUIZ CHALLENGE

6. Against which country did Terry Venables have his final game as England team coach?

WERE Spurs the last amateur team to win the FA Cup?

THE JUDGE: Tottenham were Southern League professionals when winning the Cup in 1901. Old Etonians were the last all-amateur winners in 1882.

DID Sir Tom Finney ever play in the European Cup?

THE JUDGE: Sir Tom, a one-club loyalist with Preston, made a brief comeback with Distillery in 1963 and played in the team that drew 3-3 with Benfica in a European Cup tie.

MANY record books name Jackie Robinson as the youngest England cap at 17 years 9 months against Finland in 1938. So how comes Michael Owen is now being called the youngest ever England player?

THE JUDGE: It was later discovered that Robinson had cut two years off his age. When transferred from Sheffield Wednesday to Sunderland in 1946 his fee was reduced because of the wrong information.

IS it true that Tottenham played Barnsley at White Hart Lane on Derby Day 1947.

THE JUDGE: True. The season was disrupted by a bad winter, and it was June 14 before Liverpool clinched the championship.

IN which position did Tony Dunne play in Manchester United's 1968 European Cup winning team, and which player crossed the ball for Bobby Charlton's headed goal?

THE JUDGE: Tony Dunne played at left-back, and David Sadler crossed the ball from the left for Bobby Charlton to head United into a 1-0 lead.

WHEN did Arsenal first introduce floodlit football matches at Highbury Stadium?

THE JUDGE: Herbert Chapman argued for floodlit football in the 1930s, but the authorities refused to sanction it. A Boxers v Jockeys match in 1950-51 attracted a 40,000 crowd to Highbury, and this encouraged Arsenal to play Hapoel of Israel in the autumn of 1951 (50,000). Soon after Rangers were the visitors for a floodlit friendly, and the gates were shut with 10,000 people turned away.

THE '250' QUIZ CHALLENGE

7. What is the name of the ground where Barnsley play their home Football League matches?

WHO captained Blackpool in the famous 1953 Matthews FA Cup Final?

THE JUDGE: Centre-half Harry Johnston, who later that year won his 10th and final England cap in the earth-shaking 6-3 defeat by Hungary at Wembley.

WHAT was the scoring record for Ron Davies, the Welsh international centre-forward – and for which League clubs did he play?

THE JUDGE: Davies, capped 29 times by Wales, consistently found the net with Chester (44 goals), Luton (21), Norwich (58), Southampton (134) and Portsmouth (18). A large percentage of his goals came from his head. He wound down his career with Manchester United and Millwall without adding to his goal collection.

HAS any club gone through an entire League season without a single home win?

THE JUDGE: No, but Cambridge United went close in 1984-85. They lost a record 18 of 20 home games in the Third Division.

WHICH non-Premiership (or old First Division) clubs have won the FA Cup since the war?

THE JUDGE: Sunderland (1973), Southampton (1976) and West Ham (1980), all Second Division clubs.

FOR which clubs did Allan Clarke play, and what was his goal-scoring record?

THE JUDGE: 'Sniffer' Clarke played for Walsall (41 League goals), Fulham (45), Leicester City (12), Leeds (110) and Barnsley (15). He also scored 10 goals in 19 matches for England, including a penalty in his debut against Czechoslovakia in the 1970 World Cup finals in Mexico.

WAS manager John Gregory the oldest England debutant when he won his first cap?

THE JUDGE: John Gregory was 29 years 32 days old when he won the first of his six caps under Bobby Robson in 1983. The oldest debutant was Arsenal centre-half Leslie Compton, who made his bow at the age of 38 years 64 days in 1950.

THE '250' QUIZ CHALLENGE

8. Which player, later a famous manager, was involved in the swap deal that took Ron Davies to Manchester United from Portsmouth?

WHEN did Jimmy Greaves play in Italy, and how many goals did he score for his Italian club?

THE JUDGE: Greavsie made his debut for AC Milan on June 7 1961, and played his first match for Spurs on December 16 1961. Home-sick Jimmy scored nine goals in 14 appearances for Milan. He was brought back into English football by Tottenham manager Bill Nicolson, who paid £99,999 to save Greavsie carrying the burden of being the first £100,000 footballer. He celebrated his return home with a hat-trick against Blackpool in his Spurs debut.

WHAT were Scotland's results in the 1978 World Cup finals in Argentina?

THE JUDGE: Scotland, managed by the ultra-confident Ally MacLeod, lost 3-1 to Peru, were held 1-1 by Iran and then beat eventual runners-up Holland 3-2. The victory over Holland, too late to save them from an early exit, included a magnificent solo goal by Archie Gemmill.

WHO was in goal for Crystal Palace when Liverpool hammered them 9-0?

THE JUDGE: Perry Suckling was the goalkeeper beaten nine times in a First Division match at Anfield on September 12 1989.

IN the classic 1948 FA Cup final in which Manchester United beat Blackpool 4-2 who was in goal for Blackpool – Robinson or Farm?

THE JUDGE: Joe Robinson was the goalkeeper in his last major appearance before joining Hull City. George Farm was in goal for Blackpool in the 1951 and 1953 FA Cup finals.

FOR which clubs did Brian Clough play and which did he manage?

THE JUDGE: Cloughie, born in Middlesbrough on March 21 1935, scored 197 League goals (213 games) for Boro and 54 goals for Sunderland (61 games) before a knee injury ended his career at 28. He managed Hartlepool, Derby, Brighton, Leeds and Forest, winning the League title with Derby in 1971-72. With Forest, he won the League title in 1977-78, the European Cup twice in successive seasons and captured the League Cup four times.

THE '250' QUIZ CHALLENGE

9. What was the name of Brian Clough's managerial partner who shared in much of his success, starting at Hartlepool?

FOOTBALL

WHEN was the £20 a week maximum wage abolished?

THE JUDGE: The PFA, led by then chairman Jimmy Hill and secretary Cliff Lloyd, won their case for the maximum wage to be kicked out in 1961. Fulham made Johnny Haynes the first £100 a week footballer.

WHO succeeded Billy Wright as Wolves captain?

THE JUDGE: When Billy hung up his boots in 1959, Bill Slater took over his number five shirt and the club captaincy.

WAS David Pleat on Nottingham Forest's books as an amateur player?

THE JUDGE: Pleat, an England schoolboy and youth international, joined Forest as a junior. He played six League games for Forest before later joining Luton (70 League games), Shrewsbury (12), Exeter (68) and Peterborough (28).

WHAT was the real name of Pongo Waring, and what was his goal-scoring record?

THE JUDGE: Thomas Waring scored 245 League goals while playing as a dashing centre-forward for Tranmere, Aston Villa, Barnsley, Wolves and Accrington between the wars. He netted three goals in five games for England while with Villa for whom he still holds the club record of 49 First Division goals in a season.

IS it true that Portsmouth were unbeaten FA Cup holders for a longer period than any other club?

THE JUDGE: Pompey won the FA Cup in 1939, and because of the war the competition was not played again until 1946.

HAVE a father and son played together in the same League team?

THE JUDGE: There have been two instances in post-war football: Alec and David Herd for Stockport County against Hartlepool in 1951, and Ian and Gary Bowyer for Hereford against Scunthorpe in 1990. The Easthams, George senior and junior, played together for an entire season for Ards in Northern Ireland before young George started his League career with Newcastle, and later followed his father into the England team.

THE '250' QUIZ CHALLENGE

10. With which club did George Eastham Junior play a leading role in a League Cup final victory in 1972?

THE JUDGE

WAS Tottenham winger George Robb the last amateur to play in a full international for England?

THE JUDGE: Arsenal defender Bernard Joy, later a distinguished journalist, was the last amateur to win an England cap against Belgium in 1936. Schoolteacher Robb was a part-time professional when he won his only cap against the 1953 Hungarians.

WHY was Johnny Crossan banned from British football?

THE JUDGE: The ban was imposed by the Irish League in 1959-60 after the then 20-year-old amateur inside-foward had been paid while playing for Coleraine. Crossan moved to Holland and then Belgium before the suspension was lifted in 1962. He played with Sunderland, Man City and Middlesbrough, and won 24 Northern Ireland caps.

WAS Alan Hudson in England's squad for the 1970 World Cup finals?

THE JUDGE: Hudson was an 18-year-old uncapped Chelsea midfielder when Sir Alf Ramsey named him in his World Cup 40 squad for Mexico. He did not make the final pool of players, and it was Don Revie who gave him his first of two caps in 1975.

WHO did Paul Gascoigne tackle when he seriously injured himself in the 1991 FA Cup Final?

THE JUDGE: It was Forest defender Gary Charles in the 15th minute. Gazza fouled him with a scything tackle during which he was so badly injured that he was carried off and taken to hospital for complicated cruciate ligament surgery. Tottenham won the Cup Final 2-1 thanks to an extra-time own goal by Forest defender Des Walker.

WHICH was the first Third Division side to win a final at Wembley?

THE JUDGE: Queen's Park Rangers in 1967. Inspired by a magical goal from Rodney Marsh, Rangers came from behind to beat First Division West Brom 3-2 in the League Cup Final.

DID Glenn Hoddle ever miss a penalty for England?

THE JUDGE: Hoddle had a penalty saved when playing for England against the United States in 1985. England won 5-0 in Los Angeles.

THE '250' QUIZ CHALLENGE

11. From which London club did Rodney Marsh join Queen's Park Rangers in 1965-66?

18

IS it true that England used to have a goalkeeper who played wearing glasses?

THE JUDGE: Manchester City goalkeeper Jim Mitchell wore glasses when winning his only England cap in 1924. Two years earlier he played in the FA Cup Final for Preston when he was beaten from the penalty spot for the only goal of the match to Huddersfield.

DID an inside-forward called Mason play for Wolves in the 1950s?

THE JUDGE: Tipton-born Bobby Mason scored 44 goals in 146 League games for Wolves from 1955 until 1961 before playing for Orient and then Chelmsford City.

WAS there a Christmas Day First Division programme when there were more than 50 goals scored?

THE JUDGE: It was actually on Boxing Day 1963, and there were a total of 66 goals scored in ten First Division games. Three players – Graham Leggat (Fulham), Andy Lochhead (Burnley) and Roger Hunt (Liverpool) – netted four goals each. League champions Ipswich were the biggest losers of the day, going down 10-1 at Fulham. Ipswich chairman John Cobbold, one of football's greatest characters, said: "Our problem was that only our goalkeeper was sober!"

WHO have been the oldest players to appear in the League and the FA Cup Final?

THE JUDGE: New Brighton manager Neil McBain (51 years 120 days) made an emergency appearance as a goalkeeper away to Hartlepool in a Third Division North match in 1947. Sir Stanley Matthews was the oldest First Division player when appearing for Stoke five days past his 50th birthday in 1965. Goalkeeper John Burridge (43) became the oldest Premiership player when coming on as substitute for Man City in 1995. Billy Hampson was 41 years 8 months when collecting an FA Cup winners' medal with Newcastle in 1924.

WHAT was the day of the week when Celtic became the first British club to win the European Cup?

THE JUDGE: The match against Inter Milan kicked off in Lisbon at 5.30pm on Thursday May 25 1967.

THE '250' QUIZ CHALLENGE

12. Who was captain of the Celtic team that won the European Cup in 1967?

THE JUDGE

HOW many times did John Atyeo (Bristol City) and Geoff Bradford (Bristol Rovers) play for England?

THE JUDGE: Atyeo scored five goals in six England games between 1955 and 1957. Bradford scored England's fifth goal in a 5-1 win against Denmark in his only international match in 1955. Atyeo followed a career as a teacher while playing and later became a headmaster.

DID a player called Pickering score a hat-trick in his England debut, and had this ever been achieved before?

THE JUDGE: England debut hat-tricks have been scored by no fewer than 14 players, including in 1964 by former Everton and Blackburn centre-forward Fred Pickering in a 10-0 win against the USA in New York City.

IN which match against Scotland did Frank Swift suffer damaged ribs?

THE JUDGE: It was the 1948 match at Hampden, won 2-0 by England. Swiftie played on after being knocked out in a collision with 'Flying Scot' Billy Liddell. He later collapsed on the Manchester railway platform on his way home, and was wheeled off on a porter's trolley for an examination which revealed two broken ribs.

DID Jimmy Armfield, Alan Ball and Emlyn Hughes play together in the same League team for Blackpool, and who was manager at the time?

THE JUDGE: Armfield and Ball were away on England duty when Hughes made his Blackpool debut at the end of the 1965-66 season. Ball was transferred during the summer to Everton, and so Hughes played only with Armfield. Ron Suart was manager.

WHO was manager of Man United when Laurie Cunningham played for them, and for which other clubs did he play?

THE JUDGE: Ron Atkinson was manager when the quick and clever Laurie Cunningham played five League matches for United in 1983. His other clubs were Orient, West Brom, Real Madrid, Marseille, Leicester City, Charleroi, Wimbledon and Rayo Vallencano. He was killed in a car crash in 1989, aged 33.

THE '250' QUIZ CHALLENGE

13. Which team did Emlyn Hughes skipper to victory in the 1980 League Cup final at Wembley?

WHERE did Charlton play their home League matches when The Valley was being rebuilt?

THE JUDGE: Selhurst Park and Upton Park.

IS it right that one of today's Premiership teams used to be known as the Black Watch?

THE JUDGE: Everton were briefly nicknamed the Black Watch when they wore black shirts with a white sash before changing to their royal blue strip in 1901.

HOW did Manchester United line up for the 1957 and 1958 FA Cup finals?

THE JUDGE: 1957 v Aston Villa: Wood; Foulkes, Byrne; Colman, Blanchflower, Edwards; Berry, Whelan, Tommy Taylor, Charlton, Pegg. 1958 v Bolton: Gregg; Foulkes, Greaves; Goodwin, Cope, Crowther; Dawson, Ernie Taylor, Charlton, Viollet, Webster. United were beaten 2-1 by Aston Villa in the pre-Munich 1957 final and lost 2-0 to Bolton three months after the Munich air disaster.

WHO scored the goals in the 1972 League Cup semi-final between Chelsea and Tottenham?

THE JUDGE: First leg: Osgood, Garland and Hollins (pen) for Chelsea, Naylor and Chivers for Spurs; second leg: Chivers and Peters (pen) for Spurs, Garland and Hudson for Chelsea. Hudson's free-kick goal two minutes from time gave Chelsea a 5-4 victory on aggregate. Stoke City beat Chelsea 2-1 in the final at Wembley.

WHAT was the Liverpool line-up when they won the FA Cup without any English players?

THE JUDGE: Liverpool's winning team in the 1986 FA Cup Final against Everton was Grobbelaar, Lawrenson, Beglin, Nicol, Whelan, Hansen, Dalglish, Johnston, Rush, Molby, MacDonald. Eire international Mark Lawrenson was born in Preston.

DID Middlesbrough have an Italian goalkeeper playing for them in the late '40s or early '50s.

THE JUDGE: Italian-born Rolando Ugolini joined Middlesbrough from Celtic in 1948 and played 320 League games before moving to Wrexham.

THE '250' QUIZ CHALLENGE

14. Who skippered the 1958 Bolton Wanderers team that beat Manchester United in the FA Cup final?

WHEN was the first penalty scored in a Football League match?

THE JUDGE: James Heath, of Wolves, scored from the spot against Accrington Stanley on September 14 1891. The introduction of the penalty kick caused great controversy, and the leading amateur teams refused to recognise it for many years because they felt it was a slur on their sportsmanship.

HAS David Unsworth made a full England international appearance?

THE JUDGE: Unsworth, then with Everton, won his only cap in the 2-1 England victory over Japan in the Umbro Cup at Wembley in 1995.

HAS any footballer played at every League football ground in England?

THE JUDGE: There is a 92 Club formed by fans who have watched football at every ground. Honorary members include Jim Smith who has visited every ground in a managerial role, and Alan Durban who played all 92 venues while with Cardiff City, Derby County and Shrewsbury Town between 1959 and 1977.

WAS the first match played under floodlights between two non-League teams?

THE JUDGE: The first-ever game under floodlight was staged at Bramall Lane, Sheffield, on October 14 1878 between two representative teams selected from local clubs. The electric power was generated by two portable engines that drove Siemens dynamo lamps at the four corners of the pitch. The first Football League match played under floodlight was between Portsmouth and Newcastle at Fratton Park on Feburary 22 1956.

WHAT was Arsenal's position in the table when they signed Ronnie Rooke from Fulham and what was the fee?

THE JUDGE: The December 1946 transfer cost Arsenal, then bottom of the table, £1,000 and two players in part-exchange for 35-year-old Rooke. His 21 goals in 24 games helped lift the Gunners to an end-of-season 13th place.

THE '250' QUIZ CHALLENGE

15. Which Portsmouth player represented England in 48 international matches?

WHAT was the line up of the England team that played Switzerland at Stamford Bridge in 1946?

THE JUDGE: It was an unofficial international won 4-1 by England against the uncrowned European champions. England: Swift (Man City); Scott (Arsenal), Hardwick (Middlesbro); Wright (Wolves), Franklin (Stoke), Johnson (Charlton); Matthews (Stoke), Carter (Derby), Lawton (Chelsea), Brown (Charlton), Smith (Aston Villa). Carter (2), Brown and Lawton were the scorers after the Swiss had taken a 1-0 lead. Even the Swiss applauded when Frank Swift changed direction in mid-air to stop a certain goal. It was described as the 'Save of the Century'.

DID Garth Crooks ever play and score for Manchester United?

THE JUDGE: Crooks scored two goals in seven League appearances for Man United during a brief spell on loan from Tottenham in 1983-84.

HAVE West Ham ever won the FA Cup with a team of all-English players?

THE JUDGE: Yes, twice - in 1964 and 1975.

HOW many games did George Best play for Man United in all competitions?

THE JUDGE: Best played 464 first-team matches – 361 Football League, 45 FA Cup, 24 League Cup, 34 European competition matches and two World Club Championship games.

HOW many times was Alan Hansen capped by Scotland?

THE JUDGE: While with Liverpool, Hansen won 26 full caps. Surprisingly, Scotland manager Alex Ferguson decided not to select him for the 1986 Scottish World Cup squad for the finals in Mexico.

DID Jimmy Greaves once score five goals for Chelsea and finish on the losing side?

THE JUDGE: Greavsie notched five goals in three First Division matches while playing for Chelsea at the start of his career, and each time he finished on the winning side – v Wolves (6-2), West Brom (7-1) and Preston (5-4).

THE '250' QUIZ CHALLENGE

16. With which south-coast club did George Best play five matches at the back end of his career?

THE JUDGE

IS it true that two referees officiated during an England international at West Bromwich.

THE JUDGE: There was an experiment with two referees sharing control during the England v The Rest match at West Brom on March 27 1935. It was tried again in a game between a Football League representative side and West Brom two months later, and was then scrapped as an 'unworkable' idea.

WHO, out of Peter Osgood and Brian Talbot, was first to collect FA Cup winners' medals with different clubs?

THE JUDGE: Osgood was first (1970 with Chelsea, 1976 Southampton). Talbot achieved it with Ipswich (1978) and Arsenal (1979). Raich Carter was the first post-war player to complete the two-club double, collecting an FA Cup winners' medal with Derby in 1946 to go with the one he won as Sunderland's captain in 1937.

WHO scored Holland's goal against England at Wembley in Euro 96?

THE JUDGE: Patrick Kluivert netted for Holland in the 77th minute, with England already leading 4-0 with goals from Alan Shearer (2) and Teddy Sheringham (2).

WHERE was former Manchester United goalkeeper Gary Bailey born?

THE JUDGE: Gary, son of ex-Ipswich goalkeeper Roy Bailey, was born in Ipswich and brought up in South Africa. He won two England caps.

WHAT are the most number of goals scored in a single League match by one team since the war?

THE JUDGE: Thirteen, by Newcastle against Newport at St James' Park in a Second Division match in October 1946. Len Shackleton was making his Newcastle debut and scored six goals in a 13-0 victory.

WAS Tommy Trinder still alive when Fulham reached the FA Cup Final in 1975?

THE JUDGE: Comedian Tommy 'You lucky people' Trinder was club chairman when Fulham were beaten 2-0 by West Ham at Wembley. He died in 1989 at the age of 80.

THE '250' QUIZ CHALLENGE

17. Against which club did Peter Osgood score for Chelsea in the 1971 European Cup-Winners' Cup final?

FOOTBALL

WITH which clubs was Gary Lineker playing when he won his England caps?

THE JUDGE: Leicester City (7), Everton (11), Barcelona (24), Tottenham (38). He scored 48 goals in 80 internationals.

WHAT is the best that a Welsh club has done in the FA Cup and the Welsh national team in the World Cup?

THE JUDGE: Cardiff were the only team to take the FA Cup out of England when they beat Arsenal 1-0 in the 1927 Final at Wembley. Wales reached the World Cup quarter-finals in 1958, losing 1-0 to Brazil and a first World Cup goal scored by a 17-year-old 'unknown' called Pele. It was the only time Wales had qualified for the finals, and they got in through the back door after being eliminated in the qualifying rounds. They earned their place by beating Israel in a play-off after other countries had declined to play Israel for political reasons.

WHICH defender missed his tackle out on the touchline to let Poland in for their goal against England in the 1974 World Cup qualifier?

THE JUDGE: Norman Hunter of all people, and then Peter Shilton dived over Domarski's shot at Wembley on October 17 1973. Allan Clarke equalised from the penalty spot for England but a 1-1 draw meant Poland and not England qualified for the finals. Poland eventualy finished third.

WHAT was the date when George Best scored six FA Cup goals against Northampton Town, and who scored United's other goals?

THE JUDGE: Best, playing in his first match after a month's suspension, scored six goals at Northampton in the fifth round of the FA Cup on February 7 1970. Brian Kidd netted United's other two goals in an 8-2 victory. Kim Book, brother of Man City's Tony, was in the Northampton goal.

WITH which foot did Peter Lorimer score most of his goals?

THE JUDGE: 'Hot Shot' Lorimer used to wear the Leeds number seven shirt and cut in from the wing to score with thunderbolt right-footed shots. He scored 168 goals in 526 League matches.

THE '250' QUIZ CHALLENGE

18. Which Arsenal player captained Wales in the 1958 World Cup finals in Sweden?

WHICH managers did the deal when Jamie Redknapp joined Liverpool from Bournemouth?

THE JUDGE: Harry Redknapp was the selling manager and Kenny Dalglish signed Jamie just weeks before his resignation in 1991. Graeme Souness selected him for his League debut.

AGAINST which team and in which competition did Gary Lineker make his final appearance for England?

THE JUDGE: Lineker was controversially substituted by manager Graham Taylor in his 80th and last match against Sweden in the Euro 92 finals in Stockholm. England lost 2-1. He finished his international career on 48 goals, one short of Bobby Charlton's all-time record.

WAS Derby's 16-1 aggregate UEFA Cup victory over Finn Harps in 1977 a record for Europe?

THE JUDGE: Chelsea hold the record. They beat the Luxembourg part-timers of Jeunesse Hautcharage 21-0 in the 1971-72 Cup Winners' Cup (8-0 away and then 13-0 at Stamford Bridge). Peter Osgood helped himself to eight of the goals. The 21-0 record was equalled the following season when Feyenoord flattened another Luxembourg team, US Rumelange, 9-0 at home and 12-0 away.

WHAT trophies did Bobby Robson win when manager of Ipswich. Did they win the League title under him?

THE JUDGE: Alf Ramsey was manager when Ipswich won the League title in 1961-62. Robson's Ipswich won the FA Cup (1978) and the UEFA Cup (1981).

HAVE England ever selected eight Liverpool players in the same team?

THE JUDGE: The record is seven, selected by Ron Greenwood in his first match as England manager against Switzerland at Wembley in 1977: Clemence, Neal, McDermott, Hughes, Keegan, Kennedy and Callaghan. The game finished goalless.

DID Ally McCoist play League football in England?

THE JUDGE: McCoist played for Sunderland in 1981-82, scoring eight goals in 56 League games before returning to Scotland with Rangers.

THE '250' QUIZ CHALLENGE

19. From which Scottish League club did Ally McCoist join Sunderland?

WHO has scored the fastest own goal in a League match?

THE JUDGE: Pat Kruse put the ball into his own Torquay net in eight seconds against Cambridge United in a Fourth Division match in 1977. Alan Mullery once put the ball past his own Fulham goalkeeper at a snail pace 28 seconds.

WHICH goalkeepers have captained England? Do they include Gordon Banks?

THE JUDGE: Gordon Banks did not captain England. The goalkeepers who have: Frank Swift, Peter Shilton, Ray Clemence and David Seaman.

WHEN were Tottenham last relegated and promoted?

THE JUDGE: Tottenham were relegated from the old First Division in 1976-77, and bounced straight back the following season.

WHO scored England's goals in the 3-2 1970 World Cup defeat by West Germany?

THE JUDGE: England led 2-0 through goals by Alan Mullery and Martin Peters. West Germany won 3-2 after extra-time.

WHO were the British footballers who got into trouble for playing in Bogota in the 1950s?

THE JUDGE: Neil Franklin (Stoke), Charlie Mitten (Man United), George Mountford (Stoke) and Bill Higgins (Everton) were the best known of a posse of players who were branded mercenaries for going to Bogota in 1950 to play in the then outlawed Colombian league.

WHICH England player was nicknamed The Crab?

THE JUDGE: The then Manchester United manager Ron Atkinson gave Ray Wilkins his nickname, saying: 'He can't run, can't tackle, can't head the ball and always plays the ball sideways. The only time he goes forward is to toss the coin. He is The Crab of football.' Ray won 84 England caps, Atko none.

DID Kevin Keegan play for England while at Newcastle?

THE JUDGE: Kevin won his 63 England caps while with Liverpool, Hamburg and Southampton. Bobby Robson declined to select him when he moved to Newcastle.

THE '250' QUIZ CHALLENGE

20. For which club did Ron Atkinson play 384 League games in the days when he was nicknamed The Tank?

HAS Bobby Charlton ever managed a League club?

The Judge: Sir Bobby was briefly player-manager of Preston (1973-75) before concentrating on his business activities.

HOW many League goals did George Graham score and for which clubs?

THE JUDGE: Graham's League scoring record: Aston Villa (2 goals in 8 games), Chelsea (35 in 72), Arsenal (59 in 227), Man United (2 in 43), Portsmouth (5 in 61), Crystal Palace (2 in 44).

HOW old was Stanley Matthews when he played his final League match for Stoke City, and had he been knighted by then?

THE JUDGE: Matthews was 50 years and five days old when he played his final League game for Stoke – a home First Division match against Fulham on February 6 1965. He was knighted in the 1965 New Year's Honours List.

HAS a Premiership team ever conceded more than 100 goals in a season?

THE JUDGE: The record was set by Swindon Town, who conceded exactly 100 goals in 1993-94.

WHICH is the fastest League sending off on record?

THE JUDGE: Crewe goalkeeper Mark Smith got his marching orders after just 19 seconds in a Third Division match at Darlington on 12 March 1994.

HAS a Scottish club ever reached the final of the English FA Cup?

THE JUDGE: Queen's Park, of Glasgow, were beaten in successive finals by Blackburn Rovers in 1884 and 1885 (2-1 and 2-0). Both matches were played at the Oval.

DID Welsh international strikers Wyn Davies and Ron Davies both play for Manchester United?

THE JUDGE: Wyn Davies played 16 times for United after joining them from Man City in 1972. Ron Davies made eight appearances for United, all as substitute, two years later.

THE '250' QUIZ CHALLENGE

21. Against which team did Stanley Matthews collect his only FA Cup winners' medal?

WHAT is the name of the stadium shared by AC and Inter Milan?

THE JUDGE: It is officially the Giuseppe Meazza Stadium, named in memory of Italy's winning 1938 World Cup captain. But many still refer to it by its original name of San Siro, which is the district in which the ground stands.

FOR which clubs did Dennis Wilshaw play, how many goals did he score and how many times was he capped?

THE JUDGE: Wilshaw played for Wolves (105 goals in 211 League games), Walsall (27 in 74) and, finally, with his hometown club Stoke (40 in 94). He scored 10 goals in 12 England matches between 1953 and 1956.

AGAINST which country was Pele injured during the 1966 World Cup finals?

THE JUDGE: Pele was injured in Brazil's opening game with Bulgaria, missed the second match against Hungary and was then viciously hacked out of the third game against Portugal.

WHAT were the line-ups when Tottenham played Aston Villa in the 1971 League Cup final?

THE JUDGE: Tottenham: Jennings; Kinnear, Knowles; Mullery, Collins, Beal; Gilzean, Perryman, Chivers, Peters, Neighbour. Sub: Pearce. Aston Villa: Dunn; Bradley, Aitken; Godfrey, Turnbull, Tiler; McMahon, Rioch, Lochhead, Hamilton, Anderson. Sub: Gibson. Spurs won 2-0 with two goals by Martin Chivers.

FROM which club did Jim Baxter join Rangers the first time around?

THE JUDGE: Jim Baxter joined Rangers from Raith Rovers. He later played in England with Sunderland and Nottingham Forest before winding down his career at Ibrox. 'Slim Jim' retired at the age of 30.

IS it true that more than 70 goals were scored on the same day in just two matches in Scotland?

THE JUDGE: Seventy-one goals were scored in one day in two first round Scottish Cup ties on 5 September 1885. Arbroath beat Bon Accord 36-0 and Dundee Harp beat Aberdeen Rovers 35-0.

THE '250' QUIZ CHALLENGE

22. Who was manager of the Tottenham team that won the League Cup final in 1971?

WHAT is the story behind Arsenal and the colour of their shirts?

THE JUDGE: As Woolwich Arsenal, the club was so hard-up that they could not afford a strip. They contacted Nottingham Forest for the loan of some old shirts and were sent a full kit free of charge. Arsenal have worn the same red as Forest ever since, with Herbert Chapman adding white sleeves in 1933.

WAS Glenn Hoddle appointed manager of Chelsea before his old Tottenham team-mate Ossie Ardiles took over at White Hart Lane?

THE JUDGE: Hoddle was appointed Chelsea player-manager on 4 June 1993, ten days before Ardiles returned to Tottenham as manager.

WHO scored the goals for Sheffield Wednesday in the 1993 Coca Cola-Cup and FA Cup finals against Arsenal?

THE JUDGE: John Harkes scored Wednesday's goal in the Coca-Cola Cup final. David Hirst netted in the 1-1 draw in the FA Cup final, and Chris Waddle scored in the 2-1 replay defeat.

WHO were the first substitutes fielded by England in World Cup finals?

THE JUDGE: Tommy Wright and Peter Osgood were the first England substitutes in the World Cup, replacing Keith Newton and Francis Lee in the 1970 group match against Romania in Guadalajara.

WHEN was the first League match shown in colour on British television?

THE JUDGE: The First Division game at Anfield between Liverpool and West Ham United on 15 November 1969 was the first colour transmission. The first FA Cup final screened in colour was the 1968 match between West Brom and Everton.

IS it correct that Stan Mortensen is the only player to have scored an FA Cup final hat-trick?

THE JUDGE: Billy Townley (Blackburn, 1890) and Jimmy Logan (Notts County, 1894) scored hat-tricks. Mortensen's in 1953 for Blackpool against Bolton is the only one since.

THE '250' QUIZ CHALLENGE

23. Who was manager of the Sheffield Wednesday team that reached the Coca-Cola and FA Cup finals in 1993?

DID George Best ever play World Cup football for Northern Ireland?

THE JUDGE: George Best, sadly, never played in the World Cup finals. His talent deserved to be seen on the greatest of all stages. He did, however, play for Northern Ireland in 12 World Cup qualifying matches for the finals of 1966 (6), 1970 (2), 1974 (2) and 1978 (4). Northern Ireland manager Billy Bingham resisted demands by the media to recall him for the 1982 finals in Spain.

WITH which clubs was Liam Brady a player?

THE JUDGE: Brady passed with honours for Arsenal, Juventus, Sampdoria, Ascoli, West Ham United and Celtic.

HOW many League matches did Ian Callaghan play for Liverpool, and to what club did he move?

THE JUDGE: Ian Callaghan played a club record 640 League matches for Liverpool before winding down his career with Swansea City, where his old Anfield clubmate John Toshack was the manager.

HOW many League games in total did Tommy Hutchison play?

THE JUDGE: Tommy played 797 Football League matches with Blackpool (165), Coventry (314), Manchester City (46), Burnley (92) and Swansea (180). The total reaches 865 if you count his 68 Scottish League appearances with Alloa before moving to Blackpool in 1968.

WHO refereed the famous 1960 European Cup final at Hampden Park?

THE JUDGE: Jack Mowat, one of the most respected of all Scottish League refs, was in charge of the 1960 European Cup final in which Real Madrid beat Eintracht Frankfurt 7-3 in front of a record 135,000 crowd.

HAS any team ever been reduced to nine players by having two players sent off in a Wembley final?

THE JUDGE: Stockport had two players, Mike Wallace and Chris Beaumont, sent off aganst Burnley in a Play-off final at Wembley in 1994.

THE '250' QUIZ CHALLENGE

24. Which player scored four goals for Real Madrid in the 1960 European Cup final against Eintracht Frankfurt?

WHAT is the highest number of goals scored by any one player in a League football match?

THE JUDGE: Joe Payne set the record with ten goals for Luton against Bristol Rovers in a Third Division South match on April 13 1936. Ted Drake set a First Division record with seven goals for Arsenal at Aston Villa on December 14 1935.

WHICH Spanish football club is known as the Mattress Makers, and why?

THE JUDGE: Atletico Madrid. Their Vicente Calderon stadium is nicknamed the Mattress Makers' ground because it is decorated with red and white stripes.

WHAT was the name of the League referee in the immediate post-war years who had only one arm?

THE JUDGE: This was Alf Bond, of Fulham, who refereed the 1956 FA Cup final between Manchester City and Birmingham City.

WHO was the first substitute to come on in League football?

THE JUDGE: Keith Peacock, father of Gavin, was the first player to make a League appearance wearing a number 12 shirt when he came on for Charlton against Bolton on 21 August 1965.

HAVE Liverpool been League champions more times than Manchester United?

THE JUDGE: Liverpool hold the record with 18 title victories, 14 of them in post-war football. Manchester United have been champions 13 times, including six Premier League titles.

WHO was the first manager to lead out three winning teams in the FA Cup final at Wembley.

THE JUDGE: Bill Nicholson was the first to complete this hat-trick, leading out winning Tottenham teams in 1961, 1962 and 1967.

WHO has been England's tallest goalkeeper in post-war football – Dave Beasant or David Seaman?

THE JUDGE: Both Beasant and Seaman, at 6ft 4in, are inched out of it by 6ft 5in giants Joe Corrigan and David James.

THE '250' QUIZ CHALLENGE

25. With which club did goalkeeper Joe Corrigan win a League championship medal?

IS Kenny Dalglish the only player to have been voted Footballer of the Year in both Scotland and England?

THE JUDGE: Dalglish was never voted Footballer of the Year in Scotland, but won the award twice in England. Gordon Strachan (with Aberdeen 1980 and with Leeds 1992) is the only player to have achieved the double.

FOR which clubs did Sammy Lee play after leaving Liverpool?

THE JUDGE: Queen's Park Rangers, Southampton, Osasuna (Spain) and Bolton. He became a key member of the Liverpool and England backroom teams.

WHAT was Leslie Compton's record as an all-rounder, and was he younger or older than Denis?

THE JUDGE: Born in Woodford, Essex, on September 12, 1912, Leslie was six years older than brother Denis. He signed for Arsenal from Hampstead in 1932, but did not establish himself in the first team until after the war. He played 253 League games as a commanding centre-half and was the oldest player to make his England debut at the age of 38 in 1950, the same year in which he and Denis played together in the FA Cup final triumph over Liverpool. Les played for Middlesex for 19 years, mainly as a wicket-keeper, and became an outstanding County bowls champion after retiring from cricket. He had a foot amputated when in his late 60s, and died in 1984 aged 72.

WHEN did Andy Cole make his debut for Man United?

THE JUDGE: Cole made his full League debut in the 1-0 victory over Blackburn at Old Trafford on January 22 1995. He had signed ten days earlier, but part of the deal was that he would miss the match against his old club Newcastle on January 15.

WHAT was the Leeds United squad when they were relegated from the First Division in 1982?

THE JUDGE: Leeds used 23 players: Lukic, Hird, Flynn, Hart, Cherry, Harris, Graham, Parlane, Barnes, Greenhoff, Stevenson, Firm, Connor, Hamson, Arins, Thomas, Balcombe, Burns, Butterworth, Aspin, Worthington and brothers Frank and Eddie Gray.

THE '250' QUIZ CHALLENGE

26. With which club was Andy Cole playing when he made his full England international debut?

WHERE and when was Glenn Hoddle born?

THE JUDGE: Glenn was born on October 27 1957 at Hayes, Middlesex, and brought up in Harlow, Essex.

FOR which clubs did George Best play?

THE JUDGE: Manchester United, Stockport County, Cork Celtic, Fulham, Hibernian and Bournemouth. While in the United States, he played for Los Anegels Aztecs, Fort Lauderdale Strikers, San Jose Earthquakes and Golden Bay.

DID Liverpool have a vicar in their team before the war?

THE JUDGE: Newcastle-born Jimmy Jackson signed for Liverpool from Aberdeen in 1926 and became club captain. He was nicknamed Parson because he was studying for the ministry, and was ordained in 1933.

HOW many goals did Jack Stamps score for Derby County in the 1946 FA Cup final against Charlton?

THE JUDGE: Stamps scored two goals in a 4-1 victory. Peter Doherty was the other Derby player to score, while Herbert Turner netted an own goal and also a goal for Charlton.

WHAT was the full England squad in the 1966 World Cup finals?

THE JUDGE: The winning team, and their appearances in the finals: Banks (6), Cohen (6), Wilson (6), Stiles (6), J. Charlton (6), Moore (6), Ball (4), Hunt (6), R. Charlton (6),. Hurst (3), Peters (5). Rest of the squad: Springett, Bonetti, Armfield, Byrne, Flowers, Hunter, Paine (1), Callaghan (1), Connelly (1), Eastham, Greaves (3).

WHICH club was known as the Bank of England?

THE JUDGE: This was the nickname given to Sunderland in the immediate post-war years when they paid out what were then huge transfer fees for the likes of Len Shackleton, Trevor Ford and Ivor Broadis.

HAS a manager ever won the FA Cup with two different clubs?

THE JUDGE: Billy Walker led out the winning FA Cup teams of Sheffield Wednesday (1935) and Nottingham Forest (1959).

THE '250' QUIZ CHALLENGE

27. For which club was Ray Wilson playing when he collected a World Cup winners' medal with England in 1966?

EXACTLY how many caps did Bobby Charlton receive rather than win?

THE JUDGE: Bobby played in the era when only one Home Championship cap was awarded each season, with the initials of the teams played against embroidered on the peak. He actually received 89 of his 106 caps.

DID Stanley Matthews play in most FA Cup ties?

THE JUDGE: Sir Stanley used to hold the record with 86 FA Cup appearances. But he was overtaken by marathon man Ian Callaghan, who played in 88 ties with Liverpool, Swansea and Crewe.

WHAT was the fast-scoring record set by West Bromwich Albion centre-forward W.G. Richardson?

THE JUDGE: W.G. Richardson, who called himself Ginger to avoid confusion with a team-mate with the same name, scored four goals in five minutes in a First Division game at West Ham in 1931. In that same season, he scored the two goals in a 2-1 FA Cup final victory over deadly local rivals Birmingham City.

FOR which clubs fdid Frank Worthington play during his eventuful career?

THE JUDGE: Worthington played for Huddersfield (1966-71), Leicester City (72-77), Bolton (77-79), Birmingham City (79-81), Leeds United (81-82), Sunderland (82), Southampton (83), Brighton (84), Tranmere (85-86), Preston (86-87) and Stockport County (87).

WERE Keith and Henry Newton related, and which of them won most England caps?

THE JUDGE: Keith (Blackburn, Everton and Burnley) won 27 England caps. Henry (Forest, Everton, Derby and Walsall) was not capped at senior level. They were not related.

HOW many League games did Martin Buchan play for Manchester United, and did he score any goals at League or international level?

THE JUDGE: Buchan scored four goals in 376 League matches for Man United. He did not find the net in 34 appearances for Scotland.

THE '250' QUIZ CHALLENGE

28. Who were the opponents when Martin Buchan collected the FA Cup as Manchester United captain?

THE JUDGE

FOR which clubs did Ian St John play?

THE JUDGE: The Saint joined Liverpool from Motherwell, and later played for Coventry City, Tranmere Rovers and Hellenic in South Africa.

WHICH club came up with Liverpool when they last won promotion from the old Second Division, and was Malcolm Musgrove one of their players?

THE JUDGE: Leyton Orient, managed by Johnny Carey, were runners-up when Liverpool won the Second Division title in 1961-62. Musgrove joined Orient from West Ham the following season.

HOW many England players have won more than 100 caps?

THE JUDGE: Four – Billy Wright (105), Bobby Charlton (106), Bobby Moore (108) and Peter Shilton (125).

WHAT was the line-up of the teams for the classic 1948 FA Cup final in which Man United beat Blackpool 4-2?

THE JUDGE: Manchester United: Crompton; Carey, Aston; Anderson, Chilton, Cockburn, Delaney, Morris, Rowley, Pearson, Mitten. Blackpool: Robinson; Shimwell, Crosland; Johnston, Hayward, Kelly; Matthews, Munro, Mortensen, Dick, Rickett.

WHAT is the longest sequence of matches England have played in which they have managed at least one goal?

THE JUDGE: England scored in every one of 52 successive matches from 1884 to 1902 until a goalless draw with Wales (England missed a penalty). They then scored in their next 32 games. The 52-match run was a European record until Hungary took over in the 1950s.

DID England play any matches at White City Stadium during the 1966 World Cup finals?

THE JUDGE: England played all their six matches at Wembley. Uruguay v France was the only match staged at White City.

WHO was manager when Cliff Bastin joined Arsenal?

THE JUDGE: Bastin was signed by Herbert Chapman, who spotted him at the age of 16 playing for Exeter City. 'Boy' Bastin had won every honour in the game before he was 21.

THE '250' QUIZ CHALLENGE

29. Against which team did Bobby Charlton win his 106th and final England international cap?

36

HAS goalkeeper Dave Beasant been capped?

THE JUDGE: Beasant, then with Chelsea, was capped twice by England in 1989 by Bobby Robson when substituting in successive matches for Peter Shilton.

WHO was the first black England international and the first to captain the team?

THE JUDGE: Viv Anderson was the first black player to win a full England cap (v Czechoslovakia 1978). Paul Ince was the first black captain (v USA 1993). Laurie Cunningham won an Under-23 cap in 1977.

DID Jimmy Greaves play in a World Cup quarter-final?

THE JUDGE: Greavsie did not play in the 1966 World Cup quarter-final because of injury. But four years earlier, he was in the England team beaten 3-1 by Brazil in the 1962 quarter-finals in Chile.

HAS an Englishman ever played in and then managed post-war FA Cup and League title winning teams?

THE JUDGE: Joe Mercer is the only Englishman to achieve it. He captained the Arsenal League title winners (1948 and 1953) and the FA Cup winners (1950), and later managed Man City when they won the League (1968) and FA Cup (1969). Scots Kenny Dalglish and George Graham are the only others to achieve the distinction.

WHO was the British referee in charge of the 1950 World Cup final between Uruguay and Brazil?

THE JUDGE: George Reader, who later became chairman of Southampton. The game (not officially a final, but the deciding match) was watched by a record 199,854 crowd.

WHAT was the first £5-million transfer transaction between English clubs?

THE JUDGE: Chris Sutton (Norwich to Blackburn) in July 1994.

WHERE is the Berwick Rangers ground situated – in England or Scotland?

THE JUDGE: Berwick Rangers play at Shielfield Park, which is situated on English soil. The Borderers are the only English-based team in the Scottish League.

THE '250' QUIZ CHALLENGE

30. For which club was Viv Anderson playing when he became England's first black international?

WHO won most caps for Scotland out of Andy Gray and Alan Hansen?

THE JUDGE: Hansen won 26 caps while with Liverpool. Gray was capped 20 times with Aston Villa, Wolves and Everton.

WHAT is the League record for spot-kick saves in a season?

THE JUDGE: Paul Cooper set the record when playing for Ipswich in the old First Division in 1979-80. He saved eight out of ten penalties.

WHAT is the record for most successive League game appearances?

THE JUDGE: The record stands at 401 consecutive League games (459 in all competitions). It was set by Harold Bell with Tranmere between 1946 and 1955.

WHEN was the away-goals rule first introduced into European club competitions?

THE JUDGE: Dynamo Zagreb were the first team to benefit from the rule after a 4-4 draw with Dunfermline Athletic in the 1966-67 Fairs Cup.

WHAT was the line up of the England team that beat Italy 3-2 in the infamous Battle of Highbury?

THE JUDGE: The match was played on Wedneday Feburary 14 1934. England had seven Arsenal players (Moss, Male, Hapgood, Copping, Bowden, Drake, Bastin), plus Britton (Everton), Barker (Derby), Matthews (Stoke) and Brook (Man City). Italy, reigning world champions, did not appreciate England's perfectly legal shoulder-charging game and it developed into a battle in which players of both sides were more intent on kicking each other than the ball. Eric Brook scored twice after having a first minute penalty saved, and Ted Drake put England 3-0 clear before the skilful Italians got their game together and pulled back to 3-2.

HAS a team ever gone a whole season in the Football League without winning a single home game?

THE JUDGE: Five teams have won once at home throughout the season: Loughborough, First Division, 1899-1900; Notts County, First Division, 1904-5; Woolwich Arsenal, First Division, 1912-13; Blackpool, First Division, 1967-68; Rochdale, Third Division, 1973-74.

THE '250' QUIZ CHALLENGE

31. From which Scottish League club did Alan Hansen join Liverpool in April 1977?

FOOTBALL

WAS Leslie Compton the oldest player capped by England?

THE JUDGE: Stanley Matthews (42) and Peter Shilton (40) were the oldest when winning their last caps. Compton, at 38 years 71 days, was the oldest player to make his debut for England.

WHAT is Arthur Rowley's goal scoring record?

THE JUDGE: Rowley scored a League record 434 goals between 1947 and 1964 while playing for West Brom (4), Fulham (27), Leicester (251) and Shrewsbury (152).

WAS it Joe Mercer or Ron Greenwood who picked seven Liverpool players for England against Switzerland in 1977?

THE JUDGE: It was Ron Greenwood, although Kevin Keegan had moved to Hamburg by the time the game was played. So there were officially only six Liverpool players in the side: Clemence, Neal, McDermott, Hughes, Ray Kennedy and Callaghan.

WHY did Scotland qualify for the World Cup finals in France ahead of Yugoslavia, who had the same number of points but a better goal average?

THE JUDGE: The results against the weak bottom team in each group were not taken into account when assessing which team automatically qualified as best runners-up.

WITH which club did Gerry Francis start his career?

THE JUDGE: His first club as a player was Queen's Park Rangers, and his first club as a manager was Bristol Rovers. He also played for Crystal Palace, Coventry, Exeter, Cardiff, Swansea, Portsmouth and Bristol Rovers. He was capped 12 times by England.

WAS an Englishman involved in the foundation of either AC Milan or Juventus?

THE JUDGE: Associazione Calcio Milan were founded in 1899 as the Milan Cricket and Football Club, with English residents heavily involved in the early years. Encouraged by British residents in Turin, Juventus were formed by a group of Italian students in 1897. They adopted their famous black and white striped shirts after seeing Notts County play.

THE '250' QUIZ CHALLENGE

32. Who was England manager when Gerry Francis was appointed captain for eight international matches?

WHO captained Brazil in the 1970 World Cup finals?

THE JUDGE: Right-back Carlos Alberto was skipper. He will always be remembered for the stunning fourth and last goal against Italy in the final when he finished off a length-of-the-pitch movement with an angled right-foot drive after Pele had stroked the ball into his path..

WHAT was the original name of Newcastle United?

THE JUDGE: They were formed as Stanley in 1881, and became Newcastle East End a year later before switching to Newcastle United in 1892.

Did West Ham field their 'Big Three', Moore, Hurst and Peters, in the 1964 FA Cup final against Preston?

THE JUDGE: Hurst scored the second of West Ham's goals in a 3-2 victory over Second Division Preston. Peters was then a young reserve player. Skipper Bobby Moore collected the first of his three trophies at Wembley in three successive years after Ron 'Ticker' Boyce had netted a late winner. Team: Standen; Bond, Burkett; Bovington, Brown, Moore; Brabrook, Boyce, Byrne, Hurst, Sissons.

WHAT has been the biggest crowd for any League match in England, and give the attendance records for Charlton and Tottenham.

THE JUDGE: Man United and Arsenal drew 83,260 spectators to Maine Road for their First Division match on January 17 1948 (bomb-damaged Old Trafford was under repair). Charlton's record: 75,031 (v Aston Villa in a 5th round FA Cup tie on February 12 1938); Tottenham's: 75,038 (v Sunderland in a 6th round FA Cup tie on March 5 1938).

WHAT was the name of the black goalkeeper who played for Manchester City in the 1980s?

THE JUDGE: Alex Williams, who was the first black goalkeeper to play in the old First Division. He appeared in 114 League games for Man City and 35 for Port Vale.

WHAT has been the highest scoring penalty shoot-out?

THE JUDGE: Argentinos Juniors beat Racing Club 20-19 in 1988-89. There were 44 penalties taken before the deadlock was broken after a 2-2 draw.

THE '250' QUIZ CHALLENGE

33. Which team did Newcastle United beat in the 1969 European Fairs Cup final?

HOW old was Dixie Dean when he scored his record 60 First Division goals, and how many did he score with his head?

THE JUDGE: Everton centre-forward Dixie was 21 when he overtook George Camsell's 59-goal record in the 1927-28 season. Twenty of his 60 goals in 39 games came from headers. He netted 31 away from home, and completed seven hat-tricks including in the final match of the season against Arsenal at Goodison.

WHO scored for Queen's Park Rangers in the 1982 FA Cup final?

THE JUDGE: Terry Fenwick struck for QPR, and Glenn Hoddle scored for Tottenham in a 1-1 draw. Hoddle netted the only goal of the replay from the penalty spot.

DID Alvin Martin once score a hat-trick for West Ham against three different goalkeepers?

THE JUDGE: Yes, when West Ham won a First Division match 8-1 against Newcastle United at Upton Park on April 21 1986. Alvin Martin got his first goal against Martin Thomas, who went off with a shoulder injury. His second goal was conceded by outfield player Chris Hedworth and his third was against Peter Beardsley.

WHO were the scorers and what was the attendance when England drew 1-1 with Scotland at Hampden Park in 1968?

THE JUDGE: Martin Peters scored for England, and John Hughes equalised for Scotland in front of 134,000 spectators.

WHICH footballers have played for and against England, played in the Premiership and managed in the Premiership?

THE JUDGE: This is a catch question that has been doing the rounds in pubs and clubs for several years. Ex-Everton defender Dave Watson achieved this (the game against England was for a Hong Kong XI and he was caretaker manager at Goodison). Bryan Robson and Glenn Hoddle come into the category because they played for England against Wales when Mike England was in charge.

THE '250' QUIZ CHALLENGE

34. From which club did England international defender Dave Watson join Everton in August 1986?

WHY do the Scottish League half-time results always seem to come through ahead of the English half-times on Saturday afternoons?

THE JUDGE: They still have a ten minute half-time interval in Scotland. In the Premiership and Nationwide it is 15 minutes.

WHAT was Derek Dooley's League goal-scoring record before his tragic accident?

THE JUDGE: Derek scored two goals in two matches for Lincoln City and 62 in 61 League matches for Sheffield Wednesday. He broke his right leg in a collision with the goalkeeper at Preston on February 14 1953, and had to have it amputated. Derek later became chairman of Sheffield United.

IS Alex Ferguson the only knight to have managed an English league club?

THE JUDGE: Matt Busby was knighted while in charge at Man United, and Sir Stanley Matthews was general manager of Port Vale. Sir Alf Ramsey was briefly in charge at Birmingham City, but in a director capacity. Sir Bobby Robson was knighted while in charge at Newcastle.

WHAT are Millwall supporters talking about when they refer to their 'perfect' record?

THE JUDGE: This was set in the 1973-74 season when they finished 12th in the Second Division with this remarkable record: P42 W14 D14 L14 F51 A51 Pts 42.

HOW many of Alan Shearer's England goals were scored from the penalty spot?

THE JUDGE: Six of Shearer's 30 goals in 63 games were from the spot – v Holland (1996), 2 v Luxembourg (1998), Argentina (1998), Hungary (1999), Romania (2000). Alan missed a spot-kick against Poland.

WHICH clubs have appeared in most FA Cup semi-finals, not including replays?

THE JUDGE: The top 10: Everton (23), Man United (22), Arsenal (22), Liverpool (21), Aston Villa (19), West Brom (19), Spurs (17), Blackburn (16), Newcastle (16), Sheffield Wednesday (16).

THE '250' QUIZ CHALLENGE

35. With which club did manager Sir Alex Ferguson win his first major European trophy?

WHO has been the youngest ever winner of the European Footballer of the Year award?

THE JUDGE: Michael Owen was the youngest European-born winner of the award, collecting it the week after his 22nd birthday. Brazil's Italian-based Ronaldo won it in 1997 at the age of 19.

WHAT was the fee when Ronny Rosenthal moved from Liverpool to Spurs?

THE JUDGE: Tottenham paid £250,000 to take Ronny to White Hart Lane in January 1994.

NAME the player and clubs involved in the first £1 million transfer.

THE JUDGE: Giuseppe Savoldi (Bologna to Napoli for £1,100,000, 1975) was the world's first million-pound player. Nottingham Forest manager Brian Clough made Trevor Francis Britain's first million-pound man when he paid Birmingham City £975,000 on February 14 1979. VAT plus Trevor's signing on fee took the total up to £1,180,000.

WHO was the most expensive player in England's 1966 World Cup-winning squad?

THE JUDGE: Just 15 days after the Final, Alan Ball joined Everton from Blackpool for what was then a British record fee of £110,000.

WAS Michael Owen on Manchester United's books before joining Liverpool?

THE JUDGE: Michael joined Liverpool as an associate schoolboy in 1991, and signed as a professional on his 17th birthday on December 14 1996. Liverpool beat a cluster of clubs including Man United, Chelsea and Everton for his signature.

WAS Garth Crooks capped by England?

THE JUDGE: Garth played in four England Under-21 internationals, but did not win a full cap.

WHICH team provided the opposition in Barcelona's inaugural match at the Nou Camp stadium?

THE JUDGE: Warsaw were the first opponents on September 24 1957, and Paraguayan Eulogio Martinez scored the first goal.

THE '250' QUIZ CHALLENGE

36. Who was the Everton manager who bought Alan Ball from Blackpool in 1966?

HOW many pairs of brothers have appeared in post-war FA Cup finals?

THE JUDGE: Five - Denis, Leslie Compton (Arsenal 1950), George, Ted Robledo (Newcastle 1952), Ron, Allan Harris (Chelsea 1967), Jimmy, Brian Greenhoff (Man United 1977), Gary, Phil Neville (Man United 1996 and 1999).

GEOFF Hurst scored the LAST goal in the 1966 World Cup finals. But who was the FIRST England player to have the ball in the net during the tournament?

THE JUDGE: Roger Hunt netted in the 35th minute of the second match against Mexico, after a goalless draw with Uruguay. But the goal was disallowed. Two minutes later, Bobby Charlton scored with a thunderbolt shot from 30 yards to put England on the way to a 2-0 victory.

WHICH is the oldest club in the current Premiership?

THE JUDGE: Aston Villa (1874). Bolton had their roots in the same year as Christ Church, but did not officially become the Wanderers until 1877.

DID Celtic beat Inter Milan in the 1967 European Cup final at Lisbon's Stadium of Light?

THE JUDGE: The game was played in the Portuguese National Stadium in Lisbon.

WHAT has been the closest finish to a post-war League championship season?

THE JUDGE: Michael Thomas scored an injury-time winner for Arsenal against Liverpool at Anfield in the last match of the 1988-89 season. It meant the clubs finished level on points and goal difference, Arsenal taking the title because they had scored six more goals.

WHO scored England's one goal when they were beaten 7-1 by Hungary in Budapest in 1954?

THE JUDGE: Newcastle inside-forward Ivor Broadis scored the consolation goal with the score at 6-0. The Magical Magyars, inspired by Puskas and Hidegkuti, scored 13 goals against the old masters in two games, including their historic 6-3 win at Wembley in October 1953.

THE '250' QUIZ CHALLENGE

37. Who skippered the England team beaten by Hungary at both Wembley and in Budapest?

WHERE and when was Craig Johnston born?

THE JUDGE: Craig was born in Johannesburg on June 25 1960, and was brought up in Australia.

IS it correct that the Rangers-Eintracht Frankfurt match at Ibrox in 1961 attracted a record British crowd for a friendly match.

THE JUDGE: The game was played at Hampden to mark the new floodlights, and drew a British friendly match record crowd of 104,679.

WHO has been the oldest footballer capped by England?

THE JUDGE: Stanley Matthews was 42 years 103 days old when he last played for England against Denmark in Copenhagen on May 15 1957. England won 4-1. He collected his first cap at the age of 19.

WHICH club, in post-war football, has suffered most defeats while on the way to winning the League championship?

THE JUDGE: The record is shared by three clubs, each with 11 defeats Portsmouth (1949-50), Burnley (1959-60) and Liverpool (1963-64).

WHO had the longest association with Liverpool out of Bob Paisley and Ronnie Moran?

THE JUDGE: Bob Paisley was associated with Liverpool for 57 years, first as a player in 1939. Ronnie Moran joined the staff as a player in 1952, and retired from the Anfield coaching staff in 1998-99.

ARE Notts County the oldest football club?

THE JUDGE: It is generally accepted that the oldest football club in the world is Sheffield, formed in 1857. Their charity match against Hallam in 1862 was the first serious competitive game ever played. Notts County have their roots in 1862 and are the oldest of the Football League clubs.

CHELSEA have had how many post-war managers?

THE JUDGE: There have been 18: Billy Birrell, Ted Drake, Tommy Docherty, Dave Sexton, Ron Suart, Eddie McCreadie, Ken Shellito, Danny Blanchflower, Geoff Hurst, John Neal, John Hollins, Bobby Campbell, Ian Porterfield, David Webb, Glenn Hoddle, Ruud Gullit, Gianluca Vialli, Claudio Ranieri.

THE '250' QUIZ CHALLENGE

38. Who was Chelsea manager when they won the FA Cup and European Cup-Winners' Cup in 1970 and 1971?

THE JUDGE

WHO was the first foreign footballer to play for an English League team?

THE JUDGE: Max Seeburg, born in Leipzig in 1884 and raised in London. He played for Chelsea before they joined the League in 1905 and then for Spurs, Leyton, Burnley, Grimsby and, finally, Reading, where he was later landlord at the Travellers' Rest pub on the Bath Road. As a German, he was arrested at the start of the First World War and briefly interned.

WHEN did the great Bryn Jones sign for Arsenal from Wolves, and what was the fee?

THE JUDGE: Jones joined Arsenal for a then record £14,500 in August 1938. "The world has gone mad," said the critics. Wolves manager Major Frank Buckley had plucked the clever and creative Jones out of the relative obscurity of Welsh League football.

WHO captained the Tottenham team that won the FA Cup in 1967, and what was the line-up?

THE JUDGE: Dave Mackay was skipper. The team: Jennings, Kinnear, Knowles, Mullery, England, Mackay, Robertson, Greaves, Gilzean, Venables, Saul. Sub. Jones.

IS it true that the Nazi swastika once flew at White Hart Lane.

THE JUDGE: This was when Germany played England at Tottenham in 1935. German fans carried the swastika. England won 3-0. Three years later the England players gave the 'heil Hitler' salute before an international in Berlin that they won 6-3.

IS it true that Billy Wright has had one of his England caps taken away, and no longer holds the captaincy record?

THE JUDGE: FIFA have down-graded England's 1953 match against a Rest of Europe side to 'an exhibition game'. But the Football Association continue to recognise it as a full international. So Billy's record of 105 caps and 90 times captain of England (equal with Bobby Moore) still stands. The game was played at Wembley to mark the FA's 90th anniversary and a last-minute Alf Ramsey penalty made it a 4-4 draw.

THE '250' QUIZ CHALLENGE

39. Which team did Tottenham Hotspur beat 5-1 in the 1963 European Cup-Winners' Cup final in Rotterdam?

WITH which club did George Eastham have his long-running dispute in the 1960s?

THE JUDGE: Newcastle United when, in 1960-61, Eastham won an historic High Court victory against the restraint of trade "soccer slave" transfer system. It paved the way for the players to kick out the £20 a week maximum wage, the club bosses giving in just 72 hours before a threatened player strike. By then, Eastham had transferred to Arsenal after staging a one-man protest.

WHAT were the aggregate scores when Aberdeen played Ipswich Town in a European competition?

THE JUDGE: They met in the UEFA Cup in 1981-82. The first leg at Portman Road was a 1-1 draw, and Aberdeen won the second leg at Pittodrie 3-1.

WHICH player collected English, Scottish, Northern Ireland and Republic of Ireland cup medals?

THE JUDGE: Jimmy 'Old Bones' Delaney created this unique record with Celtic (1937), Man United (1948), Derry City (1954) and Cork Athletic (a runners' up medal in 1956).

HAVE all the matches in a full programme of either the old First Division or Premiership finished drawn?

THE JUDGE: Nine out of 11 First Division matches were drawn on September 18 1948. The record for the Premiership is seven out of ten over the weekend of December 2 to 4, 1995.

FOR which League clubs did Justin Fashanu play and how many goals did he score?

THE JUDGE: Justin played for Norwich (35 League goals), Forest (3), Southampton (3), Notts County (20), Brighton (2), Man City (0), West Ham (0), Orient (0) and Torquay (15).

WHOSE shot did the Colombian goalkeeper stop with his famous Scorpion kick against England at Wembley?

THE JUDGE: Rene Higuita produced his stunning save from a midfield lob by Jamie Redknapp in a goalless draw at Wembley on September 6 1995.

THE '250' QUIZ CHALLENGE

40. With which club did Jamie Redknapp make his Football League debut in 1989-90?

WHO scored Nottingham Forest's goals in their victory over Luton in the 1959 FA Cup Final?

THE JUDGE: Roy Dwight, Elton John's cousin, scored the first goal and Tom Wilson made it 2-0 inside the first 15 minutes before Dwight was carried off with a broken leg. David Pacey pulled one back for Luton but Forest's 10 men held out for a 2-1 victory.

WHERE and when was Nobby Stiles born, and how many games did he play for club and country?

THE JUDGE: Norbert Stiles, born in Manchester on May 18 1942, played 311 League games for Man United between 1960 and 1970. He later played for Middlesbrough (57 League games) and Preston (46). Nobby won 28 England caps and was the midfield anchorman in England's 1966 World Cup winning team.

CONFIRM that Huddersfield Town had the narrowest ever League championship win when pipping Cardiff to the first of their hat-trick of titles in 1923-24.

THE JUDGE: In those days goal average was the decider, and Huddersfield were champions by 0.0241 of a goal. Cardiff, who missed a penalty in their final goalless game, would have been champions under the current decider of goal difference, having scored one more goal.

IN which years did Derby sign Dave Mackay, Roy McFarland and Colin Todd?

THE JUDGE: Brian Clough signed McFarland from Tranmere in 1967 and Mackay from Tottenham in 1968. Colin Todd came from Sunderland in February 1971 to replace Mackay, who at the end of the season became player-manager of Swindon.

WHICH British clubs have won European trophies?

THE JUDGE: European Cup – Celtic (1967), Man United (1968-99), Liverpool (1977-78-81-84), Nottingham Forest (1979-80), Aston Villa (1982); Cup-Winners' Cup – Tottenham (1963), West Ham (1965), Man City (1970), Chelsea (1971-98), Rangers (1972), Aberdeen (1983), Everton (1985), Man United (1991), Arsenal (1994); UEFA Cup (originally, Fairs Cup) – Leeds (1968-71), Newcastle (1969), Arsenal (1970), Tottenham (1972-84), Liverpool (1973-76-2001), Ipswich (1981).

THE '250' QUIZ CHALLENGE

41. Which England manager selected Roy McFarland for his international debut?

DID Jimmy Greaves play for England during his brief spell with AC Milan?

THE JUDGE: Greavsie played against Portgual, Italy and Austria after agreeing in May 1961 to move to AC Milan from Chelsea, but was not considered during his four month stay in Italy.

WHEN were Bobby Moore's first and last games for England?

THE JUDGE: Bobby made his full international debut in place of Bobby Robson in the final warm-up match before the 1962 World Cup finals against Peru in Lima. England won 4-0, and Jimmy Greaves scored a hat-trick. Bobby bowed out after his 108th match, a 1-0 defeat against Italy at Wembley Stadium on November 14 1973.

WAS Anfield used as a venue during the 1966 World Cup and did the pitch have to be altered?

THE JUDGE: The grounds used in the North West group were Old Trafford and Goodison. Everton's pitch had to be widened by two yards and lengthened by three yards to meet FIFA regulations.

DID Alan Gowling used to play for Manchester United as an amateur in the 1960s?

THE JUDGE: Alan, an economics graduate from Manchester University, was on United's books as an amateur. But he had signed professional forms by the time of making his first-team debut with a goal at Stoke on March 30 1968. He later scored for Huddersfield, Newcastle, Bolton and Preston.

WHO scored the first ever hat-trick in a League match?

THE JUDGE: Walter Tait was the first three-goal hero, netting a hat-trick for Burnley in a 4-3 victory over Bolton on the second Saturday of the first League season, September 15 1888.

FOR which League clubs did Geoff Hurst play and score?

THE JUDGE: Sir Geoff played for West Ham (180 League goals, 411 games), Stoke City (30 goals, 108 games) and West Brom (2 goals, 10 games).

THE '250' QUIZ CHALLENGE

42. Against which country did Geoff Hurst score his first goal in a World Cup finals match?

HOW much more did the old leather football weigh than today's lightweight ball?

THE JUDGE: Surprisingly, the modern ball (14 ounces minimum, 16 maximum) is an ounce heavier than the old pre-war leather ball. It seems lighter due to the plastic coating and improved manufacturing techniques that mean virtually no water retention.

WHAT bonus did the England players receive for winning the 1966 World Cup?

THE JUDGE: Each member of the 22-man squad was paid £1,000, and skipper Bobby Moore had to threaten court action on behalf of the players to stop the taxman taking a cut.

AGAINST which team did goalkeeper Peter Shilton once score a League goal?

THE JUDGE: Making use of a following wind, Shilts scored with a clearance against Southampton at The Dell in October 1967. Two months earlier, Pat Jennings scored a similar goal for Tottenham in the Charity Shield match against Man United at Old Trafford.

HOW many times have England conceded four or more goals in post-war international matches?

THE JUDGE: Eleven times – FIFA Select (4-4, 1953), Hungary (3-6 and 1-7, 1953-54), Belgium (4-4, 1954), Uruguay (2-4, 1954), Yugoslavia (0-5, 1958), Peru (1-4, 1959), France (2-5 1963), Brazil (1-5, 1964), Austria (3-4, 1979), Wales (1-4, 1980).

HOW many hat-tricks did Gary Lineker score for England?

THE JUDGE: Gary scored five hat-tricks, including four-goal hauls against Spain and Malaysia. Only my Sun team-mate Jimmy Greaves (6) has scored more hat-tricks for England.

WHAT is the record number of draws by one club in any season of League football?

THE JUDGE: Four clubs share the record of 23 draws – Norwich City (old First Division, 1978-79), Cardiff and Hartlepool (Third Division, 1997-98) and Exeter City (Fourth Division, 1986-87).

THE '250' QUIZ CHALLENGE

43. In which country did Gary Lineker play the final matches of his distinguished club career?

HOW many England goals did Trevor Brooking score?

THE JUDGE: Trevor scored five goals in 47 England appearances.

WHO was the first British player sold for a five-figure fee?

THE JUDGE: David Jack, when joining Arsenal from Bolton for £10,890 in October 1928. It took 11 hours to thrash out the deal, and it was the day they said that football had gone mad!

DID the Froggatts, Redfern and Jack, ever form a left-wing partnership for England?

THE JUDGE: Portsmouth utility player Jack, previously capped as a centre-half, partnered his cousin Redfern (Sheffield Wednesday) on the left wing against Scotland and the USA in 1953.

WERE Aston Villa wearing claret and blue shirts before West Ham?

THE JUDGE: Villa were wearing claret and blue as founder members of the Football League in 1888. West Ham did not come on the scene until 1900 after the folding of Thames Ironworks F.C.

FOR which League clubs did Derek Hales and Mike Flanagan play?

THE JUDGE: Hales: Luton, Charlton (twice), Derby, West Ham and Gillingham. Flanagan: Charlton (twice), Crystal Palace, QPR and Cambridge United. They were famously sent off for fighting each other when Charlton team-mates.

WHICH player holds the record for the fastest hat-trick in the Premiership?

THE JUDGE: Robbie Fowler for Liverpool against Arsenal at Anfield on Sunday August 28, 1994 (26, 29 and 31 mins).

WHO has scored the quickest goal for England in a post-war international match?

THE JUDGE: Tommy Lawton was reported to have scored in 17 seconds in the 10-0 rout of Portugal in Lisbon in 1947, but this was never officially accepted. The official record is Bryan Robson's 27-seconds goal against France in the 1982 World Cup finals.

THE '250' QUIZ CHALLENGE

44. Who scored two goals for Aston Villa against Manchester United in the 1957 FA Cup final?

DID goalkeepr Frank Swift play in more than one FA Cup final for Manchester City?

THE JUDGE: Swift played in just the 1934 FA Cup final at the age of 20, fainting from nervous exhaustion at the end of the match in which they beat Portsmouth 2-1. The greatest goalkeeper of his generation, he died in the 1958 Munich air disaster while travelling as a newspaper reporter.

WHEN did Carlisle United play in the old First Division, and did they win promotion in successive seasons?

THE JUDGE: Carlisle had one season in the old First Division in 1974-75 when they were relegated in 22nd position. They were promoted as Fourth Division runners-up in 1963-64, and won the Third Division title the following season.

WERE Luton the first professional football club in the south of England?

THE JUDGE: Luton became the first professional club south of Birmingham when founded in 1885 following the merger of Wanderers and Excelsior.

IN what year did Bradford City win the FA Cup, and who were the beaten finalists?

THE JUDGE: Bradford City, then in the old First Division, beat FA Cup holders Newcastle United 1-0 in a replayed final at Old Trafford in 1911 after a goalless draw at Crystal Palace.

WHO holds the record for scoring in the most consecutive games in English league football?

THE JUDGE: Chester's Bill Prendergast set the record in 1938 by scoring in 13 successive Third Division matches.

HOW many goals did Pele score?

THE JUDGE: Pele scored 1,283 first-class goals, including 97 in 111 international matches for Brazil. His most productive year was 1958 when, at the age of 17, he had a haul of 139 goals, including six in the World Cup finals. He spent most of his career with Santos (1955-74) and wound down with New York Cosmos.

THE '250' QUIZ CHALLENGE

45. Against which team did Pele score a wonder goal in his first World Cup final?

WHO managed Aston Villa when they won the European Cup in 1982?

THE JUDGE: Tony Barton, who had taken over from Ron Saunders, manager of the League championship winning team.

WHICH football club is nicknamed the Shakers?

THE JUDGE: Bury, so called because their club chairman in the 1890s was fond of saying: 'We're going to really shake the opposition today.'

WHICH players have scored in every round of the FA Cup including the final?

THE JUDGE: Twelve players have achieved this: Archie Hunter (Aston Viilla, 1887), Sandy Brown (Tottenham, 1901), Harry Hampton (Aston Villa, 1905), Harold Blackmore (Bolton, 1929), Ellis Rimmer (Sheff. Wednesday, 1935), Frank O'Donnell (Preston, 1937), Stan Mortensen (Blackpool, 1948), Jackie Milburn (Newcastle, 1951), Nat Lofthouse (Bolton, 1953), Charlie Wayman (Preston, 1954), Jeff Astle (West Brom, 1968), Peter Osgood (Chelsea, 1970).

FOR which clubs has Graeme Le Saux played?

THE JUDGE: Graeme joined Chelsea from St Pauls in Jersey, and played 129 League games for Blackburn before returning to Chelsea.

IN which year was the goalkeeper first banned from picking up a back pass, and when was the rule first introduced in the World Cup finals?

THE JUDGE: FIFA introduced the back pass rule in 1992, and it was established in time for the 1994 World Cup.

FOR which League clubs did Stewart Houston play?

THE JUDGE: Chelsea (9 League games), Brentford (77), Man United (205), Sheffield United (94), Colchester (107). He joined Chelsea from Port Glasgow and was capped once by Scotland.

WAS Geoff Hurst the first player to score a hat-trick for England in a Wembley international?

THE JUDGE: No. That honour went to Chelsea centre-forward Roy Bentley. He scored all three goals when England beat Wales 3-2 on November 10 1954.

THE '250' QUIZ CHALLENGE

46. Who was manager at Blackburn Rovers when Graeme Le Saux joined them in 1993?

WAS Dino Zoff the first goalkeeper to captain a World Cup winning team?

THE JUDGE: It was first achieved in 1934 by Zoff's countryman Giampiero Combi.

THERE were portraits of 11 players on the tickets for the 2000 FA Cup final: Fred Keenor, Dixie Dean, Billy Wright, Stanley Matthews, Bert Trautmann, Nat Lofthouse, Billy Bremner, Dave Watson, Billy Bonds, Pat Rice and Ricky Villa. Who was Fred Keenor?

THE JUDGE: One of the great Welsh international centre-halves, Fred Keenor was the only man ever to take the FA Cup out of England as captain of the Cardiff City team that beat Arsenal 1-0 in the 1927 FA Cup final.

HOW many players have scored 30 or more goals for England in international matches?

THE JUDGE: Alan Shearer became the latest member of the 30-club with his penalty against Romania in Euro 2000. He joins Bobby Charlton (49), Gary Lineker (48), Jimmy Greaves (44), Tom Finney (30), Nat Lofthouse (30).

WHO was the first British-born player to score a goal in a World Cup finals match?

THE JUDGE: Scots-born forwards Bart McGhee and James Brown scored for the United States on the way to the semi-final in the inaugural World Cup finals in Uruguay in 1930.

WHEN and against which team did Joe Payne score 10 goals in a League match?

THE JUDGE: Payne scored his record 10 goals for Luton against Bristol Rovers in a home Third Division South game on April 13, 1936. Luton won 12-0 and Payne was playing his first League match at centre-forward after switching from midfield.

HOW old was Ian Wright when he started his League playing career?

THE JUDGE: Ian was 21 when he joined Crystal Palace from Sunday club side Greenwich Borough in August 1985.

THE '250' QUIZ CHALLENGE

47. With which Football League club did Ian Wright have the final shots of his career?

54

WHEN was the first televised Match of the Day?

THE JUDGE: BBC2 showed recorded highlights of Liverpool 3, Arsenal 2 on August 22 1964. ITV experimented with live coverage of Blackpool v Bolton on Friday September 9, 1960, but did not take up the option to make it a regular series.

WHAT did Johnny Haynes achieve as a player?

THE JUDGE: During his 18 years at Fulham, Johnny scored 146 goals in a club record 594 League games (1952-70). He captained England in 22 of his 56 games. Over to my *Sun* team-mate Jimmy Greaves, who was his favourite playing partner: 'Haynsie was as good a passer as Beckham, difference being that he could do it with either foot. Johnny was the first £100 a week footballer. By today's crazy standards he would be worth paying a hundred grand a week. He was that good.'

DID Bobby Robson cap more England players than Sir Alf Ramsey?

THE JUDGE: Ramsey capped 95 players in 113 matches, Robson 86 players in 95 matches. Peter Shilton (16 caps with Ramsey, 83 with Robson) and Ray Clemence (2 with Ramsey, 2 with Robson) were the only players to bridge both eras.

WHO took the free-kick that went into the Dutch net in the last moments of England's 1990 World Cup finals match against Holland?

THE JUDGE: Stuart Pearce hammered a last-minute free-kick straight into the Dutch goal, but it was disallowed because the referee had ruled an indirect free-kick. The game ended 0-0.

WHO were the goal scorers in the 1966 FA Cup final between Everton and Sheffield Wednesday?

THE JUDGE: Jim McCalliog gave Wednesday a fourth minute lead, and David Ford made it 2-0 in the 57th minute. Goals from Mike Trebilcock (2) and Derek Temple lifted Everton to a 3-2 victory.

WHAT is the nickname of Leeds United?

THE JUDGE: It's according to which generation you ask. Old-timers still refer to them as the (proud as) Peacocks. They have also been known as The Whites (when Don Revie kitted them out to look and play like Real Madrid), and more popularly as simply United.

THE '250' QUIZ CHALLENGE

48. For which club did Sir Bobby Robson play between two spells with Fulham?

HAVE Liverpool ever had any players capped by Northern Ireland?

THE JUDGE: Not in post-war football. Elisha Scott, one of the great pre-war goalkeepers, was one of three Liverpool players capped by Northern Ireland in the 1920s.

WHO was Manchester United manager immediately before Sir Matt Busby?

THE JUDGE: Walter Crickmer, United's long-serving secretary, was caretaker manager following Scott Duncan's move to Ipswich in 1937. Busby was appointed on February 15 1945. Old Trafford was being rebuilt after suffering bomb damage, and so Sir Matt went to Maine Road for his earliest home games. He had, of course, played for Manchester City before the war, and so he felt at home.

WHO scored six goals in an FA Cup tie and finished on the losing side?

THE JUDGE: Denis Law scored six goals for Manchester City at Luton in a fourth round FA Cup tie in 1961 before the game was abandoned because of a waterlogged pitch. He also scored in the replayed match, which Luton won 3-1.

HOW many times was Carlton Palmer capped and did he captain England?

THE JUDGE: Palmer won 18 caps and was never skipper.

WHICH Third Division (old style) match drew the biggest attendance?

THE JUDGE: The three biggest crowds were: 51,621 for Cardiff v Bristol City (Third Division South, 1946-47), 49,655 for Hull City v Rotherham (Third Division North, 1948-49), and 48,110 for Aston Villa v Bournemouth (Third Division, 1971-72).

WHO were England's opponents along with Holland and the Republic of Ireland in the first stage of the Italia 90 World Cup finals?

THE JUDGE: Egypt, who finished bottom of the group after drawing with Holland (1-1) and the Republic of Ireland (0-0). England beat them 1-0, thanks to Mark Wright's first goal in international football.

THE '250' QUIZ CHALLENGE

49. With which club was Carlton Palmer playing when he made his international debut for England?

WHICH Third Division clubs (old style) have reached the FA Cup semi-finals?

THE JUDGE: There were six: Millwall (1937), Port Vale (1954), York City (1955), Norwich City (1959), Crystal Palace (1976), Plymouth Argyle (1984).

DID Sir Alf Ramsey ever play League football for Portsmouth?

THE JUDGE: Ramsey signed amateur forms with Portsmouth in 1939, but war broke out before he could make the breakthrough into the first-team. He was 26 before making his League debut with Southampton in the first post-war season. An elegant and powerful right-back nicknamed The General, he won the first of 32 caps while with Southampton. He moved on to Tottenham and became a key member of the famous Spurs push-and-run team that won the Second and First Division titles in successive seasons at the start of the 1950s.

WHAT were the attendances when Barnsley appeared in two FA Cup finals, and are they the only Yorkshire team to win the FA Cup in Yorkshire?

THE JUDGE: Barnsley drew two FA Cup finals at Crystal Palace (v Newcastle 1910, and West Brom 1912) when the attendances were 77,747 and 54,556. Newcastle won the 1910 replay at Everton in front of 69,000 fans. Barnsley won the replay against West Brom at Bramall Lane, Sheffield, to become the only team to win the FA Cup in Yorkshire.

WHEN did London amateurs Walthamstow Avenue hold mighty Manchester United to a draw in the FA Cup?

THE JUDGE: It was in the fourth round at Old Trafford in 1952-53. Avenue drew 1-1 and lost the replay at Highbury 5-2.

DID Welsh international full-back Rod Thomas win a championship medal with Derby County in 1974-75, and in what position did David Nish play that season?

THE JUDGE: Rod Thomas played 22 matches for Dave Mackay's championship team, taking over at right-back from Ron Webster after three appearances at left-back and one in the No 5 shirt. David Nish played 38 matches at left-back.

THE '250' QUIZ CHALLENGE

50. Against which country did Sir Alf Ramsey have his first match as England manager, which ended in a 5-2 defeat?

WHO was top scorer in the 1982 World Cup finals in Spain, and was Kerry Dixon in the England squad?

THE JUDGE: Paolo Rossi was top scorer with six goals that helped Italy clinch the World Cup. Dixon, then with Reading, did not go to Spain, and made one substitute appearance in the 1986 finals.

WERE the Walters, who played for Germany in the 1954 World Cup Final, related?

THE JUDGE: Fritz Walter, the captain, and Ottmar Walter were brothers.

IN the immediate post-war years, Stoke regularly fielded 11 locally-born players. Can any other club match this?

THE JUDGE: That outstanding Stoke team included local-born internationals Stanley Matthews, Neil Franklin and Freddie Steele. But I think Jock Stein's great European Cup-winning Celtic team top the local heroes parade. Their players were all born within a 30-mile radius of Parkhead! No European team that has captured a major trophy can match that.

WHICH two teams contested the 100th FA Cup final?

THE JUDGE: Leeds and Arsenal contested the Centenary FA Cup final in 1972, but the 100th actual match was the 1981 final between Tottenham and Manchester City.

FOR which League clubs did England centre-forward Tommy Lawton play?

THE JUDGE: Tommy started his career with Burnley and then travelled the football roundabout with Everton, Chelsea, Notts County, Brentford and Arsenal. During the war, he also turned out for Tranmere, Aldershot and Morton (playing for the Scottish club while on honeymoon). On one war-time Christmas Day, he played for Everton in the morning and Tranmere in the afternoon.

HAS any League player beaten the Ron Harris Chelsea record of playing 795 matches in all competitions for one club?

THE JUDGE: John Trollope remains the one-club appearances king. He added more than 70 cup games to his record 770 League matches for Swindon Town.

THE '250' QUIZ CHALLENGE

51. Who scored the only goal of the match for Leeds in the 1972 FA Cup Centenary final against Arsenal?

DID Allan Clarke captain the Leicester City side beaten 1-0 by Manchester City in the 1969 FA Cup Final?

THE JUDGE: No. Leicester left-back David Nish, at 21, was the youngest player to lead out an FA Cup team.

WHERE and when was Bob Paisley born?

THE JUDGE: The great Liverpool manager was born in Hetton-le-Hole, Co Durham, on January 23 1919.

DID Tony Cascarino play any part in Chelsea's FA Cup final against Manchester United at Wembley in 1994?

THE JUDGE: Cascarino came on as a second-half substitute for Mark Stein. Unirted won 4-0, including two Eric Cantona penalties.

WHICH member of England's 1966 World Cup winning team played most League matches?

THE JUDGE: The team and their League appearance records: Gordon Banks (510), George Cohen (408), Ray Wilson (409), Nobby Stiles (414), Jack Charlton (629), Bobby Moore (668), Alan Ball (743), Roger Hunt (480), Bobby Charlton (644), Geoff Hurst (529), Martin Peters (722). So Ballie, at 21 the 'baby' of the winning team, comes out on top.

WHEN were Gateshead relegated from the Football League and who replaced them?

THE JUDGE: Gateshead were replaced by Peterborough when demoted in 1959-60.

WERE Hereford in the Football League when they eliminated First Division Newcastle from the FA Cup?

THE JUDGE: Hereford were in the Southern League when they beat Newcastle in 1972, and were promoted to the Fourth Division at the end of the season.

IN which 'old' First Division match did television pundit Jimmy Hill take over as a linesman?

THE JUDGE: It was the goalless draw between Arsenal and Liverpool at Highbury on September 16 1972. Jimmy, a qualified referee, was at the ground working for LWT's Big Match. He took over from linesman Dennis Drewitt, who pulled a muscle.

THE '250' QUIZ CHALLENGE

52. Who famously scored the winning goal for Hereford that put Newcastle United out of the FA Cup in 1972?

WHAT was the playing record of that grand old centre-half Syd Owen?

THE JUDGE: Owen, a giant-hearted centre-half, won the first of his three England caps at the age of 31. He joined Luton in 1951 after just five games for his hometown club Birmingham City. At the age of 36, his captaincy inspired Luton to an FA Cup final appearance against Nottingham Forest (2-1 winners). Owen was elected Footballer of the Year in what was his last season before briefly becoming Luton manager and then a respected coach with Leeds United.

HOW many times did goalkeeper Colin McDonald play for England?

THE JUDGE: McDonald, born in Summerseat, Lancs, in 1930, had just established himself in the England team when his career was wrecked by a broken leg. He played 186 League games for Burnley and was capped eight times, including in the 1958 World Cup finals. He made a comeback with non-League Altrincham before scouting for Bolton and taking on administrative duties with Bury.

DID Alan Taylor score in every round of the FA Cup when West Ham won it in 1975?

THE JUDGE: Taylor, a bargain buy from Rochdale six months before the final, scored only in the last three matches – six goals in all, including two in the final against Fulham.

DID Peter Osgood or Rodney Marsh win most England international caps.

THE JUDGE: Rodney Marsh won nine caps (one with QPR and eight with Man City). Ossie was capped four times while with Chelsea.

IS the Maracana Stadium in Rio the world's biggest football ground?

THE JUDGE: The Maracana has several times had near-200,000 attendances, including for the 1950 World Cup decider between Brazil and Uruguay and the league matches between Flamengo and Fluminense. But recent ground refurbishment has cut the capacity to 120,000. Bigger grounds now include Benfica's Stadium of Light (130,000), Nou Camp, Barcelona (130,000) and Sao Paulo's Morumbi ground that has held 150,000.

THE '250' QUIZ CHALLENGE

53. Who skippered the West Ham United side that captured the FA Cup against Fulham in 1975?

WAS Charlie George voted Man of the Match when Arsenal beat Liverpool 2-1 in the 1971 FA Cup final to clinch the double?

THE JUDGE: Charlie scored a spectacular winning goal in extra-time, but it was future manager George Graham who got the man of the match vote. He was outstanding in midfield, and claimed a touch on the first goal which was later credited to substitute Eddie Kelly.

HOW many times was Kevin Keegan on the winning side in a European Cup final?

THE JUDGE: Once – with Liverpool in 1977. He was a runner-up with Hamburg against Forest in 1980.

WHO was the referee who ordered off Man United's Kevin Moran in the 1985 FA Cup final against Everton and did he ever officiate again?

THE JUDGE: Peter Willis, who was President of the Referees' Association and a year off retirement. He was the first referee to send off a player in an FA Cup final.

WHICH teams were promoted and relegated in the last year of the old First Division?

THE JUDGE: Up: Ipswich Town, Middlesbrough, Derby County. Down: Luton Town, Notts County, West Ham.

NAME the captains who have lifted the World Cup.

THE JUDGE: Jose Nasazzi (Uruguay 1930), Gianpiero Combi (Italy 1934), Giuseppe Meazza (Italy 1938), Obdulio Varela (Uruguay 1950), Fritz Walter (Germany 1954), Luiz Bellini (Brazil 1958), Mauro (Brazil 1962), Bobby Moore (England 1966), Carlos Alberto (Brazil 1970), Franz Beckenbauer (West Germany 1974), Daniel Passarella (Argentina 1978), Dino Zoff (Italy 1982), Diego Maradona (Argentina 1986), Lothar Matthaus (West Germany 1990), Dunga (Brazil 1994), Didier Deschamps (France 1998), Cafu (Brazil 2002).

ARE Robbie Keane of Leeds and Manchester United's Roy Keane related?

THE JUDGE: Roy (born in Cork) and Robbie (Dublin) are not related.

THE '250' QUIZ CHALLENGE

54. What number shirt did Lothar Matthaus wear when lifting the World Cup as West Germany skipper in Italia 90?

HOW many African teams qualified for the World Cup finals in France in 1998?

THE JUDGE: Five – Cameroon, Morocco, Nigeria, South Africa and Tunisia.

WHICH individual has made most FA Cup final appearances?

THE JUDGE: Lord Alfred Kinnaird played in nine of the first 12 finals for Old Etonians and Wanderers, winning five times before becoming the Football Association's top administrator. Captain (later Major) Francis Marindin played in two of the first three finals for Royal Engineers and later refereed eight finals. He became FA President.

WHAT has been the biggest attendance for any match at a British football ground?

THE JUDGE: An all-ticket crowd of 149,547 jammed Hampden Park for the 1937 international in which Scotland beat England 3-1. It was estimated that more than 150,000 spectators saw the first Wembley FA Cup final between Bolton and West Ham. Thousands forced their way into the ground through broken gates. The official attendance was 126,047.

WHICH League team conceded ten goals at Anfield in the 1980s?

THE JUDGE: Liverpool beat Fulham 10-0 in the first leg of their second round League Cup tie at Anfield on September 23 1986. Fulham went down 3-2 in the return leg.

WHO captained the Great Britain team that played the Rest of the Europe at Hampden Park in 1947?

THE JUDGE: The match was staged to celebrate the Home Nations rejoining FIFA. Britain, wearing Scottish blue shirts, won 6-1. Team: Swift; Hardwick (captain), Hughes; Macaulay, Vernon, Burgess; Matthews, Mannion, Lawton, Steel, Liddell. Johnny Carey skippered the European team. British scorers: Mannion (2), Steel, Lawton (2), Paroloa (og).

WHO holds the Liverpool League goal-scoring record?

THE JUDGE: Roger Hunt, with 245 goals in 404 League matches between 1959 and 1969.

THE '250' QUIZ CHALLENGE

55. For which Lancashire club did Roger Hunt sign after leaving Liverpool in 1969?

WHAT is the full name of Brazlian master Ronaldo?

THE JUDGE: Luiz Nazario da Lima.

DID George Graham ever captain Manchester United playing against Tottenham?

THE JUDGE: Graham skippered the United team beaten 2-1 by Tottenham at White Hart Lane on November 3 1974. George Best scored United's only goal. It was the season United went down to the old Second Division under Tommy Docherty, who made Graham his first signing as manager.

WITH which clubs did Peter Shilton set his all-time appearances record?

THE JUDGE: Shilts reached 1,005 League appearances with Leicester City (286), Stoke City (110), Nottingham Forest (202), Southampton (188), Derby County (175), Plymouth (34), Bolton (1), Orient (9).

WHAT have been the results of third place play-off matches in the World Cup?

THE JUDGE: 1934 (the first time third-place was decided): Germany 3, Austria 2; 1938: Brazil 4, Sweden 2; 1950: Sweden finished third in the deciding league table; 1954: Austria 3, Uruguay 1; 1958: France 6, West Germany 3; 1962: Chile 1, Yugoslavia 0; 1966: Portugal 2, Russia 1; 1970: West Germany 1, Uruguay 0; 1974: Poland 1, Brazil 0; 1978: Brazil 2, Italy 1; 1982: Poland 3, France 2; 1986: France 4, Belgium 2; 1990: Italy 2, England 1; 1994: Sweden 4, Bulgaria 0; 1998: Croatia 2, Holland 0; 2002: Turkey 3, South Korea 2.

WERE the record books rewritten to give a Czechoslovakian international footballer the fastest World Cup finals goal?

THE JUDGE: FIFA recognised Vaclav Masek's goal for Czechoslovakia against Mexico in the 1962 finals in Chile as the fastest. It was re-timed in a film of the match at 15 seconds. They originally presented England skipper Bryan Robson with a watch to mark what was thought to be the quickest World Cup finals goal in 27 seconds against France in 1982. They were overtaken in 2002 when Hakan Sukur made an instant hit for Turkey with a goal in 10.8 seconds against South Korea in the third-place play-off match.

THE '250' QUIZ CHALLENGE

56. Against which country did goalkeeper Peter Shilton make his 125th and final appearance for England?

WHO were Northern Ireland's scorers in a World Cup qualifying match against Cyprus in 1973 and why was the match staged at Craven Cottage?

THE JUDGE; Northern Ireland won 3-0 with goals from Terry Anderson (2) and Sammy Morgan. The game came during a period when most of Northern Ireland's games were played on English grounds because of the troubles in Ulster.

WHICH England goalkeeper let in 45 goals in just 23 games in the 1950s?

THE JUDGE: This was Gil Merrick, Birmingham City goalkeeper and later their manager. He had the misfortune to play in the two matches in which the Hungarians hammered 13 goals into the England net in two games. He had been beaten only 15 times in his first 13 matches, the first 12 without defeat.

WHY were the kick-offs to both the 1974 and 1978 World Cup finals delayed?

THE JUDGE: The 1974 final in Munich was delayed because the organisers had forgotten to put out the corner flags following the pre-match entertainment. Four years later, the hold up in Buenos Aires was caused when Argentina complained about the protective covering on the arm of Dutch forward Rene Van de Kerkhof.

WAS the 1968 Manchester United-Benfica European Cup final screened in colour on television?

THE JUDGE: No, it was shown live in black and white. An edited colour version was shown later on the Movietone cinema newsreel.

WHO was the first man to manage Birmingham's 'Big Three', Aston Villa, West Bromwich Albion and Birmingham City?

THE JUDGE: Birkenhead-born Ron Saunders was first to manage all three Birmingham clubs.

WHICH club has won the FA Cup most times?

THE JUDGE: Manchester United hold the record, with ten victories. Tottenham and Arsenal are joint second on eight.

THE '250' QUIZ CHALLENGE

57. Which club did manager Ron Saunders guide to a League championship triumph?

HAS an English or Scottish referee ever been in charge of a European Cup Final?

THE JUDGE: Arthur Ellis refereed the first European Cup Final in 1956. There have since been three more English referees in charge, all from the Football League - Arthur Holland (1963), Jack Taylor (1971), and Philip Don (1994). Scotland's Jack Mowat handled the 1960 10-goal classic between Real Madrid and Eintracht Frankfurt at Hampden Park.

DID Charlton manager Alan Curbishley ever play for West Ham?

THE JUDGE: Alan started his career with West Ham, playing 85 League matches before later service with Birmingham City, Aston Villa, Brighton and Charlton.

IS it true that Gordon Banks used to put chewing gum on his hands to make the ball stick?

THE JUDGE: I went to the great man himself for this answer: 'Yes, there were times when I did rub a mixture of chewing gum and soil on to the palms of my hands to make the ball easier to handle. I also used to spit on my hands. This was early in my career before goalkeeping gloves became much better manufactured.'

WHICH post-war League club had seven former England captains in their squad, and all playing under the same manager?

THE JUDGE: The club Southampton, the manager Lawrie McMenemy, the players Peter Shilton, Mick Mills, Dave Watson, Mark Wright, Kevin Keegan, Mike Channon and Alan Ball.

WHAT was the background to a side called London which was beaten by Barcelona in the first Fairs Cup final in 1958?

THE JUDGE: This forerunner of the UEFA Cup was an inter-cities competition and staged over three years in conjunction with trade fairs. London entered a combined team including players of the calibre of Jimmy Greaves (Chelsea), Johnny Haynes (Fulham) and Danny Blanchflower (Tottenham). They held Barcelona to a 2-2 draw at Stamford Bridge and, with a weakened team, lost the away leg 6-0.

THE '250' QUIZ CHALLENGE

58. Against which team did goalkeper Gordon Banks get an FA Cup runners-up medal at Wembley in 1961?

HAS Ruud Van Nistelrooy ever missed from the penalty spot while playing for Manchester United?

THE JUDGE: Ruud had his 63rd minute penalty saved by the Olympiakos goalkeeper in a Champions League group match at Old Trafford in October 2001.

WHO has scored most goals in a single season since the Premiership started?

The JUDGE: Alan Shearer, 34 goals for Blackburn in 1994-95, the season they won the Premiership.

IS it true that an England player once came off the bench to play for Wales?

THE JUDGE: The great 'Blackpool Bomber' Stan Mortensen made his international debut as a substitute for Wales in a wartime match against England. Wales had an injury problem, and were allowed to call Stan into their team from England's reserve bench. Morty, an RAF pilot who survived a bomber crash in which he received head injuries, went on to score 23 goals in 25 games for England.

DID manager Barry Fry ever play League football?

THE JUDGE: Barry, an England schoolboy star, started as an apprentice with Man United and briefly played League football with Bolton, Luton and Leyton Orient. Most of his playing career as an inside-forward was spent with non-League clubs.

HAS any player in a League match ever scored a hat-trick of own goals?

THE JUDGE: Never. Aston Villa defender Chris Nicholl came close in an extraordinary First Division match in which he scored all four goals in a 2-2 draw at Leicester in 1976. Jamie Carragher twice put the ball into his own net in Liverpool's 2-3 home defeat by Manchester United in a Premiership match in September 1999.

DID England winger Terry Paine play in the old First Division for Southampton?

THE JUDGE: Yes, from 1966 to 1974 on his way to 713 League appearances for the Saints.

THE '250' QUIZ CHALLENGE

59. From which club did Sir Alex Ferguson sign striker Ruud Van Nistelrooy for Manchester United?

HOW many times have there been all-English finals or semi-finals in the major European competitions?

THE JUDGE: Four times (all aggregate scores): Tottenham 3, Wolves 2 (UEFA Cup final, 1971-72); Chelsea 2, Man City 0 (Cup Winners' Cup semi-final, 1970-71); Leeds 1, Liverpool 0 (UEFA Cup semi-final, 1970-71); Liverpool 2, Tottenham 2 (UEFA Cup semi-final, 1972-73 – Liverpool won on away goals rule).

WERE Liverpool or Celtic first to adopt 'You'll Never Walk Alone' as their anthem?

THE JUDGE: It became Kop choir property when Scouser Gerry Marsden and the Pacemakers had a No 1 hit with the song from Carousel, co-inciding with a mood of mourning following the November 1963 assassination of John F. Kennedy. It was the 1970s before Celtic fans sang it regularly.

HAS any footballer played in Glasgow, Merseyside, Manchester and London derbies?

THE JUDGE: Ray Wilkins played in West London, Manchester, Milan, Glasgow and Edinburgh derbies, and Paul Gascoigne has featured in North London, Rome, Glasgow and Merseyside games. But nobody has got this specific 'full house.' Paul Stewart is often wrongly credited with the feat, but he did not manage to play in either Manchester or Glasgow derbies.

WHAT is the record number of draws by one club in any season of League football?

THE JUDGE: Four clubs share the record of 23 draws – Norwich City (old First Division, 1978-79), Cardiff and Hartlepool (Third Division, 1997-98) and Exeter City (Fourth Division, 1986-87).

WHICH club used to be at home at Pink Bank Lane and Reddish Lane?

THE JUDGE: Ardwick FC, which grew out of the amalgamation of West Gorton and Gorton, and then became Manchester City in 1894. They have had six grounds on the way to Maine Road: Clowes Street, Kirkmanshulme Cricket Ground, Clemington Park, Pink Bank Lane, Reddish Lane, Hyde Road, Maine Road (1923-). As I write, the move to the ultra-modern new stadium at Eastlands is imminent.

THE '250' QUIZ CHALLENGE

60. From which west country club did England international winger Mike Summerbee join Manchester City?

WHAT was the date and result of Man United's first match at Old Trafford and from which ground did they move?

THE JUDGE: A crowd of 45,000 saw Liverpool beat Man United 4-3 at Old Trafford on February 19 1910. In their final match at their old Bank Street ground at Clayton four weeks earlier, United drew just 7,000 spectators. The original Old Trafford was designed by Scottish architect Archie Leitch, who also had a hand in designing Hampden, Ibrox and White Hart Lane.

WHICH Premiership/old First Division goalkeeper has kept the most clean sheets in one season?

THE JUDGE: Goalkeeper Ray Clemence kept 28 clean sheets in 42 matches for Liverpool when they won the old First Division championship in 1978-79.

HAS any team when getting promotion from Division One to the Premier League got 100 points and 100 goals in a season?

THE JUDGE: Bolton scored 100 goals but finished on 98 points when winning promotion in 1996-97. Sunderland (105) and Fulham (101) got a century of points but not of goals when lifting the First Division title.

HAS any English team ever won a major cup competition and been relegated in the same season?

THE JUDGE: Norwich City won the League Cup and went down from the old First Division in 1985. Reading won the Simod Cup in 1988 and were relegated to the Third Division.

WAS Denis Law dropped for the 1968 European Cup final?

THE JUDGE: Denis was having a knee operation, and watched United beat Benfica from his hospital bed.

COUNTING the Premier League and old First Division, which six clubs have won the title most times?

THE JUDGE: 1. Liverpool (18); 2. Man United (13); 3. Arsenal (12); 4. Everton (9); 5. Sunderland (8); 6. Aston Villa (7).

THE '250' QUIZ CHALLENGE

61. With which club did goalkeeper Ray Clemence start his career before joining Liverpool?

FOOTBALL

WHO were England's scorers when England went a goal down to San Marino in the first minute of their 1994 World Cup qualifying match?

THE JUDGE: Ian Wright (4), Paul Ince (2), Les Ferdinand (1). England won 7-1 in front of 2,378 spectators in Bologna – the lowest crowd ever to watch England play. The opening goal by San Marino was scored in nine seconds, the quickest in World Cup qualifying-round history.

WITH all the millions being spent on players, has there ever been a post-war team that has won a major trophy and cost nothing?

THE JUDGE: Bolton were home-grown winners of the FA Cup in 1958. The team cost just £110. Each player, including skipper Nat Lofthouse, received a £10 signing-on fee.

HOW old was the great Welsh international Billy Meredith when he played his final game?

THE JUDGE: Meredith, the Stanley Matthews of his day, was 49 when he played his last game for Man City – an FA Cup semi-final against eventual Cup winners Newcastle in 1924.

WHICH club won the original Anglo-Italian Tournament, and did Blackpool ever win it?

THE JUDGE: Swindon Town (1970) were the first winners, and Blackpool won the tournament the following year.

WHO has been the oldest footballer, not including goalkeepers, to have played in the old First Division or Premiership?

THE JUDGE: Sir Stanley Matthews was 50 years and five days old when he played for Stoke City against Fulham on February 6 1965.

HOW many teams have won the FA Cup in successive seasons since the war?

THE JUDGE: The back-to-back double has been completed three times in post-war finals, first by Newcastle United (2-0 v Blackpool 1951, 1-0 v Arsenal 1952), and twice by Tottenham (2-0 v Leicester 1961, 3-1 v Burnley 1962, and 3-2 v Man City 1981, 1-0 v QPR 1982, both victories in replays).

THE '250' QUIZ CHALLENGE

62. What was the name of the Bolton Wanderers ground before they moved to the Reebok Stadium?

HOW much are referees paid in Premiership and Nationwide matches?

THE JUDGE: The match fee for a Premiership referee is £500. In the Nationwide he receives £210 per game.

WHICH two teams hold the League record for the highest scoring drawn match?

THE JUDGE: There have been two 6-6 draws – Leicester City v Arsenal in a First Division match on April 21 1930 (Dave Halliday scored four goals for Arsenal and was left out of the FA Cup Final team five days later); Charlton v Middlesbrough in a Second Division game on October 22 1960 (Brian Clough scored a hat-trick for Boro).

HAS a team in the Premiership or the old First Division ever scored more than 100 goals and also let 100 into their own net?

THE JUDGE: Manchester City managed this extraordinary double in the First Division in 1957-58 - scoring 104 and conceding 100. They finished fifth. Billy Wright's Wolves retained the title, scoring 103 goals and letting in just 47.

WHAT was David Hirst's League goal scoring record with Sheffield Wednesday?

THE JUDGE: He scored 106 goals in 261 League games, plus 33 appearances as a substitute between 1986 and 1997.

DID Manchester United take their place in the 1958 European Cup semi-final after the Munich air crash?

THE JUDGE: United had qualified for the semi-finals with a 3-3 draw against Red Star Belgrade, and it was on the way back from that match that they lost eight players in the Munich air disaster. Just weeks later, patched-up United beat AC Milan 2-1 in the first leg of the semi-final, but lost the return 4-0.

WHICH is the only team ever to have won the FA Cup and promotion in the same year?

THE JUDGE: West Bromwich Albion set this record in 1931, beating neighbours Birmingham City 2-1 in the FA Cup final and gaining promotion from the Second Division in the same season.

THE '250' QUIZ CHALLENGE

63. Who scored the goal for West Bromwich Albion when they won the FA Cup by beating Everton 1-0 at Wembley in 1968?

FOOTBALL

WHY do Italy wear blue shirts when their flag is red, white and green?

THE JUDGE: The tricolor was only adopted as the national flag after the Second World War. The football team stuck to the Azzurri blue of Savoia, the ruling house of Italy from 1861 to 1946.

IN which match did Steve McManaman make his England debut, and who was manager?

THE JUDGE: Terry Venables sent him on as substitute for injured Rob Lee against Nigeria at Wembley on November 16 1994. England won with a 40th minute headed goal by David Platt.

WOULD Man United have been relegated in 1974 even if Denis Law had not scored his famous back-heeled goal at Old Trafford?

THE JUDGE: Law's goal for Man City against Man United in the 82nd minute was the only goal of the match, which the referee abandoned following a pitch invasion by United fans. It was decided to let the result stand because relegation rivals Birmingham and West Ham won the necessary points to stay up.

HOW many League games did Clive Allen play for Arsenal?

THE JUDGE: None. Clive joined Arsenal from QPR for £1,250,000 in June 1980 as the first teenage million-pound footballer. He moved on to Crystal Palace in a £1,350,000-rated swap deal for Kenny Sansom two months later.

WHEN did Norwich City move to Carrow Road and who was their manager at the time?

THE JUDGE: A 29,779 crowd saw Norwich beat West Ham 4-3 in their first match at Carrow Road in the 1935-36 season. Former England right-back Tom Parker was their manager.

HOW many goals did Steve Bull score for England?

THE JUDGE: Four in 13 matches. Including a goal in his debut when coming on as a substitute for John Fashanu against Scotland at Hampden on May 27 1989. He also scored two against Czechoslovakia and another against Tunisia when coming on for Gary Lineker.

THE '250' QUIZ CHALLENGE

64. To which Spanish league club did Steve McManaman move from Liverpool?

71

WHICH Charlton footballer played for two teams in the same match?

THE JUDGE: Left-back Jimmy Oakes played for Port Vale against Charlton in a Second Division match on Boxing Day 1932. The game was abandoned in the second-half because of poor visibility, and by the time it was replayed Oakes had been transferred to Charlton.

WHO was the first England international transferred abroad?

THE JUDGE: Peter O'Dowd, an England international centre-half, and Chelsea clubmate Alec Cheyne moved to France in 1935 in protest at the £8-a-week maximum wage. There were no transfer fees paid, and both had a miserable time in pre-war France because of the poor rate of exchange. Neil Franklin was the most renowned of the rebel players who joined the outlawed Colombian league in 1950, but again there were no transfer fees involved. England team-mates Jimmy Greaves, Joe Baker and Gerry Hitchens all joined Italian clubs in the summer of 1961. Greavsie was the first to agree to a move, signing an option for a transfer from Chelsea to AC Milan on April 12 1961. They all followed in the footsteps of Welsh football king John Charles, who first joined Juventus in 1957.

HOW many League goals did Ralph Coates score for Spurs, and did he emigrate to Australia?

THE JUDGE: Ralph scored 14 goals in 188 League appearances for Spurs after joining them from Burnley for whom he netted 26 goals in 216 League games. He won two caps while with Burnley and another two with Tottenham. After a brief spell as a player in Australia, he returned to England to set up a catering business in Hertfordshire.

WHICH clubs have won the Premiership?

THE JUDGE: Man United (1992-93, 93-94, 95-96, 96-97, 98-99, 99-00, 2000-01), Blackburn (1994-95), and Arsenal (1997-98, 2001-02). Leeds were last winners of the old First Division in 1991-92.

FROM which club did Forest sign Stuart Pearce?

THE JUDGE: Pearce, who started his career with Wealdstone, joined Forest from Coventry in June 1985 for a £200,000 fee.

THE '250' QUIZ CHALLENGE

65. What was Stuart Pearce's nickname at the peak of his career, when his tackling was always firm bordering on fierce?

WHO was the first footballer to score a goal live on television?

THE JUDGE: There were several experimental broadcasts in Germany and England before the first major televised match. This was the 1937 FA Cup final in which Frank O'Donnell put Preston in the lead in the 38th minute. Sunderland came back to win 3-1. The BBC TV audience was estimated at 10,000.

DID Arsenal's Lee Dixon ever score for England?

THE JUDGE: Lee Dixon scored one goal in his 22 England appearances – in the 1-1 draw against the Republic of Ireland at Wembley on March 27 1991.

IN which match did Joe Mercer break a leg while making his final appearance for Arsenal, and who tackled him?

THE JUDGE: Joe broke his right leg in two places in a collision with Arsenal team-mate Joe Wade against Liverpool at Highbury on April 10 1954. While being carried off on a stretcher, 39-year-old Joe waved to the hushed 33,000 crowd who then gave him a roaring send-off as they realised that Joe was waving goodbye.

WHAT did an old-time footballer called Syd Puddefoot achieve?

THE JUDGE: East London-born Syd Puddefoot has legendary status at West Ham, with whom he started and finished his career either side of the First World War. He scored 87 goals in 150 League matches for the Hammers, and in between two spells with them played for Falkirk and Blackburn, helping Rovers beat Huddersfield in the 1928 FA Cup final. Capped twice by England, his transfer to Falkirk in 1922 was the first £5,000 deal.

WHO was England's third-choice goalkeeper in the 1970 World Cup finals?

THE JUDGE: The three goalkeepers in the 22-man squad were Gordon Banks, Peter Bonetti and Alex Stepney. Peter Shilton was called in as the fourth goalkeeper in the squad that travelled to Mexico in place of Everton's Gordon West who asked to be released. Shilts was one of the six players left out of the final pool.

THE '250' QUIZ CHALLENGE

66. Who were England's first opponents when they started their defence of the World Cup in Mexico in 1970?

DID Gary Lineker miss a penalty for Tottenham in the 1991 FA Cup final?

THE JUDGE: Lineker had a penalty saved by Nottingham Forest goalkeeper Mark Crossley, but had the consolation of finishing on the winning side thanks to an equalising goal by Paul Stewart and an own goal decider in extra-time by Des Walker.

HOW many of Tottenham's 1960-61 Double team were capped?

THE JUDGE: All but three. The team: Brown (Scotland), Baker, Henry (England), Blanchflower (NI), Norman (England), Mackay (Scotland), Jones (Wales), White (Scotland), Smith (England), Allen, Dyson. Reserves Terry Medwin and Mel Hopkins were also capped during a period when it was common for Spurs to have nearly their entire first-team squad on international duty.

DID Gary Mabbutt score an own goal in a Euro 92 qualifying match in Poland?

THE JUDGE: Poland's Szewczyk claimed the goal, although the ball deflected into the net off Mabbutt. Gary Lineker equalised to clinch England's place in the finals.

IS it true that Manchester United once bought a player in return for some ice-cream?

THE JUDGE: Stockport County received three freezers of ice-cream in exchange for amateur half-back Hugh McLenahan in 1927. The ice cream was sold to raise funds for the club.

WHAT was the real first name of Fatty Foulke, England's enormous goalkeeper in the 1890s?

THE JUDGE: William Henry Foulke weighed more than 20 stone during his peak playing years with Sheffield United and Chelsea. His other nickname was Little Willie. He was capped just once in 1897. He died in tragic circumstances, catching pneumonia while scraping a living as a penny-a-shot target at a Blackpool side show. He was 42.

WHEN was the first all-English £100,000 transfer deal?

THE JUDGE: Tony Hateley, father of Mark, joined Chelsea from Aston Villa for £100,000 in October 1966.

THE '250' QUIZ CHALLENGE

67. Which manager paid £100,000 to take Tony Hateley to Stamford Bridge from Villa Park?

DID ex-Luton midfielder Ricky Hill win full England international honours?

THE JUDGE: Hill was Bobby Robson's first new cap in 1982 and won his third and last cap three years later.

WHAT nationality was the great Alfredo di Stefano?

THE JUDGE: Argentinian-born Di Stefano took out Spanish citizenship while with Real Madrid and won 31 caps for Spain from 1957. He had earlier won three caps with Argentina and three with Colombia.

DID Alan Devonshire play in the West Ham team that won the FA Cup by beating Arsenal in 1980?

THE JUDGE: Devonshire did play in this line-up: Parkes, Stewart, Lampard, Bonds, Martin, Devonshire, Allen, Pearson, Cross, Brooking, Pike. Trevor Brooking headed the only goal of the game.

WAS Tony Kay or Roy Vernon captain of Everton when they won the League championship in 1963?

THE JUDGE: Welsh international Vernon was the skipper.

WHICH British players have been voted European Footballer of the Year?

THE JUDGE: Stanley Matthews (the first ever winner in 1956), Denis Law (1964), Bobby Charlton (1966), George Best (1968), Kevin Keegan (1978/79), Michael Owen (2001).

FROM which club did Chelsea buy that great ball player Charlie Cooke?

THE JUDGE: Chelsea manager Tommy Docherty bought Cooke from Dundee for £72,000 in April 1966. He came as a replacement for Terry Venables, who was sold to Tottenham.

WHERE was John Barnes born?

THE JUDGE: John was born in Jamaica on November 7 1963.

DID Jack Charlton and the great John Charles ever play in the same Leeds United team?

THE JUDGE: Yes, when Charlton first broke into the Leeds team in the 1950s and again when Charles briefly returned from Juventus.

THE '250' QUIZ CHALLENGE

68. With which club did John Barnes start his professional football career before joining Liverpool?

DID goalkeeper Alex Stepney ever play for Chelsea?

THE JUDGE: Alex played just one League game for Chelsea before moving to Manchester United for £55,000 in September 1966. He spent four months at Stamford Bridge after joining the Blues from Millwall. His departure to Old Trafford left Peter Bonetti as the undisputed number one Chelsea goalkeeper.

WAS John Charles the top scorer in the First Division when Leeds were relegated to the Second Division in the late 1950s?

THE JUDGE: Charles was never relegated with Leeds. He was with Juventus when Leeds went down in 1959-60. His record goal scoring season with Leeds was in 1953-54 when he netted 42 Second Division goals in 39 matches.

IS it correct that Jack Charlton retired from League football 20 minutes before his brother Bobby?

THE JUDGE: Both Bobby and Jack retired on the final Saturday of the 1972-73 season, April 28 1973. Bobby was playing his 606th League match for Man United at Chelsea and Jack number 629 for Leeds at Southampton (where he came off in the second-half with a pulled hamstring). Bobby later played 38 League games as player-manager of Preston.

FOR which League clubs did former England international Ronnie Allen play?

THE JUDGE: Port Vale, West Brom and Crystal Palace. He scored two goals in five England appearances, and netted two goals including a penalty in West Brom's 1954 3-2 FA Cup final victory over Preston.

WHAT was the League playing record of Clyde Best?

THE JUDGE: His only club was West Ham (186 League games and 47 goals between 1969 and 1975). Born in Bermuda, he was one of the first black players to make a major impact in the First Division.

WHO scored more goals for England out of Bryan Robson and Bobby Robson?

THE JUDGE: Bryan Robson scored 26 goals in 90 internationals, Bobby Robson four goals in 20 games.

THE '250' QUIZ CHALLENGE

69. Against which country did Bryan Robson score a hat-trick in an away international in 1984?

DID Reg Lewis score six goals for Arsenal in two Wembley cup finals?

THE JUDGE: Yes, if you include the 1943 wartime South League cup final. Lewis scored four goals in a 7-1 defeat of Charlton, and netted both Arsenal goals in the 1950 final against Liverpool.

WAS the 1966 World Cup televised in colour, and was it live on both BBC and ITV? If so, who were the commentators?

THE JUDGE: The match was shown live on both BBC and ITV in black and white. Kenneth Wolstenholme was the BBC commentator, and Hugh Johns was at the microphone for ITV. The only colour version was the official film called GOAL!

CONFIRM that Jackie Milburn scored a hat-trick for England in a World Cup match?

THE JUDGE: Wor Jackie scored three goals in England's 4-1 victory over Wales in the first ever World Cup qualifier played by British teams at Ninian Park in 1949.

FOR which clubs did Tommy Harmer play and was he ever capped?

THE JUDGE: Harmer 'The Charmer' played for Tottenham (205 League games), Watford (63) and Chelsea (8). This Tom Thumb of football, standing 5ft 6in tall and weighing under nine stone, was one of the most gifted ball players ever to appear in the League but his only international honours were at England-B level. He was famous for penalty kicks that he approached with a casual half moon walk before chipping the ball into the net.

HOW many times was Colin Grainger capped by England?

THE JUDGE: Colin, who was discovered playing for a Yorkshire colliery team, won seven caps while with Sheffield United and Sunderland, and scored three goals. He netted two goals in his debut against Brazil at Wembley in 1956 in a 4-2 victory. Colin later played for Leeds United, Port Vale and Doncaster Rovers. Away from the world of football, he was a popular nightclub singer.

THE '250' QUIZ CHALLENGE

70. At which First Division club did Jackie Milburn take over as manager in 1962-63?

DID Denis Law play three matches in a week at Wembley for Man United, Scotland and the Rest of the World?

THE JUDGE: The Rest of the World match against England was staged five months after Denis helped United win the 1963 FA Cup final against Leicester City.

WHAT was the line-up of Team America against England in the Bicentennial Tournament in Philadelphia in 1976, and who were the scorers?

THE JUDGE: England won 3-1. Scorers Keegan (2) and Francis. Stewart Scullion scored for Team America, who were captained by Bobby Moore. The team, made up of players from the North American Soccer League: Rigby, Smith (B), Jump, Eddy, England, Bobby Moore, Vee, Tommy Smith, Chinaglia, Pele, Clements. Subs: Kowalik, Scullion, Chandler.

IN how many Football League matches did cricketer Ian Botham play?

THE JUDGE: Botham made 11 League appearances in defence for Scunthorpe United between 1980 and 1984, four as substitute. He was offered a trial by Crystal Palace when a teenager, but preferred to concentrate on his cricket career with Somerset.

WHAT were the results of Manchester United's matches immediately before and after the Munich air disaster of February 6 1958?

THE JUDGE: The Busby Babes won a classic First Division match 5-4 against Arsenal at Highbury on February 1 1958. Team: Gregg; Foulkes, Byrne; Colman, Jones, Edwards; Morgans, Charlton, Tommy Taylor, Viollet, Scanlon. Their first match after the crash was a fifth round FA Cup tie in which they beat Sheffield Wednesday 3-0 at Old Trafford on February 19. Team: Gregg; Foulkes, Greaves; Goodwin, Cope, Crowther; Webster, Ernie Taylor, Dawson, Pearson, Brennan.

WHICH clubs did Herbert Chapman manage?

THE JUDGE: Northampton (player-manager 1907), Leeds City (1912), Huddersfield (1921, leading them to the FA Cup in 1922 and the start of their hat-trick of First Division titles in 1924), Arsenal (1925, dying in 1934 with the Gunners on the way to a hat-trick of First Division titles).

THE '250' QUIZ CHALLENGE

71. With which English League club did Denis Law make his League debut at the age of 16?

WHO scored Man United's first ever League goal under the management of Alex Ferguson?

THE JUDGE: Defender John Sivebaek in a 1-0 win over QPR at Old Trafford on November 15 1986.

WHEN and why was I'm Forever Blowing Bubbles adopted as the West Ham theme song?

THE JUDGE: It was an old music hall song popularised by a nationwide campaign for Pears soap. West Ham supporters picked on it as their anthem when following their team to the first FA Cup final at Wembley in 1923 ... when their bubble was burst by Bolton!

WHO was the first British footballer sold for a five-figure fee?

THE JUDGE: David Jack, when joining Arsenal from Bolton for £10,890 in October 1928. It took 11 hours to thrash out the deal, and it was the day they said that football had gone mad! With the rich full name of David Bone Nightingale Jack, he had the distinction of scoring the first goal in a Wembley final in 1923. He was a scheming and scoring inside-forward who was too much of an individualist for the taste of some selectors and he won only nine England caps, four of them as captain. Born in Southend-on-Sea, he joined Bolton from Plymouth where his father was the manager.

WITH which club did Neil Webb start his League playing career?

THE JUDGE: Webb followed his father as a professional at Reading, and then moved to Portsmouth before joining Forest for £250,000 in May 1985.

WITH which club did Ray Houghton make his League debut, and was he born in Ireland?

THE JUDGE: Houghton, born in Glasgow in 1962, moved to London with his Irish father when he was ten. He made his League debut as a substitute for West Ham, who gave him a free transfer after his one appearance in 1982. Malcolm Macdonald then signed him for Fulham, and he later played with distinction for Oxford United, Liverpool, Aston Villa, Crystal Palace, Reading and the Republic of Ireland.

THE '250' QUIZ CHALLENGE

72. Against which European country did Ray Houghton score a classic winning goal in Ireland's opening game of USA 94?

HOW many goalkeepers have been voted Footballer of the Year?

THE JUDGE: Four goalkeepers have won the coveted Football Writers' Association award: Bert Trautmann (1956), Gordon Banks (1972), Pat Jennings (1973) and Neville Southall (1985).

HAS any player won the World Cup both as a captain and as a manager?

THE JUDGE: Franz Beckenbauer completed this unique double when he managed the West Germany team that beat Argentina in the 1990 World Cup final in Italy. Sixteen years earlier he had skippered the West German side that beat Holland 2-1 in the 1974 final in Munich.

HOW many goals did England concede on the way to winning the World Cup in 1966?

THE JUDGE: Three. The first came from a Eusebio penalty in the semi-final against Portugal, and Helmut Haller and Wolfgang Weber scored for West Germany in the final. England's defence played in all six matches: Banks, Cohen, Wilson, Stiles, Jack Charlton, Moore.

WHICH FA Cup match has taken the longest to decide?

THE JUDGE: Alvechurch and Oxford City took six matches (11 hours) before Alvechurch went through after their 1972 qualifying round. In the competition proper, Stoke City went through at the fifth time of asking after 9 hours 22 minutes of a third round replay against Bury in 1955.

WHAT is the quickest hat-trick by an England player in a full international?

THE JUDGE: The record was set by Tottenham goal master Willie Hall, who completed a hat-trick in just three and a half minutes when playing for England against Ireland at Old Trafford on November 16 1938.

WAS the great Michel Platini French or Italian by birth?

THE JUDGE: Platini was born to Italian parents in Joeuf, France, on 21 June 1955. His father, Aldo, had emigrated to France as a maths teacher, but was drawn to his first love of football and he was the coach at Nancy when his son joined him first as an amateur and then professional. He became a star with St Etienne and then Juventus, where he was voted European Footballer of the Year for three successive seasons.

THE '250' QUIZ CHALLENGE

73. With which club was Pat Jennings playing when he was voted Footballer of the Year in 1973?

HOW many times was Frank McLintock on the losing side in Wembley finals?

THE JUDGE: I went to Frank McLintock for this answer: 'I lost twice with Leciester City in FA Cup finals and then in two League Cup finals with Arsenal. I was beginning to think I would never win there when I was privileged to captain the Arsenal team that clinched the double in the 1971 final against Liverpool. A year later we lost in the FA Cup centenary final against Leeds. I have to confess that Wembley was not my favourite ground!'

WHO scored the goals when England hammered Scotland 9-3 at Wembley in 1961?

THE JUDGE: Jimmy Greaves (3), Johnny Haynes (2), Bobby Smith (2), Bobby Robson and Bryan Douglas. Dave Mackay and Davie Wilson scored for the Scots to make it 3-2 just after half-time before Scotland's defence fell apart. The teams – England: Springett, Armfield, McNeil, Robson, Swan, Flowers, Douglas, Greaves, Bobby Smith, Haynes, Bobby Charlton. Scotland: Haffey, Shearer, Caldow, Mackay, McNeill, McCann, McLeod, Law, St John, Quinn, Wilson.

AGAINST which team did Ted MacDougall score nine goals in the FA Cup?

THE JUDGE: MacDougall's record nine goal haul was for Bournemouth against Margate in the first round of the FA Cup on November 20 1971. The individual record for a preliminary round of the FA Cup is 10 goals by Chris Marron for South Shields against Radcliffe in 1947.

WHAT has been the greatest number of spot-kicks needed to decide a penalty shoot-out in Britain?

THE JUDGE: This was in a Freight Rover Trophy quarter-final (Southern section) between Aldershot and Fulham on 10 February 1987. It took 28 alternate penalties, with just seven missed, before Aldershot finally won 11-10.

HAS there ever been a crowd of less than 5,000 to watch an international football match in Britain?

THE JUDGE: The lowest attendance was the 2,315 spectators who paid to watch Wales v Northern Ireland at the Racecourse Ground, Wrexham on 27 May 1982.

THE '250' QUIZ CHALLENGE

74. With which club was Ted MacDougall playing when he won his seven Scottish international caps?

WHO was manager of Arsenal when they signed Charlie Nicholas?

THE JUDGE: Terry Neill was in charge at Highbury when Nicholas joined Arsenal from Celtic for £750,000 in June 1983.

WHICH footballer was first to win the PFA Player of the Year award?

THE JUDGE: This honour went to Leeds United defender Norman 'Bites Yer Legs' Hunter when the award was first introduced in 1974.

WAS Ruud Gullit ever the captain of the Dutch international team?

THE JUDGE: Gullit skippered the Dutch team that won the European Championship in 1988. He was elected European Footballer of the Year in 1987, and was a key man for AC Milan when they captured the European Cup in 1989.

IS it right that John Aldridge started his League career in Wales?

THE JUDGE: Aldridge was a full-time toolmaker and a part-time player with South Liverpool when Newport County launched his professional career in 1979. He scored 69 goals for Newport and then 72 League goals for Oxford before returning home to Liverpool in 1987. Aldridge filled in for Ian Rush with 50 goals, and then added 23 to his collection during a spell with Real Sociedad. He later topped a century of goals at Tranmere to join the exclusive club of players who have broken the 300 goal barrier.

HOW old was Trevor Francis when he made his debut, and for how many clubs did he play?

THE JUDGE: Francis made his debut for Birmingham City at the age of 16, and two months before his 17th birthday he scored four goals in a League game against Bolton. His clubs: Birmingham City (1970-79), Nottingham Forest (1979-81), Manchester City (1981-82), Sampdoria (1982-86), Atalanta (1986-87), Glasgow Rangers (1987-88), Queen's Park Rangers (1988-90). He played 29 full League games as player-manager of Sheffield Wednesday, and made another 47 appearances as substitute.

THE '250' QUIZ CHALLENGE

75. Which England manager selected Trevor Francis for his international debut against Holland in 1977?

DID Brian Clough sign Francis Lee when he joined Derby County?

THE JUDGE: No. Dave Mackay had taken over from Clough as manager and bought Lee from Manchester City. He linked up with another Mackay signing, Bruce Rioch, and between them they scored 27 goals in the 1974-75 season as Derby recaptured the League title won three years earlier by Clough's team.

WHICH non-League side once put six goals into the Derby County net in an FA Cup tie?

THE JUDGE: Boston United, fielding six former Derby players, beat Third Division Derby 6-1 in an FA Cup second round tie at the Baseball Ground in December 1955. Ex-Derby striker Geoff Hazeldine scored a hat-trick, and Boston right winger Reg Harrison had helped Derby win the Cup nine years earlier.

DID Ferenc Puskas win an Olympic gold medal with Hungary?

THE JUDGE: Puskas captained the team that beat Yugoslavia in the 1952 Olympic final in Helsinki. The following year he skippered the 'Magical Magyars' side that hammered England 6-3 in their first ever defeat at Wembley.

FOR which overseas clubs did Mark Hughes play?

THE JUDGE: Two – Barcelona and Bayern Munich (on loan) before his return to Manchester United, who sold him to Barcelona for £2.3 million in 1986.

HOW old was Stan Collymore when he made his League debut?

THE JUDGE: Collymore, born in Stone in 1971, had been released by Wolves and was playing non-League football with his local Stafford club when discovered by Crystal Palace, who gave him his first League game at the age of 20 in a goalless draw with QPR. Palace sold him to Southend for £100,000 after one goal in 20 League games. Then 15 goals in 30 games attracted Nottingham Forest, who bought him for £200,000 in 1993 before selling him to Liverpool for an £8.3 million profit in 1995.

THE '250' QUIZ CHALLENGE

76. Which club did Mark Hughes join after scoring a goal against them in an FA Cup final at Wembley?

DID Gary Lineker ever miss from the penalty spot while playing for England?

THE JUDGE: Yes, in his 76th appearance for England. He needed one goal to equal Bobby Charlton's all-time record of 49 goals for England when he missed his spot-kick against Brazil at Wembley on May 17 1992. His international career ended four matches later when pulled off by manager Graham Taylor in the Euro 92 match against Sweden. Lineker was left stranded on 48 England goals.

WHY was Arsenal and England winger Cliff Bastin known as 'Boy'?

THE JUDGE: It was a nickname that stuck from when he won every honour in the game while still in his teens. 'Boy' Bastin, who joined Arsenal from his local club Exeter City, had won five League championship medals, two FA Cup winners' medals and 21 England caps when his career was halted by the Second World war. He was still only twenty-seven. A fast, direct outside-left who was equally adept at inside-forward, Bastin scored 156 goals in 367 League games – a prodigious scoring rate for a winger.

HOW many goals did Wolves striker Steve Bull score for England?

THE JUDGE: Four in 13 matches, including a goal in his debut when coming on as a substitute for John Fashanu against Scotland at Hampden Park on May 27 1989. He was the first Third Division player capped since Peter Taylor in 1976.

WHAT was the longest that Gary Lineker went without scoring a goal for England?

THE JUDGE: Lineker had a run of seven barren matches from June 1988 until April 1989. He ended his drought with a headed goal against Albania in a World Cup qualifying match at Wembley. He also laid on two goals for Peter Beardsley in the 5-0 victory.

WITH which club was striker Cyrille Regis playing before starting his League career?

THE JUDGE: Regis was discovered playing for Hayes in the Isthmian League. West Bromwich Albion bought him for £5,000 in 1977.

THE '250' QUIZ CHALLENGE

77. With which club did Midlands favourite Steve Bull start his Football League career?

DID Vinnie Jones ever play for an overseas club?

THE JUDGE: Jones had a season on loan with Swedish club IFK Holmsund before joining Wimbledon from Wealdstone for £10,000 at the start of his League career in 1986.

DID Brian McClair start his career with Aston Villa?

THE JUDGE: Brian joined Villa straight from school, but returned to Scotland after a year to study for a maths degree at Glasgow University. He made his Scottish League debut with Motherwell before going on to greater things with Celtic and Manchester United. He scored two goals in 30 international appearances for Scotland.

WITH which club was Dean Saunders playing when he made his international debut for Wales?

THE JUDGE: Saunders was playing for Third Division Brighton when he made his first appearance for Wales as a substitute against the Republic of Ireland in 1986.

HAS any player been leading scorer in successive seasons in the top two divisions?

THE JUDGE: Kerry Dixon went one better, top scoring in three successive seasons – with Reading in the Third Division in 1982-83 and then with Chelsea in the following two seasons in the Second and old First Division.

WERE Rangers or Celtic founded first?

THE JUDGE: Rangers were founded in 1873, Celtic in 1887. In their first official match in May 1888, Celtic beat Rangers 5-0.

WHO has been the oldest man to captain a World Cup winning team?

THE JUDGE: Goalkeeper Dino Zoff was 40 years and three months old when he captained the Italian team that beat West Germany 3-1 to win the 1982 World Cup final in Madrid.

WHAT is the biggest attendance for an FA Cup final away from Wembley?

THE JUDGE: The crowd record was set in 1913 when 120,081 jammed Crystal Palace to see Aston Villa beat Sunderland 1-0.

THE '250' QUIZ CHALLENGE

78. With which club did goalkeeper Dino Zoff win six Italian league championships?

DID Graeme Souness play League football for Spurs?

THE JUDGE: No. Souness served his apprenticeship with Tottenham, but was impatient for first-team football. Jack Charlton took him to Middlesbrough for £30,000 in 1973 and within two years he had won a place in Scotland's team.

HOW many times did Liverpool win the old Football League First Division championship?

THE JUDGE: Liverpool had a record 18 League championship triumphs: 1901, 1906, 1922, 1923, 1947, 1964, 1966, 1973, 1976, 1977, 1979, 1980, 1982, 1983, 1984, 1986, 1988 and 1990.

WERE the two John Astons who played for Manchester United related?

THE JUDGE: John Aston was a Manchester United inside-forward who was converted into a full-back by Matt Busby. He won 17 England caps in the immediate post-war years, and later became chief scout at Old Trafford. His son, Johnny, was a winger who played a prominent role in United's 1968 European Cup winning team.

WHEN were three points for a win first introduced to League football, and which club had most points under the old two-points system?

THE JUDGE: The three-points system started in the 1981-82 season. The record of 67 points under the old two-point system was set over 42 games by Don Revie's Leeds United in 1968-69. They were unbeaten at home, winning 18 and drawing three of their matches at Elland Road. They lost just twice away, winning nine times and drawing ten games. Liverpool were six points behind in second place.

HOW many goals did Oleg Blokhin score during his peak years in Soviet football?

THE JUDGE: A star with Dynamo Kiev, Oleg became the Soviet Union's top goalscorer of all time with 302 goals, as well as scoring a record 44 goals in 108 internationals. Voted European Footballer of the Year in 1975, he featured in the World Cups of 1982 and 1986 and in 1988 was allowed to transfer to Austria's Vowarts Steyr. He eventually ended his career in Cyprus.

THE '250' QUIZ CHALLENGE

79. Which Portuguese team did Graeme Souness manage before returning to British football with Blackburn Rovers?

FOOTBALL

HAVE any former Fulham players managed the England football team?

THE JUDGE: Two – Ron Greenwood and Bobby Robson. Greenwood joined Fulham from Chelsea and played with Bobby Robson and Jimmy Hill in the Johnny Haynes inspired Fulham team of the 1950s.

DID Emlyn Hughes win a League Cup medal with Liverpool before joining Wolves?

THE JUDGE: No. Hughes was in the Liverpool team beaten 1-0 by Nottingham Forest in the 1978 League Cup final two years before leading Wolves to victory over Forest at Wembley in the 1980 final.

WHO was capped more times by England – Emlyn Hughes or Kevin Keegan, and which of them captained England most times?

THE JUDGE: Hughes won 62 caps (1969-80) and skippered England in 23 matches. Keegan collected 63 caps (1972-82), and captained the team in 29 international games.

DID Tom Finney play in all five forward positions for England?

THE JUDGE: Sir Tom won 40 caps at outside-right, 33 at outside-left and three at centre-forward. In one match he switched to inside-forward because a team-mate was injured. He was a one-club loyalist with Preston, playing in all forward positions while scoring 187 goals in 433 League games. Sir Tom netted 30 goals in his 76 England games.

HOW many times did the Charlton brothers play together for England?

THE JUDGE: Alf Ramsey picked them together in 28 international matches between 1965 and 1970, and they were on the losing side during this sequence just twice – v Austria 1965 and Scotland 1967.

TRUE or false: Johan Cruyff was signed by Ajax on the recommendation of his mother?

THE JUDGE: True. His mother was a cleaner at the Ajax stadium, and persuaded the club coaching staff to take her twelve-year-old son on their coaching staff.

THE '250' QUIZ CHALLENGE

80. Which England manager awarded Kevin Keegan his last international cap?

87

WITH which club did Danny Blanchflower start his career?

THE JUDGE: Belfast-born Danny began his career with the Irish dub Glentoran in 1945 and transferred to Barnsley in 1949 (in which year he also made his international debut for Northern Ireland). In 1951 he moved to Aston Villa and switched to Tottenham in 1954 remaining there until his retirement as a player in 1964. He skippered the Spurs side that won the League and FA Cup double in 1960-61, a second FA Cup in 1962 and the European Cup-Winners' Cup in 1963. He was voted Footballer of the Year in 1958 and 1961 and collected what was then a record 56 Northern Ireland international caps. He later established himself as a distinguished sports columnist with the *Sunday Express* before briefly managing Chelsea. His brother Jackie played for Manchester United until his career was ended by injuries received in the Munich air disaster.

EXACTLY how far out was David Beckham when he scored his famous long range goal against Wimbledon?

THE JUDGE: The Sky TV computer showed that Becks was 57.4 yards from goal when the Manchester United midfielder launched his dipping shot from just inside his own half. The stunning goal was scored on the opening day of the 1996-97 season.

FOR which clubs did Eric Cantona play before joining Manchester United?

THE JUDGE: Auxerre, Bordeaux, Montpellier, Marseille, Nimes and Leeds. He was offered a trial by Sheffield Wednesday before joining Leeds from Nimes for £900,000 on Februrary 6 1992, and switched to Manchester United for £1,200,000 on November 27 1992.

WITH which club did David Platt start his career?

THE JUDGE: Platt was an apprentice with Manchester United, but he was released before making it into the first-team and signed on a free transfer with Crewe in January 1985. He later travelled the football roundabout with Aston Villa, Bari, Juventus, Sampdoria and Arsenal for total transfer fees of around £22m. He wound down his playing career as player-manager of Nottingham Forest before taking on the job of England Under-21 manager.

THE '250' QUIZ CHALLENGE

81. On which ground did David Beckham score from the halfway line on the opening day of the 1996-97 season?

DID Franz Beckenbauer play for any club side other than Bayern Munich?

THE JUDGE: 'Kaiser Franz' was with Bayern from his youth days in 1959 until his retirement from international football in 1976 after winning 103 caps. He then played for New York Cosmos for four years before retiring in 1980, eventually becoming the World Cup winning manager of West Germany in 1990 and then the overall supremo of German football.

HOW many times did the Charles and Allchurch brothers appear together for Wales?

THE JUDGE: John and Mel Charles and Ivor and Len Allchurch appeared together in the same Welsh international team on three occasions, the first against Northern Ireland at Windsor Park, Belfast, on 20 April 1955. The Allchurch brothers played together for Wales in eight matches, and the Charles brothers were in the same Welsh team on fifteen occasions.

DID Les Ferdinand win any club honours while playing club football in Turkey?

THE JUDGE: Ferdinand collected a Turkish Cup final winners medal while on loan to Besiktas from QPR in 1988-89. He had been bought from Hayes for £15,000 in 1987, and Rangers made a huge profit when selling him to Newcastle for £6 million in 1995. He also had a three-match loan period with Brentford before he established himself as one of the most potent strikers in the League.

HOW old was Dennis Bergkamp when he made his first-team debut for Ajax?

THE JUDGE: Bergkamp was seventeen and still at school. He sat school examinations in the morning and then in the afternoon travelled to join the Ajax team for a European Cup tie against Malmo the next day. His parents were Manchester United fans and named their son after their hero, Denis Law.

WHO was the last player before Arsenal's Freddie Ljungberg to score in back-to-back FA Cup finals?

THE JUDGE: This was last achieved by centre-forward Bobby Smith for Tottenham against Leicester City (1961) and Burnley (1962).

THE '250' QUIZ CHALLENGE

82. For which club was Mel Charles playing when he won the first of his Welsh international caps?

DID Billy Bremner and Don Revie ever play together in the same Leeds United team?

THE JUDGE: Billy made his Leeds debut as a winger at the age of seventeen in 1959 alongside player-manager Don Revie, who was twice his age. Over the next 15 years Bremner was to become Revie's right-hand man and loyal captain.

WHO has been the youngest player capped by each of the home countries in the last 100 years?

Michael Owen, Liverpool (England, 18 years 59 days v Chile February 11 1998); Norman Whiteside, Manchester United (Northern Ireland, 17 years 42 days v Yugoslavia, June 17 1982); Denis Law, Huddersfield Town (Scotland, 18 years 235 days v Wales, October 18 1958); Ryan Giggs, Manchester United (Wales, 17 years 332 days v Germany, October 16 1991). Michael Owen took over from Duncan Edwards (18 years 183 days v Scotland, April 2 1955) as England's youngest modern international. James Prinsep (17 years 252 days v Scotland, April 5 1879) was the youngest England cap of all time.

WHY was Tom Finney known as the 'Preston Plumber'?

THE JUDGE: Sir Tom was called the Preston Plumber because throughout his career with Preston (187 goals in 433 League games) and beyond he ran a family plumbing and electricians' business.

IS it true that Brazil's Garrincha had two left feet?

THE JUDGE: Garrincha, a nickname meaning Little Bird, was crippled by polio when he was a child and his right leg was so badly twisted that surgeons feared he would never walk properly. An operation left him needing to wear two left boots. Garrincha (real name Manoel Francisco dos Santos) was deadly with both of them. He won the first of his 51 Brazilian caps in 1955, and was a key player in the World Cup triumphs of 1958 and 1962. Sadly, he led a reckless life off the pitch and died of alcohol poisoning at the age of 49.

WHO was the first England player to score from the penalty spot at Wembley?

THE JUDGE: Alf Ramsey, scoring the first of England's goals in a 2-2 draw with Austria on November 28 1951.

THE '250' QUIZ CHALLENGE

83. For which club did Billy Bremner play 61 League games after leaving Leeds United?

HOW many European Cup goals did Tommy Gemmell score for Celtic?

THE JUDGE: Eight, which was a remarkable haul for a full-back. The most memorable was the equaliser that he blasted against Inter Milan in the 1967 European Cup final which set Celtic up for a 2-1 victory and the honour of becoming the first British club to win the European Cup. He also scored against Feyenoord in the final three years later when Celtic were beaten 2-1.

HAS any player won more than five European Cup winners' medals?

THE JUDGE: The record is six, set by Real Madrid's flying left winger Fancisco Gento. He won them all with Real, along with twelve Spanish championship medals during an 800-game career in which he scored 256 goals. Gento had a long-running partnership on the left of the Real attack with José Hector Rial, and they rivalled Puskas and Di Stefano with their contribution to the team.

WHAT was John Greig's record with Rangers?

THE JUDGE: Greig played a club record 496 League matches for Rangers between 1962 and 1978. He established himself as one of Scotland's greats as a commander in midfield and defence. He was a driving captain for much of his sixteen years at Ibrox, and helped steer Rangers to the European Cup Winners' Cup finals of 1967 (beaten 1-0 by Bayern Munich) and 1972 (beat Moscow Dynamo 3-2). Greig played 44 times for Scotland and was an inspirational skipper. Scottish Footballer of the Year in 1966 and again in 1976, he later had a brief but relatively unsuccessful spell as manager at Ibrox.

WHAT record did Peterborough United set when gaining promotion from the Fourth Division in 1960-61?

THE JUDGE: It was their first season in the Football League and they won the Fourth Division championship with a record haul of 134 goals. Centre-forward Terry Bly scored 52 of them.

WHO was first to miss an FA Cup final penalty?

THE JUDGE: Charlie Wallace, for Aston Villa against Sunderland in the 1913 final at Crystal Palace. Villa won 1-0. Sunderland won the League championship, with Villa runners-up.

THE '250' QUIZ CHALLENGE

84. Which Football League club in the Midlands did Tommy Gemmell join from Celtic in December 1971?

WAS Bobby Moore included in the England line-up when they were beaten by Poland in the 1973 World Cup qualifier at Wembley?

THE JUDGE: England were not beaten, but the 1-1 draw was enough to eliminate them from the World Cup. Bobby Moore was on the bench having been dropped after his mistake had cost England a goal during the defeat in Poland. Team: Shilton, Madeley, McFarland, Hunter, Hughes, Bell, Currie, Peters (capt.), Channon, Chivers (Hector), Clarke. England's goal came from an Allan Clarke penalty on a night when they missed a hatful of chances and saw goalkeeper Tomaszewski pull off a dozen world-class saves. TV pundit Brian Clough famously dismissed him as a clown. England had 35 goal attempts to two by Poland.

HOW many sons have followed their father into the England international football team?

THE JUDGE: Three: George Eastham snr and George Eastham jnr, Brian Clough, Nigel Clough, Frank Lampard snr, Frank Lampard jnr.

HAS Alan Shearer scored most hat-tricks in a season in the Premiership or old post-war First Division?

THE JUDGE: Shearer scored a Premier record five hat-tricks for Blackburn in 1995-96, one behind the old post-war First Division record set by *Sun* columnist Jimmy Greaves for Chelsea in 1960-61.

FOR which clubs did Simon Stainrod play and was he ever capped by England?

THE JUDGE: Simon played for Sheffield United, Oldham, QPR, Sheffield Wednesday, Aston Villa, Stoke, Strasbourg, Falkirk and Dundee. He was capped at England youth team level.

HOW many players have been sent off playing for England, and does the list include Kevin Keegan?

THE JUDGE: Eight have been sent off in full internationals: Alan Mullery (v Yugoslavia, 1968), Alan Ball (v Poland, 1973), Trevor Cherry (v Argentina,1977), Ray Wilkins (v Morocco, 1986), David Beckham (v Argentina, 1998), Paul Ince (v Sweden, 1998), Paul Scholes (v Sweden, 1999), David Batty (v Poland, 1999). Keegan was sent off in an Under-23 match in East Germany in 1972.

THE '250' QUIZ CHALLENGE

85. For which club was Alan Mullery a key midfield player when he became the first player sent off in an England shirt?

WHO scored the goals for Manchester United in their first match after the Munich air crash on February 6 1958?

THE JUDGE: United's first match after Munich was a home fifth round FA Cup tie against Sheffield Wednesday on February 19 1958. Youth team full-back Shay Brennan, playing as an emergency outside-left, scored two goals and Alex Dawson one in a 3-0 victory.

WHO scored more goals for England, David Platt or Martin Peters?

THE JUDGE: Platt scored 27 goals in 62 international appearances, and Peters netted 20 goals in his 67 games.

WHAT happens when a team has had players sent off and the game comes down to penalty deciders?

THE JUDGE: The new rule is that "when a team finishes a match with a greater number of players than their opponents, they must reduce their numbers to equate with that of the other team."

HOW many League appearances did Derek Forster make in goal for Sunderland after his debut at 15, and with which other League clubs did he play?

THE JUDGE: Derek played for Sunderland after winning an England schoolboys cap. He appeared in 18 League games for the Wearsiders before briefly playing for Charlton in 1973 and Brighton in 1974.

DID Ian Storey-Moore ever play for Spurs?

THE JUDGE: Ian Storey-Moore played for Nottingham Forest and Man United. Ian Moores joined Tottenham from Stoke in 1976.

IS it correct that Duncan Edwards once scored more than three goals in a match while wearing an England shirt?

THE JUDGE: Duncan, playing as an emergency centre-forward for 10-man England, had the ball in the net four times during a 6-0 thrashing of Scotland in an Under-23 international in Glasgow on February 8 1955. Two months later, at 18, the Man United idol made his full England debut at left-half in a 7-2 victory over Scotland at Wembley.

THE '250' QUIZ CHALLENGE

86. Against which country did David Platt score with a last-minute volley during Italia 90?

WERE Arsenal ever relegated from the old First Division?

THE JUDGE: Arsenal, then known as Woolwich Arsenal, were relegated in 1912-13. They were re-elected to the First Division as plain Arsenal in the first season after the 1914-18 war, and have been in the top division ever since.

HOW many League games did former Scotland and Celtic skipper Bobby Evans play for Chelsea?

THE JUDGE: Centre-half Bobby joined Chelsea from Celtic in 1960 and played 32 First Division matches before winding down his career with Newport.

WHERE did QPR finish each season that they were in the Premier Division?

THE JUDGE: 1992-93 (5), 1993-94 (9), 1994-95 (8), 1995-96 (19).

HAVE England ever fielded a team with all five forwards having a surname beginning with 'M'?

THE JUDGE: Nearest to it was four when England beat Norway 4-1 in Oslo in 1949. The forward line read: Finney, Morris, Mortensen, Mannion, Mullen. It needed Matthews to complete a full house!

WHEN were squad numbers introduced into English football?

THE JUDGE: They were introduced at the start of the 1993-94 season by the Premier League, and were optional in the Football League until made compulsory in 1999-2000. Players wore names as well as numbers on their shirts for the first time in the 1993 Coca-Cola Cup and FA Cup finals, both featuring Arsenal against Sheffield Wednesday.

DID those two English football legends Jackie Milburn and Nat Lofthouse ever appear together in the same England attack?

THE JUDGE: Just once, in a 5-1 victory over Denmark in Copenhagen on October 2 1955. Lofty led the attack and scored one goal. Wor Jackie played on the right wing. Don Revie netted a hat-trick, and Bristol Rovers inside-left Geoff Bradford marked his one and only international with the fifth and final goal.

THE '250' QUIZ CHALLENGE

87. With which European city is Nat Lofthouse forever linked because of his hard-earned nickname?

FOOTBALL

DID ex-Arsenal goalkeeper Bob Wilson ever wear an England jersey?

THE JUDGE: Chesterfield-born Bob played for England schoolboys before preferring to follow his father's allegiance to Scotland. He was capped twice by the Scots while at Highbury.

WHICH player has been the most successful from the penalty spot in post-war League football?

THE JUDGE: Francis Lee scored 13 out of 13 penalties awarded to Manchester City in the First Division in 1971-72. His team-mates nicknamed him Lee One Pen.

WHICH post-war footballer played most games at Wembley?

THE JUDGE: Goalkeeper Peter Shilton made 57 Wembley appearances – 52 England matches, two League Cup finals, one FA Cup final, one Charity Shield match and a game with a Football League representative side.

WHAT is the record attendance for any match involving British clubs?

THE JUDGE: Celtic and Leeds United were watched by a crowd of 135,826 in the second leg of their European Cup semi-final at Hampden Park on April 15 1970. The aggregate attendance for the two legs was 181,331.

IN their three post-war FA Cup Final appearances, have West Ham ever fielded a non-English player?

THE JUDGE: West Ham used 30 different players in their three FA Cup final triumphs in 1964, 1975 and 1980. All but Scottish full-back Ray Stewart in the 1980 final were English.

HAS any British-born footballer played in the European Cup flnal for different clubs?

THE JUDGE: There have been two. Frank Gray was a runner-up with Leeds against Bayern Munich in 1975 and collected a winners' medal with Nottingham Forest against Hamburg in 1980. Kevin Keegan was a winner with Liverpool against Borussia Moenchengladbach in 1977, and a runner-up with Hamburg three years later.

THE '250' QUIZ CHALLENGE

88. Against which team did Bob Wilson collect an FA Cup winners' medal at Wembley in 1971?

THE JUDGE

WITH which clubs has Sir Alex Ferguson been involved as a player and manager?

THE JUDGE: Sir Alex, an aggressive centre-forward, played for Queen's Park (1958-60), St Johnstone (1960-64), Dunfermline Athletic (1964-67), Rangers (1967-69), Falkirk (1969-73), Ayr United (1973-74). He has managed East Stirling (1974), St Mirren (1974-78), Aberdeen (1978-86) and Man United (1986-).

WHY are Norwich City known as The Canaries?

THE JUDGE: Their former ground was The Nest, which was carved out of an old chalk pit. This coupled with their yellow and green shirts brought them their nickname. They moved to Carrow Road in 1935.

WHICH Hughes won most international caps - Mark for Wales or Emlyn for England?

THE JUDGE: Emlyn was capped 62 times. Mark won 72 caps before taking over as manager of Wales.

WHICH teams were involved in the first Football League match played on a Sunday?

THE JUDGE: Millwall beat Fulham 1-0 at The Den on Sunday January 20 1974 during a power crisis that caused a fixture pile-up. The following week Darlington became the first club to play back-to-back weekend League matches – against Stockport on the Saturday and then Torquay on the Sunday.

WHEN did Stanley Matthews make his international debut?

THE JUDGE: Sir Stanley made his England debut at the age of 19 in a 4-0 victory over Wales in Cardiff on September 29 1934. It was the start of a 54-match career spanning 22 years, and not including 29 unofficial wartime internationals.

WHO has scored the quickest Premiership goal?

THE JUDGE: Ledley King scored with a deflected shot after 10 seconds for Tottenham at Bradford on December 9 2000. The previous record of 13 seconds was shared by Chris Sutton (for Blackburn at Everton, April 1 1995) and Andy Cole (for Man United at Nottingham Forest, February 6 1999).

THE '250' QUIZ CHALLENGE

89. With which club did England international striker Chris Sutton start his League playing career?

HAS any team ever gone through a Premiership or old First Division season undefeated?

THE JUDGE: Only two clubs have gone through a season unbeaten: "Proud" Preston in the old First Division in 1888-89 (22 matches) and Liverpool in the old Second Division in 1893-94 (28 matches).

WHAT has been the smallest recorded attendance for a Premiership match?

THE JUDGE: Just 3,039 turned out to watch Wimbledon play Everton at Selhurst Park on January 26 1993.

WHY do Juventus players have two stars on their shirts?

THE JUDGE: Any club that wins 10 Italian league championships is awarded a star. Juventus have achieved this twice and have achieved 25 title triumphs in all. If the idea was taken up in England, Liverpool, Man United and Arsenal would have a star each.

AGAINST which countries did Gary Lineker score international hat-tricks?

THE JUDGE: Turkey twice (1985 and 1987), Poland (1986 World Cup finals), Spain (four goals in Madrid, 1987) and Malaysia (four goals in Kuala Lumpur, 1991).

FOR which League clubs did the England amateur international goalkeeper Mike Pinner play?

THE JUDGE: Aston Villa (4 matches), Sheffield Wednesday (7), QPR (19), Man United (4), Chelsea (1), Swansea (1) and Leyton Orient, as a professional (77).

NOT including own goals or replays, has any player scored two goals in an FA Cup final at Wembley and finished on the losing side?

THE JUDGE: It has happened twice - Stuart McCall for Everton against Liverpool in 1989, and Ian Wright for Crystal Palace against Man United in 1990.

WHICH British clubs have won the European Cup in back to back seasons?

THE JUDGE: Bob Paisley's Liverpool (1977/78) and Brian Clough's Nottingham Forest (1979/80)

THE '250' QUIZ CHALLENGE

90. Who was Liverpool skipper when they won their first ever European Cup final in Rome in 1977?

WHAT were the line-ups of the England teams that went down to two heavy defeats against the Hungarians in the 1950s?

THE JUDGE: At Wembley on November 25 1953 (lost 6-3): Merrick, Ramsey, Eckersley, Wright, Johnston, Dickinson, Matthews, Ernie Taylor, Mortensen, Sewell, Robb. In Budapest on May 23 1954 (lost 7-1): Merrick, Staniforth, Byrne, Wright, Owen, Dickinson, Harris, Sewell, Jezzard, Broadis, Finney.

HOW many goals in total did Dixie Dean score in his record-breaking season of 1927-28?

THE JUDGE: Dixie scored a total of 82 goals that season – 60 in 39 First Division matches, three in FA Cup ties and 19 in representative games.

WHAT is the highest number of goals scored before half-time in a Football League or FA Cup match?

THE JUDGE: Tottenham 10, Crewe Alexandra 1 in a fourth round FA Cup replay at White Hart Lane on February 3 1960 is the record. Spurs eventually won 13-2. Chester City set a League record when leading York City 8-0 at half-time in a Third Division North match on February 1 1936, going on to win 12-0.

HAS any English manager other than Alf Ramsey guided a team to the World Cup final?

THE JUDGE: George Raynor led host country Sweden to the 1958 final in which they were beaten 5-2 by Pele-inspired Brazil. Raynor was a Yorkshireman who had been a winger with Rotherham and Aldershot before becoming one of Europe's most respected coaches.

WHO was the goalkeeper involved when George Best had a goal turned down against England after kicking the ball out of his hands?

THE JUDGE: Gordon Banks was in goal for England at Windsor Park on May 15 1971. He was attempting a clearance when the quick-witted Best flicked the ball away from him and into the net. The referee disallowed the goal, much to Best's disgust, and England went on to win the match 1-0.

THE '250' QUIZ CHALLENGE

91. How many World Cup finals matches did England goalkeeper Gordon Banks play in total?

SINCE England first entered the World Cup competition in 1950 how many times have they failed to qualify for the finals?

THE JUDGE: England failed to make it to the finals in 1974 (West Germany), 1978 (Argentina) and 1994 (United States).

WHERE and when did goalkeeper Pat Jennings score against Manchester United?

THE JUDGE: It was at Old Trafford in the August 1967 Charity Shield match, which ended Man United 3, Tottenham 3. Jennings, with the wind behind him, hammered a huge clearance downfield that went first bounce over the head of United goalkeeper Alex Stepney and into the net. Most of the Spurs players had their backs to Jennings and had no idea who had scored!

WHO was the manager who took Coventry City to the top division?

THE JUDGE: Jimmy Hill took Coventry from the Third to the First Division during five years in charge of the Sky Blues. He quit on the eve of their 1967-68 debut season in the First Division to move full-time into television. Noel Cantwell was his successor.

WHAT was the name of the white horse on which the policeman cleared crowds from the Wembley pitch so that the 1923 FA Cup final could go ahead?

THE JUDGE: Pc George Scorey was riding Billy. This first Wembley final between Bolton and West Ham was watched by a crowd of more than 180,000, with 126,047 paying to get in.

FOR which clubs did Henrik Larsson play before joining Celtic?

THE JUDGE: Larsson played in Sweden for Hogaborg and Helsingborgs before moving to Dutch club Feyenoord in 1993. He signed for Celtic in 1997.

WHERE do Anderlecht play their home matches?

THE JUDGE: Royal Sporting Club Anderlecht are at home at the Constant Vanden stadium in Brussels. The ground is named after a billionaire brewer.

THE '250' QUIZ CHALLENGE

92. In which World Cup finals tournament did Pat Jennings make his 119th and last appearance for Northern Ireland?

HOW did Newell Old Boys in the Argentine league get their name?

THE JUDGE: In 1884, Kent-born English teacher Isaac Newell started a boarding school in Rosary where his son, Claudius, formed a football team. Soccer was then known in Argentina as "the crazy English game". Newell Old Boys, officially founded in 1905, developed into one of the country's major clubs.

WHICH was the first British team to win a domestic match using the penalty shoot-out system.

THE JUDGE: Man United were the first winners of a British penalty shoot-out – in the Watney Cup semi-final against Hull City in August 1970. George Best was the first player to score, Denis Law the first to miss!

WHAT was Ian Wright's longest run without scoring for England?

THE JUDGE: Ian Wright went his first nine matches without finding the back of the net. He scored his first England goal against Poland in a World Cup qualifier on May 29 1993 and finished with nine goals in 33 internationals.

WHO have been Manchester City's managers since 1970?

THE JUDGE: Joe Mercer (1965-71), Malcolm Allison (1972-73/79-80), Johnny Hart (1973), Ron Saunders (1973-74), Tony Book (1974-79), John Bond (1980-83), John Benson (1983), Billy McNeill (1983-86), Jimmy Frizzell (1986-87), Mel Machin (1987-89), Howard Kendall (1990), Peter Reid (1990-93), Brian Horton (1993-95), Alan Ball (1995-96), Steve Coppell (1996), Frank Clark (1996-98), Joe Royle (1998-2001) and Kevin Keegan.

DID David Seaman ever play in goal for Leeds United in a League game?

THE JUDGE: Rotherham-born Seaman started his career at Leeds but did not make his League debut until joining Peterborough in 1982. He later played for Birmingham and QPR before signing for Arsenal for £1.3 million in 1990.

THE '250' QUIZ CHALLENGE

93. Against which country did Ian Wright score four goals in a World Cup qualifying match?

AFTER Neil Franklin had been banned for playing 'outlawed' football in Bogota, how many centre-halves were tried by England before settling on Billy Wright?

THE JUDGE: Eleven - Bill Jones (Liverpool, 2 caps in the No 5 shirt). Laurie Hughes (Liverpool, 3), Allenby Chilton (Man U, 2), Leslie Compton (Arsenal, 2), Jack Froggatt (Portsmouth, 9), Jim Taylor (Fulham, 2), Malcolm Barrass (Bolton, 3), Harry Johnston (Blackpool, 5), Derek Ufton (Charlton, 1), Harry Clarke (Tottenham, 1), Syd Owen (Luton, 3). Wright won 46 of his 105 caps at centre-half.

WHO was Manchester United's goalkeeper in the 1948 FA Cup final?

THE JUDGE: Jack Crompton, who later became a trainer at Old Trafford. United twice came from behind to beat Blackpool (including Matthews and Mortensen) 4-2 in one of the great finals.

WHO had the best English League goal-scoring record out of Gary Lineker, Ian Wright and Ian Rush?

THE JUDGE: Ian Rush 246 goals (14 for Chester, 229 for Liverpool and 3 for Leeds), Ian Wright 235 (89 for Crystal Palace, 128 for Arsenal, 9 for West Ham, 5 for Nottingham Forest, 4 for Burnley), and Gary Lineker 192 (95 for Leicester, 30 for Everton and 67 for Spurs).

DID Denis Compton play fewer than 100 Football League games for Arsenal?

THE JUDGE: Because of cricketing commitments, the intervention of the war and the famous knee injury, Denis played just 54 League games for Arsenal over a span of 14 years. In wartime matches for the Gunners he scored 74 goals in 126 matches, helping them win the Regional League three times. He represented England in 14 wartime internationals, but never in a peacetime match.

WHAT was the England team that played Italy in the 1976 World Cup qualifier in Rome?

THE JUDGE: England, beaten 2-0, lined up in this 4-4-2 formation: Clemence; Clement (Beattie), Hughes, McFarland, Mills; Greenhoff, Bowles, Cherry, Brooking; Keegan, Channon. England won the return match 2-0 at Wembley in 1977, but failed to qualify for the 1978 finals.

THE '250' QUIZ CHALLENGE

94. With which Football League club did striker Ian Rush start his goal-scoring career?

WHAT is the worst start a League championship winning team has made to a season?

THE JUDGE: Sunderland lost five and drew two of their first seven matches in 1912-13 and went on to win the League title by winning 25 of the remaining 31 games.

WHEN West Ham played Fulham in the 1975 FA Cup final Is it true that all the players involved were English born?

THE JUDGE: All but Fulham's Dublin-born Jimmy Conway and Malta-born John Cutbush.

FOR which clubs did Peter Brabrook play, and did he represent England in any World Cup finals match?

THE JUDGE: Right winger Peter played for Chelsea, West Ham and Orient. He won three caps, making his debut in England's 1958 World Cup finals play-off defeat by Russia in Sweden.

WHERE and when did George Best score his first and last League goals for Manchester United, and how many League goals did he score in total?

THE JUDGE: George scored the first of his 137 League goals for Man United against Burnley at Old Trafford on September 14 1963. His final League goal for United was in a home match against Coventry on December 15 1973. He also scored for Stockport (2), Fulham (8) and Hibs (3), and added another 40 goals while playing in the USA.

AGAINST which team did Ryan Giggs score his first League goal for Man United, and how old was he?

THE JUDGE: His first goal came in the Manchester derby against City at Old Trafford on May 4 1991. It was the first match in which 17-year-old Giggs had started after one brief appearance as a substitute.

WHEN did players start wearing numbered shirts in English football?

THE JUDGE: Players wore numbered shirts in the 1931 FA Cup final between Everton (1 to 11) and Manchester City (12-22). It was 1939 before numbering was made compulsory.

THE '250' QUIZ CHALLENGE

95. Where did Sunderland play their home matches before moving to the Stadium of Light?

EXCLUDING replays, which player has appeared in most Wembley FA Cup finals?

THE JUDGE: Eight players share the record with five FA Cup finals at Wembley: Joe Hulme (Arsenal, Huddersfield), Johnny Giles (Man United, Leeds), Pat Rice (Arsenal), Frank Stapleton (Arsenal, Man United), Ray Clemence (Liverpool, Spurs), Mark Hughes (Man United, Chelsea), John Barnes (Watford, Liverpool, Newcastle), Roy Keane (Nottm Forest, Man United).

WHICH player created the post-war record for most League goals in a Scottish season before the New Millennium?

THE JUDGE: Joe Baker with 42 goals in 33 games for Hibernian in Scottish League Division 1, in 1959-60. Joe won the first of his eight England caps while playing for Hibs, and was the first player selected for England from a club outside the Football League.

HOW many European cup medals did Phil Neal win during his career?

THE JUDGE: Liverpool's loyal right-back won four European Cup medals (76-77, 77-78, 80-81, 83-84) and one in the UEFA Cup (75-76). He also collected eight League Championship medals and 50 England caps.

HAS any team ever finished runners up for the League championship in three successive seasons?

THE JUDGE: It has happened four times: Preston North End (1891-1893); Manchester United (1947-1949), Leeds United (1970-1972) and Arsenal (1999-2001).

WHICH were the original Premiership clubs?

THE JUDGE: The 22 clubs when the Premier League kicked off in 1992-93 were, in the order that they finished: Man United, Aston Villa, Norwich City, Blackburn Rovers, QPR, Liverpool, Sheffield Wednesday, Tottenham, Manchester City, Arsenal, Chelsea, Wimbledon, Everton, Sheffield United, Coventry City, Ipswich Town, Leeds United, Southampton, Oldham Athletic, Crystal Palace, Middlesbrough, Nottingham Forest.

THE '250' QUIZ CHALLENGE

96. From which then Fourth Division club did Phil Neal join Liverpool in 1974 after playing 187 League games?

THE JUDGE

HAS any English club ever fielded an all-Scottish team?

THE JUDGE: Liverpool fielded an all-Scottish eleven in their first-ever match in 1892 following their acrimonious split with Everton. John McKenna, the club's first manager, went north of the border for players and picked an all-Scottish team for the match against Higher Walton on September 3 1892.

DID Chelsea manager Gianluca Vialli ever select a team without a single British player?

THE JUDGE: Yes, on Boxing Day 1999, the Chelsea starting line-up at Southampton was: De Goey, Ferrer, Babayaro, Thome, Leboeuf, Petrescu, Poyet, Deschamps, Di Matteo, Flo, Ambrosetti. Two first-half goals from Flo lifted Chelsea to a 2-1 victory that was celebrated in a multitude of tongues!

IS it true that a Liverpool player once scored a hat-trick of penalties?

THE JUDGE Jan Molby slotted home all three Liverpool goals from the penalty spot in a 3-1 victory over Coventry in November 1986. The match was a Littlewoods Cup fourth round replay.

HAS a player-manager ever guided a team to the Premiership or old First Division championship?

THE JUDGE: Kenny Dalglish had this distinction in 1985-86 when he succeeded Joe Fagan as the Anfield boss. He not only guided Liverpool to the League championship but also to the FA Cup. His contribution on the pitch included 17 League appearances (four as substitute) and three goals, and on the way to Wembley in the FA Cup he scored one goal and played the full 90 minutes of the final in which Liverpool beat deadly rivals Everton 3-1. They ended their double season with 11 First Division victories in 12 games, and not surprisingly Kenny Dalglish was voted Manager of the Year. Winning the Double was an achievement that eluded all his predecessors, including Bill Shankly and Bob Paisley.

WHO scored the first hat-trick in the Premiership?

THE JUDGE: Eric Cantona, who scored three goals for Leeds United in a 5-0 win against Tottenham at Elland Road on the Tuesday evening of August 25 1992.

THE '250' QUIZ CHALLENGE

97. With which Italian club did Gianluca Vialli collect a European Cup winners' medal as a player?

FOOTBALL

WHO was the last English manager to win a major football trophy in the 20th Century?

THE JUDGE: This honour went to Brian Little, who guided Aston Villa to a 3-0 victory over Leeds in the 1996 Coca-Cola Cup final. Howard Wilkinson was the last English manager to lift the League championship with Leeds in 1992.

HAVE Arsenal or Everton spent the longest time in the top division?

THE JUDGE: Arsenal, re-elected to the First Division in the first season after the 1914-18 war, have had the longest run in the top table, but Everton have spent the most seasons at the highest level. They were founder members of the League in 1888 and have played only four seasons outside the top division (1930-31 and 1951-54).

WHICH FA Cup giant-killings have caused the biggest shocks?

THE JUDGE: This is subjective, and depends on your allegiance. For instance, I doubt if Liverpool fans have yet recovered from their 1988 FA Cup final defeat by Wimbledon; and Leeds supporters must still shake their heads in disbelief over Sunderland's 1-0 defeat of Don Revie's mighty team at Wembley in 1973. My top dozen early-round giant killings, based on the shock they caused at the time, would be: Walsall 2, Arsenal 0 (1933), Yeovil 2, Sunderland 1 (1949), Derby County 1, Boston United 6 (1956), Bournemouth 3, Tottenham 1 (1957), Wolves 0, Bournemouth 1 (1957), Norwich City 3, Man United 0 (1959), Chelsea 1, Crewe 2 (1961), Colchester 3, Leeds 2 (1971), Hereford 2, Newcastle 1 (1972), Bournemouth 2, Man United 0 (1984), Chorley 3, Wolves 0 (1987), Wrexham 2, Arsenal 1 (1992).

WAS Peter Taylor ever capped by England?

THE JUDGE: Peter was the first Third Division player capped by England (1976) since Johnny Byrne (1961), both of them with Crystal Palace. He was awarded four caps in all during Don Revie's reign as manager, and became the first player to score while making his debut as a substitute (a 2-1 victory over Wales on May 24 1976). He played for six League clubs: Southend, Palace, Tottenham, Leyton Orient, Oldham and Exeter before starting a managerial career.

THE '250' QUIZ CHALLENGE

98. Which former England centre-forward scored two goals for Colchester in their 1971 giant-killing of Leeds?

105

THE JUDGE

HAS there ever been a match without a single corner kick?

THE JUDGE: Newcastle against Portsmouth in the First Division in December 1931 finished cornerless and goalless.

WHICH Ipswich Town goalkeeper was known as the Penalty King?

THE JUDGE: Paul Cooper, who saved eight of the ten penalties he faced in the 1979-80 season. Notts County goalkeeper Roy Brown saved six penalties in a row in 1972-73. The non-league record is eight successive penalty saves by Andy Lomas for Chesham United across two seasons in 1991-93.

WHICH Football League club has had the most penalty misses in a season?

THE JUDGE: Southend United will be hard to beat. They missed seven successive penalties between 1990 and 1991, straddling two seasons.

DID Ron Atkinson ever play in the First Division and which clubs has he managed?

THE JUDGE: Ron was an apprentice with Aston Villa and played all his League football with Oxford United (384 League matches from 1962 to 1971). He was player-manager of Kettering Town and subsequently managed Cambridge United, West Bromwich Albion (two spells), Manchester United, Atletico Madrid, Sheffield Wednesday (two spells), Aston Villa, Coventry, and finally Nottingham Forest. He retired from management in May 1999 to concentrate full-time on his job as an ITV summariser.

WHO has scored the quickest hat-trick in the Football League?

THE JUDGE: Former Spurs inside-forward Jimmy Scarth scored three goals in two-and-a-half minutes for Gillingham against Leyton Orient in a Third Division South match on November 1 1952.

WHAT is the Football League record for the most successive drawn matches?

THE JUDGE: Torquay United set the record in 1968-69 with eight successive drawn Third Division matches.

THE '250' QUIZ CHALLENGE

99. Against which team did Ron Atkinson, in his role as manager, lead Manchester United to an FA Cup final victory at Wembley?

FOOTBALL

HAS an England player scored a hat-trick in successive international matches?

THE JUDGE: Dixie Dean is the only player to have achieved this while wearing an England shirt. The power-propelled Everton centre-forward scored hat-tricks in successive matches on the 1927 summer tour against Belgium (9-1) and Luxembourg (5-2). Dixie scored 18 goals in 16 Internationals. The following season he scored his all-time record 60 goals in a First Division season.

WAS there a match in the 1990s in which all six goals were headers?

THE JUDGE: This was the Second Division match between Oxford United and Shrewsbury Town on April 23 1996. Oxford won 6-0 with headed goals from Paul Moody (2), Stuart Massey, David Rush, Joey Beauchamp and Matt Murphy.

WHAT is the longest run of Football League games a team has gone without scoring a goal?

THE JUDGE: Coventry City and Hartlepool share the record with eleven successive blanks, Coventry set the record in 1919-20 in the Second Division, and Hartlepool equalled it in 1992-93. Including an FA Cup tie and a match in the Autoscreen Trophy, Hartlepool's run stretched to 13 games without scoring.

HAVE the three clubs promoted together to the Premiership all been relegated back to Division One a year later?

THE JUDGE: Yes, Bolton, Barnsley and Crystal Palace went up in 1997 and came down together at the end of the following season.

IS it true that Arsenal goalkeeper Jack Kelsey once played two games in one day, including an international?

THE JUDGE: Jack kept goal for Wales in a 2-2 draw with England at Villa Park on the afternoon of November 26 1958, and in the evening played for Arsenal against Juventus in a floodlit friendly at Highbury.

WHO was the youngest captain to collect the FA Cup?

THE JUDGE: Bobby Moore, who was 23 years 20 days old when he captained West Ham to their 1964 victory over Preston.

THE '250' QUIZ CHALLENGE

100. Who did West Ham beat in a classic European Cup-Winners' Cup final at Wembley in 1965?

WHAT is England's longest sequence without a victory?

THE JUDGE: Six matches between April and June 1993 when Graham Taylor was in charge. England drew 2-2 against Holland (Wembley), drew 1-1 against Poland (Katowice), then lost 2-0 against Norway (Oslo), all in World Cup qualifiers. They followed this with a 2-0 defeat by the United States in Boston, a 1-1 draw with Brazil in Washington and then a 2-1 defeat by Germany in Detroit.

WHAT have been the most goals scored on any one Saturday in the Football League?

THE JUDGE: A total of 209 goals were scored in 44 League matches on Saturday February 1 1936. Three players scored four goals each and there were nine hat-tricks. Chester beat York 12-0, and Chesterfield won 6-5 at Crewe!

WHO has scored the fastest ever goal?

THE JUDGE: Jim Fryatt claimed a goal in four seconds for Bradford Park Avenue against Tranmere in a Fourth Division match on April 25 1965. But he was tortoise-paced compared with a goal in 2.8 seconds by Argentinian Ricardo Olivera in December 1998. He collected the ball from the kick-off and shot into the net from the halfway line.

HAS any goalkeeper won more caps than the 125 collected by England's Peter Shilton?

THE JUDGE: Swedish goalkeeper Thomas Ravelli won 143 caps between 1981 and 1997. Lothar Matthaus overtook Ravelli as the most capped player of all time with 150 caps for Germany.

WHO was Kevin Keegan playing for when he was elected European Footballer of the Year?

THE JUDGE: Kevin is the only English player to win back-to-back European Footballer of the Year awards, each time with SV Hamburg in 1978 and 1979.

WHICH countries were the founder members of FIFA?

THE JUDGE: Belgium, Denmark, France, Holland, Spain, Sweden and Switzerland started the ball rolling in 1904. There are now more than 200 member countries. The Home Countries refused to join until 1948 following a drawn-out dispute over payment to amateurs.

THE '250' QUIZ CHALLENGE

101. Which club did Kevin Keegan join from SV Hamburg?
YOU CAN CHECK YOUR RATINGS ON PAGE 222

BOXING

WHICH boxer has recorded most knockout victories during his career?

THE JUDGE: Archie Moore knocked out 145 of his 234 opponents, but these are knockouts in the American sense and not necessarily ten-second kayos. In a career spanning more than 20 years he won another 54 contests on points and drew eight. The 'Old Mongoose' was world light-heavyweight champion for ten years.

WHICH heavyweight fighter holds the record for most consecutive knockouts?

THE JUDGE: Lamar Clark, from Cedar City, Utah, scored 44 straight knockouts against a procession of hand-picked opponents. His run finally ended in 1960 when he was stopped in ten rounds by 1956 Olympic champion Pete Rademacher. Clark was then pitched against an up-and-coming prospect from Louisville, Kentucky, called Cassius Clay. He knocked Clark out in the second round to register his sixth professional victory.

WHAT was the ring record of Dick McTaggart, and did he turn professional?

THE JUDGE: McTaggart, winner of the best stylist award when capturing the gold medal in the 1956 Olympic lightweight division, lost just 24 of 634 contests over a span of more than 20 years. He did not box professionally.

WHO was the heavyweight boxer known as the Wild Bull of the Pampas?

THE JUDGE: Luis 'Angel' Firpo, who famously knocked Jack Dempsey out of the ring before being stopped in two rounds in a savage world title fight in New York in 1923. The Argentinian had been floored six times and then knocked the champion through the ropes in a crazy first round. Press reporters helped a dazed Dempsey back into the ring and he flattened Firpo in the second round.

THE '250' QUIZ CHALLENGE

102. Which opponent did Archie Moore stop in ten rounds in his only world title defence in London in 1956?

WAS referee Roy Francis a member of the British amateur boxing team that beat the United States 10-0? What was the line-up?

THE JUDGE: Francis was an outstanding amateur but was not in the team that white-washed the Americans at Wembley on November 2 1961. The team: Alan Rudkin (flyweight), Peter Bennyworth (bantam), Frankie Taylor (feather), Dick McTaggart (light), Brian Brazier (light-welter), Jim Lloyd (welter), Derek Richards (light-middle), John Fisher (middle), Dennis Pollard (light-heavy), Billy Walker (heavy). Roy Francis, a southpaw from Brixton, knocked American Golden Gloves champion Frankie Davis cold in the first round of their televised contest at Wembley on October 25 1955. It helped the ABA team beat the USA 7-3.

DID Randolph Turpin ever fight Don Cockell, and if so was there a title at stake?

THE JUDGE: Turpin stopped Cockell in 11 rounds in a British and Commonwealth light-heavyweight title fight at London's White City on June 10 1952.

WHEN was the last scheduled 20-rounds world heavyweight championship contest?

THE JUDGE: Joe Louis knocked out Abe Simon in the 13th round of a world title fight scheduled for 20 rounds in Detroit on March 21 1941.

HOW many fights did Mike Tyson win before his first defeat, and how many opponents did he stop?

THE JUDGE: Tyson won 37 fights (33 inside the distance) before his first defeat on a 10th round knockout by James 'Buster' Douglas in Tokyo on February 11 1990.

DID Lennox Lewis ever appear in a British ring as an amateur?

THE JUDGE: Yes, when winning the Commonwealth Games heavyweight title for Canada in Edinburgh in 1986.

DID Bruce Woodcock ever fight Tommy Farr?

THE JUDGE: No. Tommy had retired by the time Bruce was at his peak, and Bruce had retired when Tommy made his 1950s comeback.

THE '250' QUIZ CHALLENGE

103. In which city did Lennox Lewis stop Frank Bruno in seven rounds in their WBC world heavyweight title fight in 1993?

WHERE and when did Kirkland Laing beat Roberto Duran?

THE JUDGE: Kirkland outpointed the legendary Duran over ten rounds in Detroit on September 4 1982.

WAS Marvin Hart ever officially recognised as the heavyweight champion of the world?

THE JUDGE: The 'Punching Plumber' from Kentucky was nominated to fight for the title by retiring champion James J. Jeffries, who refereed his fight with Jack Root for the vacant championship in Reno in 1905. Hart won on a 12th round knockout, but did not have universal recognition as champion. He was outpointed by Canadian Tommy Burns in his first defence.

HOW many opponents did Muhammad Ali stop inside the distance, and who beat him?

THE JUDGE: Ali won 37 of his 61 contests inside the distance. His five defeats were by Joe Frazier (lost points 15), Ken Norton (lost points 12), Leon Spinks (lost points 15), Larry Holmes (lost retired 11) and Trevor Berbick (lost points 10). Only Holmes stopped him and he reversed the defeats by Frazier, Norton and Spinks.

WHICH boxers managed to put Muhammad Ali on the canvas during his professional career?

THE JUDGE: Ali was on the canvas four times, against Sonny Banks, Henry Cooper, Joe Frazier and Chuck Wepner. Ali disputed the Wepner knock down and later produced photographic evidence to show that he had been tripped.

WHAT were the second names of world champions Randolph Turpin, Bob Fitzsimmons and Max Baer ... and were there fighters called Honey Mellody and Mysterious Billy Smith?

THE JUDGE: Turpin – Adolphus; Fitzsimmons – James; Baer – Adalbert. William (Honey) Mellody was world welterweight champion in 1906, and Amos (Mysterious Billy) Smith held the title at the turn of the century. He was called Mysterious because few had heard of him when he emerged as a world title challenger in the 1890s.

THE '250' QUIZ CHALLENGE

104. In which round did Muhammad Ali beat British lionheart Richard Dunn in their 1976 world title fight in Munich?

HOW many times did Sugar Ray Leonard and Roberto Duran face each other, and who won the contests?

THE JUDGE: They met twice for the world welterweight title in 1980, Duran winning on points over 15 rounds and then Sugar Ray getting revenge with an eighth round stoppage. Leonard won on points in a third fight over 12 rounds on December 7 1989 for the WBC super-middleweight title.

HOW many times did Marvin Hagler and Sugar Ray Leonard fight each other?

THE JUDGE: Once, Leonard scoring a hotly disputed 12 rounds points victory in Las Vegas on April 6 1987. It was Hagler's final fight.

WHICH heavyweight boxer had the nickname the Eastern Assassin?

THE JUDGE: Larry Holmes was known as the Easton Assassin, on account that he was based in Easton, Pennsylvania. His other nickname was Black Cloud.

HOW many times was Herbie Hide on the canvas when he had his one and only fight in the United States?

THE JUDGE: Hide defended his WBO title against Riddick Bowe in Las Vegas on March 10 1995. He was counted out in the sixth round on his ninth visit to the canvas.

WHO was the opponent when Muhammad Ali kept asking "What's ma name?" in a fight for the undisputed world championship?

THE JUDGE: It was Ernie Terrell. Ali outpointed him over 15 one-sided rounds at Houston on February 6 1967.

AT what weight did Jimmy Wilde fight?

THE JUDGE: Wilde, the Ghost with a Hammer in His Hand, never weighed more than eight stone, and was officially world flyweight champion from 1916 to 1923. The Mighty Atom from Tylorstown in Glamorgan conceded weight nearly every time he stepped into the ring, but had such shuddering power that he stopped 101 of his 153 professional opponents.

THE '250' QUIZ CHALLENGE

105. At which weight was Sugar Ray Leonard a gold medallist in the 1976 Olympics in Montreal?

PLEASE confirm that Sugar Ray Robinson won world titles at three different weights.

THE JUDGE: Sugar Ray was world welter and middleweight champion (a title he won five times), but failed in a bid for the world light-heavyweight championship when he collapsed through heat exhaustion after 13 rounds against Joey Maxim in New York in 1952.

ON the night that Randolph Turpin took the world middleweight title from Sugar Ray Robinson who won the Jack Solomons heavyweight novices competition?

THE JUDGE: Worcester heavyweight Ted Morgan, who had three one-round victories against Frank Elrington, Francis Zibai and Johnny Apee. In his next contest at Wembley, Morgan was outpointed by Fred 'Nosher' Powell.

WHAT were the circumstances surrounding the death of former world heavyweight champion Sonny Liston?

THE JUDGE: Sonny was found dead in his Las Vegas apartment on January 5 1971, and was believed to have died a week earlier. There were traces of drug substances in his blood, but the coroner ruled that death was due to lung congestion. Rumours persist to this day that he had been 'eliminated' by gangster associates.

DID 1930s film star Victor McLagen fight Jack Johnson for the world heavyweight title?

THE JUDGE: Irishman McLaglen once went the distance in a non-title fight with Jack Johnson before switching to a career as a film actor in Hollywood. He won an Oscar in 1935 for his performance in The Informer.

WHAT did the initial 'L' stand for in John L. Sullivan?

THE JUDGE: His full name was John Lawrence Sullivan.

DID the great Sugar Ray Robinson win any of his fights in Britain?

THE JUDGE: Sugar Ray stopped Nigerian Johnny Angel in six rounds at the opening show of the Anglo-American Sporting Club at the London Hilton Hotel in 1964. He had previously lost on points to Randolph Turpin (1951), Terry Downes (1962) and Mick Leahy (1964).

THE '250' QUIZ CHALLENGE

106. What was the London venue for the fight in which Randolph Turpin took the world middleweight title from Sugar Ray Robinson?

IS it true that Pete Rademacher challenged Floyd Patterson for the world heavyweight championship in his professional debut?

THE JUDGE: Rademacher was 1956 Olympic heavyweight champion, and in his first professional fight on August 22 1957 he was knocked out in six rounds by Patterson, defending his world crown.

WAS Marvin Hagler undefeated when he took the world middleweight title from Alan Minter in 1980?

THE JUDGE: Hagler had been beaten twice in 53 professional fights – 10 rounds points defeats in 1976 by Bobby Watts and Willie Monroe. He avenged both defeats.

DID Glen Murphy, star of London's Burning, ever box as a professional?

THE JUDGE: Glen represented England as an amateur while with the famous Repton Boxing Club, but never boxed for pay. His father, Terence, was a Southern Area middleweight champion.

HOW long did Max Schmeling reign as the world heavyweight champion?

THE JUDGE: Two years, 9 days – from 12 June 1930 (won the title on a disqualification against Jack Sharkey) until 21 June 1932 (outpointed over 15 rounds by Sharkey). He made one successful defence, stopping Young Stribling in the 15th round in Cleveland on July 3 1931.

IS it right that Brian London once beat the great American light-heavyweight Willie Pastrano

THE JUDGE: London stopped Pastrano in five rounds in London on September 30 1958, seven months after the American had won their first fight on points. Pastrano won the world light-heavyweight championship in 1963.

WHAT were the results of the Riddick Bowe/Evander Holyfield world title fights?

THE JUDGE: Bowe won the first on points (1992), Holyfield the return on points (1993), and Bowe stopped Holyfield in the eighth round of the rubber match (1995).

THE '250' QUIZ CHALLENGE

107. In which round did Max Schmeling knock out Brown Bomber Joe Louis in their first contest?

IS it right that Brian London knocked out Ingemar Johansson and ended his career?

THE JUDGE: It's right but wrong! London landed with a thumping right just before the end of the last round of their fight in Stockholm in 1963. Johansson crashed to the canvas, and the referee was taking up the count when the bell rang. Ingemar, named as the 12 rounds points winner, never fought again.

CONFIRM that Brian London fought both Billy Walker and Joe Bugner.

The JUDGE: London outpointed Walker over 10 rounds in 1965, and - like Henry Cooper - hung up his gloves after losing to Bugner. He was stopped in the fifth round at Wembley in 1970.

HOW many defeats did Jack Dempsey suffer apart from the two by Gene Tunney, and did he ever fight Jack Johnson?

THE JUDGE: As well as two ten rounds points defeats by Tunney, Dempsey was beaten four times in 79 contests by Jack Downey (points 4, 1915), Fireman Jim Flynn (ko 1, 1917), Willie Meehan (points 4, 1917 and 1918). He did not fight Jack Johnson.

WHERE was Bob Fitzsimmons born and what was the name of the knockout punch that he developed?

THE JUDGE: Fitzsimmons was born at Helston, Cornwall, in 1863 and moved to New Zealand at the age of eight. He won the world heavyweight title in 1897 when he knocked out James J. Corbett in the 14th round with a corkscrew right to the body that became known as the 'solar plexus' punch.

DID Henry Cooper take a count in either of his two fights against Muhammad Ali?

THE JUDGE: Sir Henry was never off his feet. He was stopped on cuts in the fifth round of their first meeting at Wembley in 1963 after dropping Ali at the end of the fourth with his left hook. Ali, then known as Cassius Clay, was on the floor with the count at four when the bell rang. Henry was again stopped on cuts in the sixth round of their world title fight at Highbury football stadium in 1966.

THE '250' QUIZ CHALLENGE

108. Under which name was Brian London boxing when he won the ABA heavyweight championship in 1954?

DID Rocky Marciano and Muhammad Ali, then Cassius Clay, ever meet in the ring?

THE JUDGE: Only in a computerised fight staged for the film cameras with Rocky wearing a wig to make him look younger. He died in an air crash just before the film was released in 1969. The producers shot three different endings to the fight, and the one shown to the public had Rocky winning by knockout in the 13th round.

HOW many times did Nigel Benn and Chris Eubank fight each other, and what were the results?

THE JUDGE: They met twice, Eubank winning the first on a ninth round stoppage in Birmingham on November 18 1990. They drew the return over 12 rounds at Manchester on October 9 1993.

HOW many times has Lennox Lewis fought Riddick Bowe?

THE JUDGE: Once, in the 1988 Olympic super-heavyweight final when Lewis stopped Bowe in the second round.

IS it right that Jack Johnson was knocked down in a world heavyweight title fight by world middleweight champion Stanley Ketchel?

THE JUDGE: It's true, but Ketchel (the Michigan Assassin) quickly regretted it. He and Johnson were pals and had agreed to a distance fight in 1909. Ketchel went back on his word and floored Johnson with a sneak right hand in the 12th round. Johnson leapt straight up and knocked Ketchel cold with a right that was so hard that his opponent's front teeth were lodged in his glove. A year later Ketchel was shot dead by a jealous farmhand whose girl he had been eyeing. His manager Joe O'Connor said: "Just count over Stanley...he'll get up. That's for sure." He was world middleweight champion at the time of his death.

HOW many times was Floyd Patterson knocked down during his professional career?

THE JUDGE: 'Freudian' Floyd was knocked down more times than any other heavyweight champion, 16 in all including seven times in the third round of his first fight with Ingemar Johansson and four times in two fights with Sonny Liston that both ended in the first round.

THE '250' QUIZ CHALLENGE

109. In which round did Floyd Patterson knock out Ingemar Johansson to regain the world heavyweight title in 1960?

WHICH world heavyweight champion has had most successful title defences?

THE JUDGE: Joe Louis, who made 25 consecutive defences of his title between 1937 and 1949, a record stretch of 11 years seven months.

HAS any boxer fought in all the main weight divisions?

THE JUDGE: Georges Carpentier, the Orchid Man, started his career as an eight-stone flyweight and ended his career as a heavyweight. He won the world light-heavyweight title and challlenged Jack Dempsey for the world heavyweight championship, going down to a fourth round defeat after having his jaw broken.

WHICH fights have drawn the biggest crowds?

THE JUDGE: 1. Tony Zale v. Billy Pryor 135,132 (an eliminator for the world middleweight title in Milwaukee, 1941); 2. Julio Cesar Chavez v. Greg Haugen 132,274 (world light-welterweight title fight in Mexico City 1993); 3. Gene Tunney v. Jack Dempsey 120,757 (their return world heavyweight title fight in Chicago, 1927, that became famous as the Battle of the Long Count).

WHO has been the youngest fighter to win a world title?

THE JUDGE: Wilfred Benitez, who was 17 years and 3 months old when he outpointed Antonio Cervantes over 15 rounds to win the world light-welterweight title in his 26th fight in 1976. He turned professional at the age of 15.

WHO was ahead on points when Joe Frazier retired at the end of the 14th round of his 'Thriller in Manila' with Muhammad Ali?

THE JUDGE: The judges' scorecards at the time of the stoppage had Ali winning comfortably with scores of 166-160, 166-162, 167-162.

WHICH British champion was known as Smiler?

THE JUDGE: This was Sammy McCarthy, an East End idol of the 1950s who always smiled in the ring whether winning or losing. A true sportsman and gentleman of the ring, Sammy took the British featherweight title from Blackpool's Ronnie Clayton in 1954 and six years later as a manager steered the Golden Boy Terry Spinks to the same nine-stone crown.

THE '250' QUIZ CHALLENGE

110. Which British boxer did Wilfred Benitez knock out in the 12th round when challenging for the world light-middleweight title?

HOW many boxers did British manager Terry Lawless guide to world titles?

THE JUDGE: Four – John H. Stracey, Maurice Hope, Jim Watt and Charlie Magri. Frank Bruno had left the Lawless camp by the time he took the WBC world heavyweight crown from Oliver McCall.

WHO was the first woman to judge a world heavyweight championship contest?

THE JUDGE: Elva Shain, who was one of three judges to award Muhammad Ali a unanimous points victory over Earnie Shavers in a 15 rounds world title fight in New York on September 29 1977. Ali continually rubbed the bald head of the fearsome-punching Shavers in the clinches, saying, 'Nice coconut you've got there, Earnie.'

WHICH two boxers hold the record for most fights against each other?

THE JUDGE: Sam Langford and Harry Wills, two great black heavyweights who were victims of the colour bar, fought each other 23 times between 1914 and 1922 over a total of 246 rounds. Most of their contests were of the 'no decision' variety over ten rounds, but Willis came out on top in the one that really mattered. He outpointed Langford over 15 rounds in a fight for the Negro Heavyweight championship of the World in Tulsa on November 5 1919. Both were ducked by the likes of Jack Dempsey and Gene Tunney at a time when black fighters were not given a chance at the championship following the stormy reign of the first black champion, Jack Johnson.

WHAT was a 'No Decision' contest that shows on many old-timer records?

THE JUDGE: Boxing was outlawed in many States in America and, to get round the ban, boxers fought without a decision being given so that it came into the 'exhibition' category. It was left to the reporters at the ringside to give their verdicts in the newspapers.

WHO was the first southpaw heavyweight champion of the world?

THE JUDGE: Michael Moorer, stopping Bert Cooper in the fifth round for the vacant WBO heavyweight title in Atlantic City on May 15 1992.

THE '250' QUIZ CHALLENGE

111. What was the famous nickname of Sam Langford, who stood just over 5ft 7in tall and had a 44-inch chest measurement?

WHICH world heavyweight title fight was the first to be broadcast live on radio?

THE JUDGE: Jack Dempsey's three round demolition of Jess Willard in Toledo, Ohio, in 1919, when he became world heavyweight champion. Willard was down seven times in the first round but was saved by the bell. Dempsey's manager Jack 'Doc' Kearns had bet the entire purse on a first round victory.

WHEN was the first fight televised anywhere in the world?

THE JUDGE: Archie Sexton (father of football manager Dave) and Laurie Raiteri featured in an exhibition contest in front of the BBC cameras at Broadcasting House on August 22 1933. The first actual bout to be televised was when Jock McAvoy outpointed Len Harvey over 15 rounds for the British middleweight title at Harringay Arena on April 4 1938. This was on closed-circuit television. The first public screening featured the classic British lightweight title fight in which Eric Boon stopped Arthur Danahar in the 14th round at Harringay on February 23 1939.

WHEN was the first fight televised in colour?

THE JUDGE: Gustav Scholz, German and later European middleweight champion, outpointed Al Andrews over ten rounds at Madison Square Garden on March 26 1954. The fight was shown live in colour on 21 TV stations through the NBC network.

WHO was the first fighter to win three world titles?

THE JUDGE: Bob Fitzsimmons, who won world championships at middleweight (1891), heavyweight (1897) and light-heavyweight (1903).

WHICH boxer was first to win a world title on a disqualifcation?

THE JUDGE: West Ham's Thomas 'Pedlar' Palmer, who became world bantamweight champion when his opponent Billy Plimmer was disqualified in the 14th round at London's National Sporting Club on November 25 1895. The title victory was not universally recognised.

WHEN was the gumshield introduced to boxing?

THE JUDGE: It was the invention of a London dentist called Jack Marks, who created it for British welterweight master Ted 'Kid' Lewis in 1912.

THE '250' QUIZ CHALLENGE

112. Which American took the world heavyweight championship from Bob Fitzsimmons?

THE JUDGE

WHICH world heavyweight champion has had the shortest reign?

THE JUDGE: Leon Spinks, who lost the world title back to Muhammad Ali seven months after taking it from The Greatest in 1978.

WHO have been the tallest and shortest world heavyweight champions?

THE JUDGE: No doubt about the shortest – Tommy Burns at 5ft 7in. The tallest is open to argument – take your pick from Jess Willard, Ernie Terrell, Henry Akinwande and Ukrainian brothers Vitali and Vladimir Klitschko (all around 6ft 6in)

IS it true that George Foreman first became world heavyweight champion on his birthday?

THE JUDGE: Foreman celebrated his 25th birthday the day he rocked and shocked Joe Frazier to a second round defeat in their world title fight in Kingston, Jamaica, on January 22 1973.

WHO have been the youngest and oldest winners of the world heavyweight championship?

THE JUDGE: Mike Tyson (21 years 2 months) was the youngest when he ripped the WBC world crown away from Trevor Berbick in two rounds in Las Vegas on November 22 1986. George Foreman was the oldest (45 years 9 months) when he knocked out Michael Moorer in the 10th round in Las Vegas on November 5 1994 to win the WBA and IBF crowns.

WHEN was the last bare-knuckle title fight?

THE JUDGE: John L. Sullivan knocked out Jake Kilrain in the 75th round in a fight lasting two hours 16 minutes at Richburg, Miss., on July 8 1889. In his next defence Sullivan was knocked out in the 21st round by James J. Corbett on September 7 1892 at the Olympic Club in New Orleans. This was the first heavyweight title fight with gloves.

HOW many boxers have won Olympic gold medals and gone on to become world heavyweight champion?

THE JUDGE: Seven – Floyd Patterson (middleweight, 1952); Cassius Clay (light-heavy, 1960); Joe Frazier (heavyweight, 1964), George Foreman (heavyweight, 1968), Leon Spinks (light-heavy, 1976), Michael Spinks (middleweight, 1976), Lennox Lewis (super-heavyweight, 1988).

THE '250' QUIZ CHALLENGE

113. In which round did Muhammad Ali knock out George Foreman in their 'Rumble in the Jungle'?

120

HOW many times did Jack Britton and Ted 'Kid' Lewis fight each other?

THE JUDGE: American Jack Britton and the Jewish Pride of London Ted 'Kid' Lewis dominated the welterweight division from 1915 to 1922. They fought each other 20 times over a total of 224 rounds and traded the world title back and forth four times. The majority of their fights were No Decision bouts. In the contests when an official verdict was given Britton won four, Lewis three and there was one draw. In their first meeting on August 31 1915, Lewis – real name Gershon Mendeloff – outpointed Britton over 12 rounds to gain universal recognition as welterweight champion. Lewis made five successful defences before Britton regained the title with a 20-rounds points decision on April 24 1916 in New Orleans. Britton then made three title defences, two against Lewis, before the British ring master took back the title, again over 20 rounds on June 25, 1917 in Dayton, Ohio. Lewis then held onto the crown for one defence before Britton knocked him out in nine rounds on March 17 1919 in Canton, Ohio. It was the only one of their title fights that did not last the distance. They became so close during their fight marathon that they used to play cards with each other in the dressing-room before climbing into the ring, often with their purse money changing hands before a punch was thrown!

WHAT has been the shortest world heavyweight title fight in history?

THE JUDGE: James J. Jeffries knocked out Jack Finnegan in 55 seconds of his title defence in Detroit on April 6 1900.

WHAT has been the shortest world title fight in any weight division?

THE JUDGE: James Warring ko'd James Pritchard in 24 seconds of their world cruiserweight title fight in Salemi, Italy, on September 6 1991.

OF post-war world champions, who has boxed the most rounds in title fights?

THE JUDGE: That honour goes to former world welter and middleweight champion Emile Griffith, from the Virgin Islands. In 25 world championship contests from 1961 to 1976, Griffith boxed his way through 339 rounds.

THE '250' QUIZ CHALLENGE

114. Which British champion did Emile Griffith outpoint over 15 rounds in a world welterweight title defence in London in 1964?

THE JUDGE

HOW many title fights did Cassius Clay/Muhammad Ali contest?

THE JUDGE: Twenty-five, of which he won 22 and lost three. Here is a full list of his title fights (opponents are American unless stated):

25-02-64	Sonny LISTON	W ret 6	Miami
25-05-65	Sonny LISTON	W ko 1	Lewiston
22-11-65	Floyd PATTERSON	W rsf 12	Las Vegas
29-03-66	George CHUVALO (Canada)	W pts 15	Toronto
21-05-66	Henry COOPER (England)	W rsf 6	London
06-08-66	Brian LONDON (England)	W ko 3	London
10-09-66	Karl MILDENBERGER (Germany)	W rsf 12	Frankfurt
14-11-66	Cleveland WILLIAMS	W rsf 3	Houston
06-02-67	Ernie TERRELL	W pts 15	Houston
22-03-67	Zora FOLLEY	W ko 7	New York
08-03-71	Joe FRAZIER	L pts 15	New York
30-10-74	George FOREMAN	W ko 8	Zaire
24-03-75	Chuck WEPNER	W rsf 15	Cleveland
16-05-75	Ron LYLE	W rsf 11	Las Vegas
01-07-75	Joe BUGNER (England)	W pts 15	Malaysia
01-10-75	Joe FRAZIER	W ret 14	Manila
20-02-76	Jean-Pierre COOPMAN (Belgium)	W ko 5	Puerto Rica
30-04-76	Jimmy YOUNG	W pts 15	Maryland
24-05-76	Richard DUNN (England)	W ko 5	Munich
28-09-76	Ken NORTON	W pts 15	New York
16-05-77	Alfredo EVANGELISTA (Spain)	W pts 15	Landover
29-09-77	Earnie SHAVERS	W pts 15	New York
15-02-78	Leon SPINKS	L pts 15	Las Vegas
15-09-78	Leon SPINKS	W pts 15	New Orleans
02-10-80	Larry HOLMES	L ret 10	Las Vegas

HOW many challenges did Jersey Joe Walcott make before he won the world heavyweight championship?

THE JUDGE: Jersey Joe won the title at the fifth time of asking. He was twice beaten by Joe Louis (15 rounds points 1947, ko'd round 11 1948) and was then twice outpointed by Ezzard Charles (1949 and 1951). He was finally crowned champion when he produced a peach of a left hook to ko Charles in the seventh round of their third title fight in Pittsburgh on July 18 1951. He defended the crown with a points victory over Charles and then ran into a truck called Rocky Marciano, who knocked him out in the 13th round with his famed and feared Suzy Q punch on September 23 1952. In a return eight months later, Walcott was ko'd in the first round. He hung up his gloves at the end of a 69-fight career.

THE '250' QUIZ CHALLENGE

115. Who refereed the world title fight in which Muhammad Ali knocked out Sonny Liston in the first round?

WHO were the first three fighters to win world titles in more than three weight divisions?

THE JUDGE: Sugar Ray Leonard (WBC welterweight, WBA light-middleweight, WBC middleweight, WBC super-middleweight, WBC light-heavyweight), Thomas Hearns (WBA welterweight, WBC light-middleweight, WBC middleweight, WBO super-middleweight, WBA light-heavyweight) and Roberto Duran (WBA lightweight, WBC welterweight, WBA light-middleweight, WBC middleweight). The remarkable Henry Armstrong simultaneously held the feather, light and welterweight titles when there were only eight weight divisions, and he drew in a challenge for the middleweight championship.

DID Muhammad Ali make any title defences against southpaw opponents?

THE JUDGE: He met and beat two left handers, both fights taking place in Germany. He stopped Karl Mildenberger in 12 rounds and Richard Dunn in five rounds.

DID Emanuel Steward ever box professionally?

THE JUDGE: Steward had 97 amateur contests and was National Golden Gloves champion at bantamweight before giving up his job as an electrician to become a full-time trainer in Detroit where he ran the famous Kronk gymnasium. He has trained four Olympic gold medal winners and a procession of world champions including Thomas Hearns, Julio Cesar Chavez, Evander Holyfield, Leon Spinks, Oscar De La Hoya and Lennox Lewis.

DID Bob Fitzsimmons meet and beat Jack Dempsey?

THE JUDGE: Yes, but not the Manassa Mauler. Fitzsimmons took the world middleweight title from the legendary Jack 'Nonpareil' Dempsey at the Olympic Club in New Orleans on January 14 1891. Dempsey, who had been champion since 1884, never weighed more than 150 pounds and, by today's standards, would be considered a welterweight. He was past his best by the time he climbed into the ring with Fitzsimmons, who battered him around the ring before knocking him out with a vicious right to the jaw at the start of the 13th round. It was the first of three world titles for Fitz, who had the upperbody of a heavyweight and the slim legs of a featherweight.

THE '250' QUIZ CHALLENGE

116. Which Puerto Rican fighter brought an end to the undefeated reign of Golden Boy Oscar De La Hoya?

WHO holds the record for the longest span between winning his first and last title?

THE JUDGE: George Foreman went 21 years, 10 months and 14 days between his first world title victory and then winning the championship again in 1994. Roberto Duran won his first world championship on June 26, 1972, when he took the WBA lightweight title by stopping Scotland's Ken Buchanan in the 13th round. Almost 17 years later, on February 24, 1989, he won the WBC middleweight title by outpointing Iran Barkley over 12 rounds.

HOW many fighters took Rocky Marciano the distance in world title fights?

THE JUDGE: Rocky made six successful title defences after knocking out Jersey Joe Walcott in the 13th round to become world heavyweight champion in 1952: Walcott (wko1), Roland LaStarza (wrsf11), Ezzard Charles (wpts15 and wko8), Don Cockell (wrsf9), Archie Moore (wko9). In 1955, he became the only world champion to retire without a single defeat on his record.

WHERE was organised boxing first staged?

THE JUDGE: The birth of organised boxing can be traced back to 18th century England. James Figg, born in Thame in Oxfordshire, is regarded as the first heavyweight champion in the sport's history. A master of quarter-staff, cudgel and sword fighting, he helped popularise boxing by opening a training academy. He taught the sport to hundreds of pupils and accepted the challenges of all comers. James retired as undefeated bare-knuckle champion in 1734. A procession of British fighters held the heavyweight crown after Figg. One of the more prominent pugilists was Jack Broughton, who fought from 1729 to 1750. He was recognised as a heavyweight champion and he too was the proprietor of a successful boxing academy. He rivals Figg as the father of boxing because he was the first to establish rules, encouraged the use of gloves and set up the bouts in an area between ropes. Broughton's rules triggered a chain of reform in boxing that led directly to the universally recognised Marquis of Queensberry rules. The Queensberry regulations, established in 1867 and the foundation of boxing as we know it today, introduced three-minute rounds and helped hurry the transition from bare knuckle fights to gloved contests.

THE '250' QUIZ CHALLENGE

117. How many fights in total did undefeated Rocky Marciano have as a professional?

BOXING

WHAT would be considered the 20 best-known ring nicknames?

THE JUDGE: The top 20 that I would select in no particular order: Brown Bomber (Joe Louis), Manassa Mauler (Jack Dempsey), The Ghost with a Hammer in His Hand (Jimmy Wilde), Ambling Alp (Primo Carnera), Bronx Bull (Jake LaMotta), Cinderella Man (James J. Braddock), Gentleman Jim (James J. Corbett), Homicide Hank (Henry Armstrong), Orchid Man (Georges Carpentier), Peerless Jim (Jim Driscoll), Sugar Ray (Robinson and Leonard), Toy Bulldog (Mickey Walker), Whitechapel Whirlwind (Jack Kid Berg), Wild Bull of the Pampas (Luis Firpo), Hands of Stone (Roberto Duran), Marvelous Marvin (Marvin Hagler), The Hit Man (Thomas Hearns), Iron Mike (Mike Tyson), The Real Deal (Evander Holyfield), and, of course, The Greatest/Lousville Lip (Muhammad Ali).

WHO are the 20 best-known world champions who adopted ring names?

THE JUDGE: The top 20 in no particular order: Walker Smith (Sugar Ray Robinson), Henry Jackson (Henry Armstrong), Anthony Zaleski (Tony Zale), Rocco Barbella (Rocky Graziano), Richard Ihetu (Dick Tiger), Arnold Cream (Jersey Joe Walcott), Joseph Barrow (Joe Louis), Rocco Marchegiano (Rocky Marciano), David Ritchie (Dave Sands), Gershon Mendeloff (Ted Kid Lewis), Barnett Rosofsky (Barney Ross), Gerardo Gonzalez (Kid Gavilan), Benjamin Leiner (Benny Leonard), Judah Bergman (Jack Kid Berg), William Guiglermo Papaleo (Willie Pep), Giuseppe Carrora (Johnny Dundee), Noah Brusso (Tommy Burns), Jacob Finkelstein (Jackie Fields), Stanley Ketchel (Stanislaus Kiecal), Giuseppe Antonio Berardinelli (Joey Maxim).

HOW many Lonsdale Belts did Sir Henry Cooper win outright, and which boxers did he meet in contests for the British heavyweight championship?

THEJUDGE: Our Enery won a record three Lonsdale Belts outright. He was involved in 12 British title fights – Joe Erskine (lpts 15, 1957); Brian London (wpts 15, 1959); Joe Erskine (wrsf12, 1959); Joe Erskine (wret5, 1961); Joe Erskine (wrsf9, 1962); Dick Richardson (wko5, 1963); Brian London (wpts15, 1964); Johnny Prescott (wret10, 1965); Jack Bodell (wrsf2, 1967); Billy Walker (wrsf6, 1967); Jack Bodell (wpts15, 1970); Joe Bugner (lpts15, 1971).

THE '250' QUIZ CHALLENGE

118. From which Spanish opponent did Henry Cooper take the European heavyweight title in his penultimate fight?

125

CRICKET

HAS any batsman ever gone more than 100 Test innings without registering a duck?

THE JUDGE: David Gower holds the record with a sequence of 119 consecutive innings without a duck.

WHAT was the span of W.G. Grace's career, and what was his highest score?

THE JUDGE: The Doctor's career lasted 43 years, from 1865 to 1908. His highest score was an undefeated 400 for the United South against a Grimsby team that fielded 22 players! His highest score in an official match was 344. He played his final innnings (69 not out) for Eltham 10 days before the outbreak of World War 1 when he was 66.

HOW many times did Len Hutton and Cyril Washbrook open for England, and what was their highest stand?

THE JUDGE: Hutton and Washbrook partnered each other in 31 Tests. They put on a then world record 359 in 310 minutes against South Africa in the Second Test at Ellis Park during the 1948-49 tour. Hutton, Yorkshire captain, averaged 56.67 runs in his 79 Tests. Washbrook, Lancashire captain, averaged 42.81 in his 37 Tests.

HOW many sons have followed their fathers into the England Test team?

THE JUDGE: In alphabetical order: Alan and Mark Butcher, Colin and Christopher Cowdrey, Joe and Joe junior Hardstaff, Len and Richard Hutton, Frank and George Mann, Jim (JH) and Jim (JM) Parks, Arnold and Ryan Sidebottom, Micky and Alec Stewart, Fred and Maurice Tate, Charlie and David Townsend.

DID Graham Gooch score more Test runs for England than David Gower?

THE JUDGE: Gooch scored 8,900 runs in 118 Tests at an average 42.58. Gower scored 8,231 runs in 117 Tests at an average 44.25.

THE '250' QUIZ CHALLENGE

119. What was Graham Gooch's highest score in a single Test match innings for England?

CRICKET

AFTER which aristocrat was the Lord's cricket ground named?

THE JUDGE: The ground is named after its founder Thomas Lord, a Yorkshireman with a farming background who organised the building of the ground in 1814.

WHAT is the highest Test team total without a single batsman reaching 50?

THE JUDGE: South Africa scored 302 against New Zealand at Wellington in 1963-64 when Peter van der Merwe top scored with 44.

WITH which County did England's bodyline captain D.R. (Douglas) Jardine play?

THE JUDGE: Jardine, who followed his father as an Oxford blue, headed the batting averages with Surrey in 1927 and 1928. He was their captain when he set off on the Bodyline tour of 1923-33. He was born at Malabar Hill, Bombay, where his father was Advocate-General.

WHO was Alec Bedser's new ball bowling partner when he was at his peak with England?

THE JUDGE: Take your pick from Bill Edrich (6 Tests), Cliff Gladwin (5), Trevor Bailey (12), Brian Statham (6), Freddie Trueman (5).

WHAT has been the lowest fourth innings total successfully defended?

THE JUDGE: This was in the famous Test match at The Oval in 1882 which inspired the mock obituary notice in the *Sporting Times* that led to the birth of The Ashes. England needed just 85 runs to win, but collapsed all out 77. Freddie 'The Demon' Spofforth did the damage for Australia with seven for 44, taking his match haul to 14 wickets for 90. It was reported that the atmosphere was so intense on the second (and final!) day that one spectator died of a heart attack and another bit through the wooden handle on his umbrella.

DID Len Hutton score more Test centuries than that other great Yorkshire opener Geoff Boycott?

THE JUDGE: Sir Leonard Hutton scored 19 centuries in 79 Tests, Geoff Boycott 22 in 108 Tests.

THE '250' QUIZ CHALLENGE

120. Sir Leonard Hutton's then world record Test score of 364 runs was set on which ground?

WHAT is the shortest completed Test match on record?

THE JUDGE: Australia beat South Africa by an innings and 72 runs in a 1931-32 Test at Melbourne that lasted just five hours 53 minutes. The play was stretched across three days because of rain. Herbert 'Dainty' Ironmonger, the Australian left-arm spinner, was virtually unplayable on a drying wicket and took 11 wickets for 24 runs. South Africa were hustled out for 36 and 45, sandwiching a total of 153 by Australia. The Aussies managed it without a contribution from Don Bradman, who twisted his ankle in the dressing-room and did not get out to bat.

HOW many Test ducks did Mike Atherton get, and is it a record?

THE JUDGE: Mike Atherton (20 ducks) reluctantly holds the England record, one ahead of Derek Underwood. Courtney Walsh is the world record holder with 43 Test ducks.

WHAT does the three-digit number under the three lion's emblem indicate on an England players' shirt?

THE JUDGE: It was introduced in 2001 by the ECB to signify what number cap a player had become, for example Ryan Sidebottom was the 604th player to represent England in Test cricket. WG Grace would have been numbered 24. Number one (on alphabetical terms) would be Tom Armitage, a Yorkshireman who specialised in lobbed underarm bowling and who appeared in the first Test against Australia in Melbourne in 1877. The registering is in the capable hands of ECB scorer Malcolm Ashton, formerly of the BBCtv statistics team and now Channel Four.

IS it right, Judge, that Denis Compton was the first man to take the wicket of Garfield Sobers in a Test match?

THE JUDGE: Tony Lock was the bowler and Compo the fielder when 17-year-old Sobers was caught for 26 in his Test debut against England at Sabina Park in 1954. Garfield had been selected as a spin bowler and batted at number nine.

WHO was the first black cricketer to play for England?

THE JUDGE: Roland Butcher was the first black cricketer of West Indian descent to play for England in 1980-81. 'Cape Coloured' Basil D'Oliveira was capped 44 times between 1966 and 1972.

THE '250' QUIZ CHALLENGE

121. With which county was Roland Butcher playing when he made his Test debut for England?

HAVE any England Test cricketers represented other countries?

THE JUDGE: The following eight cricketers represented England and one other country at Test match level (including their birth place and year of birth): John Ferris (Australia/England; Sydney, 1867), Frank Hearne (England/South Africa; Middlesex, 1858), Billy Midwinter (England/Australia; Gloucestershire 1851), Frank Mitchell (England/South Africa; Yorkshire 1872), Billy Murdoch (Australia/England; Victoria, Australia, 1854), Nawab of Pataudi, sr (England/India, India), Albert Trott (Australia/England; Melbourne 1873), Sammy Woods (Australia/England; Sydney, 1867).

WHICH England Test opening partners have averaged the most runs together?

THE JUDGE: Jack Hobbs and Herbert Sutcliffe hold the record with 38 opening partnerships averaging 87.81 (15 hundreds and 10 others of 50 or more). Of the modern openers Michael Atherton and Graham Gooch have led the way with an average of 56.84.

HAS there ever been a case of a hat-trick achieved by each batsman being stumped?

THE JUDGE: Charlie Townsend, then a 16-year-old schoolboy spinner, achieved this with Gloucestershire against Somerset at Cheltenham in 1893. His spin completely deceived three successive batsmen and wicket-keeper W.H. Brain whipped off the bails. Both Townsend and his son later played for England.

WHERE was former Northants and England fast bowler David Larter born, and how tall was he?

THE JUDGE: Larter was born in Inverness, Scotland, on April 24 1940. He stood 6ft 7in and took 37 wickets in 10 Tests before injuries forced an early retirement.

HAS there ever been a first-class match in which a bowler has taken all 20 wickets?

THE JUDGE: No. The record is the 19 wickets famously taken by Jim Laker for England against Australia in the 1956 Test at Old Trafford (9 for 37 and 10 and 53).

THE '250' QUIZ CHALLENGE

122. Who took the other wicket in the Old Trafford Test in which Jim Laker finished with 19 Australian wickets for 90?

WHICH batsman has made the highest score in a Test match without scoring a boundary?

THE JUDGE: Australian skipper Bill Lawry managed 84 runs without finding the boundary when opening the second innings against England in the first Test at Brisbane in 1970-71. A rare instance of a century without a single boundary came from Derbyshire opener Alan Hill when scoring 103 for Orange Free State against Griqualand West at Bloemfontein in 1976-77, a performance equalled by Paul Hibbert for Victoria against the Indian tourists at Melbourne in 1977-78.

WHY is a certain spinning ball called a Chinaman?

THE JUDGE: It is an off-break ball bowled by a left-handed slow bowler, and it was first developed by Ellis Achong, a Trinidadian of Chinese extraction. He played six Tests for West Indies in the 1930s.

HOW many England caps did Colin Milburn win and did he score a Test century?

THE JUDGE: The larger than life 'Ollie' Milburn played nine Tests for England before losing an eye in a car crash, and he scored one century against West Indies and another against Pakistan.

HOW many England Test batsmen have missed a century by just one run in more than one innings?

THE JUDGE: Two England batsmen have twice been dismissed for 99 in Test cricket: Michael Atherton and Mike Smith. Athers had the further frustration of being run out in pursuit of the elusive 100 while on 99.

IS it right that Sir Donald Bradman never ever scored a century at Old Trafford?

THE JUDGE: The Great Man did not even manage 100 runs in total in his three Tests at Old Trafford. He was dismissed by Ian Peebles for 14 in his first appearance at the Lancashire ground in 1930, and was caught behind by wicket-keeper Les Ames off the bowling of Walter Hammond for 30 in his next visit in 1934. On his final tour as captain in 1948 he was leg-before to Lancashire's Dick Pollard in the first innings, and 30 not out in the second when he and opener Arthur Morris remained at the same ends for 100 minutes while battling to a drawn finish. In his memoirs, The Don said he was never comfortable with the light at Old Trafford.

THE '250' QUIZ CHALLENGE

123. What was Donald Bradman's highest ever Test score, which he accumulated at Headingley in 1930 and was then a world record?

IS it true that more than ten of England's Test cricket captains were not born in England?

THE JUDGE: Fourteen have been born outside England: Lord Harris (Trinidad), Timothy O'Brien (Dublin), Plum Warner (Trinidad), Douglas Jardine (India), Gubby Allen (Australia), Freddie Brown (Peru), Donald Carr (Germany), Colin Cowdrey (India), Ted Dexter (Italy), Tony Lewis (Wales), Mike Denness (Scotland), Tony Greig (South Africa), Allan Lamb (South Africa), Nasser Hussain (India).

WHAT happens if the stumps are broken with both batsmen safely home, and then during overthrows the broken wicket is hit with the batsman stranded?

THE JUDGE: Not out, unless a fielder has the ball in his hand and has removed a stump from the ground.

DOES Walter Hammond still hold the record for most non-wicket-keeper catches in first-class cricket?

THE JUDGE: Yes – ten catches for Gloucestershire against Surrey at Cheltenham in 1928. He also scored a century in each innings. I wonder who got Man of the Match?

WHEN did the great Essex fast bowler Ken Farnes play his last Test for England?

THE JUDGE: Farnes, who stood 6ft 5in tall and bowled at scorching pace off an 11-pace run-up, won his 15th and last cap in the 'Timeless Test' in South Africa in 1939. A Worksop College master and RAF pilot, this hero of Essex was killed while flying on active service in 1941.

WHAT was Sir Donald Bradman's complete Test record?

THE JUDGE: The nearest thing to perfection in cricket – Tests: 52, Innings: 80, Not Outs: 10, Runs: 6,996, Average: 99.94, 100s: 29. He needed four runs in his final innings against England at The Oval in 1948 to take his aggregate score to 7,000 and the magical three-figure average of 100, but was bowled for a second-ball duck by spinner Eric Hollies (statisticians wept tears on to their scorebooks). He scored a century in every 2.9 innings, and his 117 first class centuries included a record 37 over 200 and six over 300. His highest score was a then world record 452 not out for NSW against Queensland at Sydney in 1930. He captained Australia in 24 Tests, losing only three of them.

THE '250' QUIZ CHALLENGE

124. Against which country did Walter Hammond take over as the world record holder with a Test score of 336 not out?

WHICH England skipper holds the record for most consecutive Test matches as captain?

THE JUDGE: The record is 52 set by Mike Atherton from 1993-98. Australian Allan Border holds the world record with 93 successive Test matches as captain from 1984 to 1994.

DID Graham Gooch start his Test career with a pair?

THE JUDGE: Gooch ducked out twice against Australia at Edgbaston in 1975. Batting at number five, he was caught behind by Rodney Marsh in both innings, first off the bowling of Max Walker and then against the pace of Jeff Thomson. He finished his Test career 20 years later with 8,900 runs at an average 42.58.

WHAT is the highest fourth innings total ever recorded in a Test match?

THE JUDGE: This was in the famous 'Timeless Test' at Durban in 1938-39. England – set 696 for victory – had reached 654-5 when rain forced the match to be abandoned as a draw on the 11th day. The England team had to leave to catch their boat home from Cape Town. The top scorers for England were Bill Edrich (219), skipper Walter Hammond (140) and Paul Gibb (120).

HAS any batsman scored six successive sixes off one over in a Test match?

THE JUDGE: The record is four by Kapil Dev off the bowling of Eddie Hemmings in the England-India Lord's Test of 1990. This feat has been achieved only twice in first-class cricket, first by Garfield Sobers off Malcolm Nash for Nottinghamshire against Glamorgan at Swansea in 1968, and in 1984-85 by Ravi Shastri off Tilak Raj for Bombay against Baroda.

DID cricket commentator Jonathan Agnew ever score a century in first class cricket?

THE JUDGE: Aggers spectacularly put together a career-best 90 from 68 balls for Leicestershire against Yorkshire at Scarborough in 1987 after coming in as a nightwatchman. His run rush included six sixes. He then proceeded to take the first five Yorkshire wickets to fall. A fast medium right-arm bowler with a high action, he played three Tests for England in 1984-85.

THE '250' QUIZ CHALLENGE

125. Which batsman did Allan Border overtake as the most prolific runmaker in Test cricket history?

CRICKET

HOW many ways can a batsman get out in cricket?

THE JUDGE: There are ten: bowled, caught, stumped, lbw, run out, hit wicket, handled the ball, hit the ball twice, obstruction of the field and timed out.

WHAT was the all-round sporting record of MJK (Mike) Smith?

THE JUDGE: MJK (Mike) Smith was England's last double international (50 Tests 1958 to 1972) and one rugby union cap in 1955-56. He was a double Blue at Oxford where, as a fly-half, he formed a notable combination with Welsh international scrum-half Onllwyn Brace.

WHY is 111 referred to as Nelson?

THE JUDGE: There are two reasons usually given, the first that it is a reference to Horatio Nelson's three major sea victories: Aboukir Bay, Copenhagen and Trafalgar. The more common reference involves one eye, one arm and one private part!

WHAT is the lowest score never ever registered by a batsman in Test cricket?

THE JUDGE: Amazingly, no batsman in the history of Test cricket has finished his innings on 228 or 229.

IS it right that Robin Smith scored 150 for England in a one-day international and finished on the losing side?

THE JUDGE: Robin scored an unbeaten 167 for England against Australia in the 1993 Texaco Trophy at Edgbaston when Australia won by six wickets.

HAVE England ever gone through an entire Test series without a single team change?

THE JUDGE: It has happened in two Test rubbers – against Australia in 1884-85 and against South Africa in 1905-06.

WHO has scored most runs in a Test match and finished on the losing side?

THE JUDGE: Andy Flower amassed 341 runs for Zimbabwe against South Africa in the first Test in Harare in 2001 (142 and 199 not out), but he ran out of partners and could not prevent South Africa from winning the match.

THE '250' QUIZ CHALLENGE

126. With which county did former England captain MJK (Mike) Smith start his first-class career?

WHAT is the highest recorded batting partnership?

THE JUDGE: Vijay Hazare (288) and Gul Mahomed (319) put on 577 for the fourth wicket for Baroda against Holkar at Baroda, India, in the final of the Ranji Trophy in March 1947. They came together with the score at 39 for three and their stand lasted 533 minutes. Baroda totalled 784 and went on to win the match by an innings and 409 runs.

WHO was the first batsman to score a century in limited-overs international cricket?

THE JUDGE: Warwickshire opener Dennis Amiss, who scored 103 for England against Australia at Old Trafford in 1972.

WHICH bowler has produced the best bowling figures in a limited-overs international?

THE JUDGE: Muttiah Muralitharan, who took seven wickets for 30 runs for Sri Lanka against India at Sharjah in 2000-01.

WHAT is the highest team total in a Test match without any of the batsmen reaching three figures?

THE JUDGE: Highest Test innings without a hundred is India's 524 for nine declared against New Zealand at Kanpur in 1976. All eleven batsmen reached double figures, Amarnath top scoring with 70.

HAVE there ever been eight-ball overs in Test cricket in England?

THE JUDGE: England experimented with eight ball overs in the 1939 series against West Indies, but reverted to six-ball overs when first-class cricket was resumed after the war. Australia brought in eight-ball overs in 1918-19, copying an idea that had been introduced into cricket in California! They switched back to six-ball overs in Australia and New Zealand in 1978-79.

WAS Tony Lewis capped by England at cricket and rugby by Wales?

THE JUDGE: Tony was a Rugby Blue at Cambridge University, but was not capped by his native Wales. He became Glamorgan and England cricket captain. A predecessor at Glamorgan and Cambridge, Maurice Turnbull, was capped twice by Wales at rugby and played nine Tests for England between 1929 and 1936.

THE '250' QUIZ CHALLENGE

127. Against which country did Dennis Amiss make a match-saving Test score of 262 not out in 1974?

WHO have been the youngest and oldest scorers of Test centuries for England?

THE JUDGE: Denis Compton (20 years 19 days old) was the youngest with a century in his first Test against Australia at Trent Bridge in 1938. Jack Hobbs (46 years 82 days) was the oldest when he made 142 at Melbourne in March 1929. It was his 15th Test hundred and his 12th against Australia. Sir Jack scored 197 centuries during his career, 98 of them after the age of 40. No wonder they called him The Master.

HOW many times did Glenn McGrath dismiss Mike Atherton in Test matches?

THE JUDGE: They came up against each other in 17 Tests matches and 34 innings, with McGrath claiming Atherton's scalp 19 times.

HOW many Scots have captained England?

THE JUDGE: Mike Denness, born in Bellshill, Lanarkshire, captained England 19 times while with Kent. Douglas Jardine could also be claimed for Scotland, even though he was born in India. He had Scottish descendants, as did South African-born Tony Greig.

WHICH bowler has taken ten or more wickets the most times in Test matches?

THE JUDGE: Sir Richard Hadlee is the record holder, taking ten or more wickets in nine of his 86 Test appearances.

HAS Darren Gough ever scored a County century?

THE JUDGE: Darren scored a career-best 128 for Yorkshire against Warwickshire at Headingley in 1996.

HOW many balls did it take Ian Botham to reach his century in the famous 1981 Headingley Test?

THE JUDGE: It took Both 87 balls to get to his century on his way to an unbeaten 149 that set England up for a miraculous victory by 18 runs against a shell-shocked Australian side. Bob Willis wrapped up the victory with a career-best eight wickets for 43.

WHAT was Peter May's highest score in Test cricket?

THE JUDGE: Peter scored an undefeated 285 for England against the West Indies at Edgbaston in 1957, putting on 411 with Colin Cowdrey for the fourth wicket.

THE '250' QUIZ CHALLENGE

128. With which partner did Mike Atherton share a first wicket stand of 159 against the West Indies at The Oval in 2000?

HORSE RACING

WHAT was Willie Carson's record as a jockey, and what is his involvement in racing away from the TV cameras?

THE JUDGE: Willie rode 17 Classic winners, topped a century of winners in 23 seasons and was first past the post in 3,828 races. Only Gordon Richards, Lester Piggott and Pat Eddery have better UK records. Away from his job as expert summariser alongside Clare Balding on BBCtv he runs his Minster House Stud and is European manager for The Thoroughbred Corporation.

WHO has ridden most winners out of the Hills twins, Richard and Michael?

THE JUDGE: Michael Hills was born 10 minutes before his brother Richard but coming into the year 2002 he was 97 winners behind, 1,565 to 1,468 by Richard. Michael has, however, been first past the post more times than Richard in the UK (1,350 to 1,194) and has even ridden a winner under National Hunt rules.

WHO was the jockey known as The Shoe?

THE JUDGE: American jockey Willie Shoemaker. A schoolboy wrestler in his home State of Texas and a Golden Gloves boxer, he became a jockey and won his first race aged 18. He rode what was then an all-time record 8,833 winners, which was surpassed in 1999 by Laffit Pincay Jr. He retired in 1990 to become a trainer but was paralysed in a 1991 motor crash.

WHEN did Pat Eddery take over Lester Piggott's total number of winners?

THE JUDGE: It was at Goodwood on June 21 2002 when Galway-born Pat rode his 4,494th winner, moving into second place on the all-time British record list behind the Gordon Richards total of 4,870 wins. On the way Pat has won 11 jockeys' championships and ridden more than a century of winners for 27 seasons, overtaking Lester's record of 25 centuries in 1999.

THE '250' QUIZ CHALLENGE

129. On which horse did Pat Eddery win the Arc de Triomphe at Longchamp in 1986, leaving six Group 1 winners in his wake?

WAS Kieren Fallon Ireland's leading apprentice when he first started riding in the UK, and when did he win his first jockeys' championship?

THE JUDGE: Kieren finished second in the Irish apprentices table in 1987 and moved to the United Kingdom the following year. He won the first of a hat-trick of jockeys' championships in 1997 and was on the way to a fourth successive title when injured in a fall at Royal Ascot. At his peak in the 1990s he rode a remarkable three double centuries of winners.

WHAT was the international treble recorded by All Along, and who was the jockey and trainer?

THE JUDGE: All Along, trained by Patrick Biancome and ridden by Walter Swinburn, won the 1983 Arc de Triomphe. The combination crossed the Atlantic to win the Washington DC International and the Canadian International.

IN which year did John Reid win his first Classic, and who was the trainer?

THE JUDGE: John Reid had his first Classic triumph aboard On the House in the 1982 1,000 Guineas which was trained by Harry Wragg.

WHO rode Generous to victory in the Derby, and did the same combination finish first in the Irish Derby?

THE JUDGE: Alan Munro won the 1991 Epsom Derby on Generous, and they were together again when winning the Irish Derby ahead of subsequent Arc winner Suave Dancer.

WHY is Frankie Dettori called Frankie when on the racecards his initial is listed as 'L'?

THE JUDGE: Frankie was named Lanfranco when born on December 15 1970, and he became Frankie to his new English friends when he came from Italy to start his apprenticeship in 1985 with Luca Cumani.

DID Frankie Dettori's father ride any classic winners in England?

THE JUDGE: Gianfranco Dettori, Italy's top post-war jockey, won the 2,000 Guineas in 1975 and 1976 on Bolkonski and then Wollow.

THE '250' QUIZ CHALLENGE

130. In which year did Frankie Dettori win the jockeys' championship for the first time?

WHAT was the Classics record of the great Steve Donoghue?

THE JUDGE: Steve Donoghue won 14 Classics from 1915 to 1937 – the Derby (6), 2,000 Guineas (3), Oaks (2), St Leger (2) and 1,000 Guineas (1).

HOW many times did Michael Hills wins the Jockey Club Gold Cup on Further Flight?

THE JUDGE: Further Flight was one of the great grey stayers and Michael rode him to a record six consecutive wins in the Jockey Gold Cup at Newmarket.

DID the master jump jockey Stan Mellor ever win races on the flat?

THE JUDGE: Stan Mellor rode three flat-race winners to go with his then record 1,049 National Hunt victories.

WHAT was the first horse race screened live on British television, and who was the commentator?

THE JUDGE: It was the 1938 Derby won by Bois Roussel and ridden by Charlie Elliott. Thomas Woodroofe and Richard North shared the commentary. BBC covered the race with three cameras. Six years earlier there was an experimental TV broadcast of the Derby to the Metropole in Victoria.

HOW many Group-race winners did Lester Piggott ride, and what was his overall record?

THE JUDGE: The Group-race system was not introduced until Lester was more than halfway through his remarkable career, but he still managed to register 465 Group race wins. From his first winner, The Chase at Haydock Park on August 18 1948 at the age of 13, to May 1993 he rode over 5,300 winners world wide, including 4,493 in Britain. There were a record 30 Classic winners between 1954 and 1992, five in the 2,000 Guineas, two in the 1,000 Guineas, six in The Oaks, eight in the St Leger and, of course, his all-time record nine in the Epsom Derby, a race with which he will always be associated by his army of admirers. He won 11 jockeys' championships and rode more than 100 winners 25 times.

THE '250' QUIZ CHALLENGE

131. What was the name of the last of Lester Piggott's nine Epsom Derby winners in 1983?

WHO was the first jockey to ride more than 4,000 winners?

THE JUDGE: Sir Gordon Richards was the first jockey in the world to break through the 4,000-winner barrier. He was jockeys' champion for 26 of his 34 seasons (1921–54). His career total of 4,870 victories was a world record until broken by Johnny Longden of the United States on September 3 1956. Gordon was the first jockey ever to be knighted in the 1953 Coronation week when he rode his one and only Derby winner on Pinza. He rode 14 Classic winners in all, and topped 200 winners in 12 seasons.

IS it true that legendary American jockey Johnny Longden was born in Yorkshire?

THE JUDGE: Johnny was born in Wakefield on February 15, 1907, but spent his formative years in Canada before becoming an American citizen in 1942. During his 40-year career (1927-66), he established a world record with 6,032 victories which was eventually overtaken in 1970 by Willie Shoemaker.

WHICH flat racing jockey was known as the Choirboy?

THE JUDGE: Walter Swinburn, because of his baby-faced looks. The son of a top Irish flat racing jockey, he had the greatest moment of his career when steering Shergar to victory in the 1981 Epsom Derby by a record ten lengths. Walter was forced to make a premature retirement following a long battle with the scales, and he has since become an eloquent summariser with the Channel 4 racing team.

WHAT was Frankie Dettori's first winner in the UK?

THE JUDGE: Lizzy Hare at Goodwood on June 9 1987. His first ever winner was on Rif at Turin on November 16 1986. At the age of 19 Luca Cumani appointed him as stable jockey to replace Ray Cochrane after Frankie had become Champion Apprentice in 1989. He had his first Group 1 triumph on Mark of Distinction in the Queen Elizabeth II Stakes at Ascot in 1990 on his way to his first 100 winners in a season.

WHO was the first woman rider in the Grand National?

THE JUDGE: Charlotte Brew, whose mount Barony Fort refused four fences from home in the 1977 Grand National.

THE '250' QUIZ CHALLENGE

132. On which horse was Walter Swinburn first past the post in the 1986 Epsom Derby?

WITH which trainer did Ray Cochrane serve his apprenticeship, and what was his first winner?

THE JUDGE: Ray Cochrane served his apprenticeship with Barry Hills, and his first contract was with Luca Cumani.

HOW many winners did Fred Archer ride?

THE JUDGE: Fred Archer won 2,748 winners from 8,084 mounts between 1870 and 1886. He won 21 Classics - The Derby (5), Oaks (4), 2,000 Guineas (4), 1,000 Guineas (2) and St Leger (6), and was Champion Jockey 13 times before committing suicide at the age of 29 when he was depressed by a combination the death of his wife and the effects of continual weight-reducing.

WHAT were the main jumping triumphs of those wonderful steeplechasers Arkle and Dawn Run, and which was considered the greater?

THE JUDGE: Dawn Run was the first to complete the Champion Hurdle/ Gold Cup double at Cheltenham (1984/1986). She won the Gold Cup in her fifth race over fences and won 18 of her 28 National Hunt races. Arkle, winner of three Gold Cups at Cheltenham, won 22 of 26 steeplechases and is generally considered the greatest of all time.

IS it true that Lester Piggott was suspended after winning his first Derby on Never Say Die in 1954?

THE JUDGE: Lester's suspension to the end of the season followed his next ride on Never Say Die in the King Edward VII Stakes at Royal Ascot. He was charged with dangerous riding, which Lester has always strenuously denied.

ON which horse did Michael Scudamore win the Grand National, and is Peter any relation?

THE JUDGE: Michael, Peter Scudamore's father, rode in 16 consecutive Grand Nationals and won in 1959 on Oxo.

WAS there a jockey riding at the same time as Gordon Richards called Cliff Richards, and were they related?

THE JUDGE: Clifford Richards was a good-class jockey between the wars and the brother of Sir Gordon.

THE '250' QUIZ CHALLENGE

133. Which jump jockey rode Arkle to three glorious Gold Cup triumphs at Cheltenham?

WHERE and when was the 11-race winning sequence by Sir Gordon Richards?

THE JUDGE: Actually it was 12 successive winners. Gordon rode the winner of the final race at Nottingham on October 3 1933, all six at Chepstow the next day and the first five at Chepstow on October 5. This was the astonishing sequence: Tuesday (Nottingham): Barnby 11-2; Wednesday (Chepstow): Manner 6-5 on, Brush Past evens, Miss B 7-4, Arcona 6-4 on. Red Horizon 7-4, Delicia 5-4 on; Thursday (Chepstow): The Covenanter evens, Kirrimuir 6-4 on, June Rose 9-4, Montrose 7-4 on, Lady Swift Filly evens. In the last race of the day Gordon was leading on Eagleray but faded in the last furlong to finish third. In all that season, Gordon rode a record 259 winners.

WHAT were Frankie Dettori's seven winners when he went through the card at Ascot?

THE JUDGE: His 'Magnificent Seven' winners at the Ascot Festival meeting on September 28 1996 were: Wall Street (Cumberland Lodge Stakes, 2-1), Diffident (Diadem Stakes, 12-1), Decorated Hero (Tote Festival Handicap, 7-1), Mark of Esteem (Q.E.II Stakes, 100-30), Fatefully (Rosemary Rated Stakes, 7-4), Lochangel (Blue Seal Conditions Stakes, 5-4) and Fujiyama Crest (Gordon Carter Handicap, 2-1). The accumalitive odds were 25,095-1. Bookmakers lost a combined total of more than £20 million and look back on it as Black Saturday.

HAVE bookmakers had a worse day than when Frankie Dettori caned them by going through the card?

THE JUDGE: Probably the biggest kick in the satchels for bookmakers came in the 1946 Epsom Derby. It was the first Derby after the end of World War II and everyone who had ever served in the Royal Air Force – or who had relatives in the RAF or paratroops – went for an outsider called Airborne. It was numbered 13 which drew further support from superstitious housewives. All the racing experts were convinved Airborne, a winner of only one previous race, was just there to make up the numbers. Ridden by Tommy Lowrey, Airborne started at odds of 50-1. He came through like an express train to overtake the Earl of Derby's Gulf Stream by a length. He later also won the St Leger at 3-1, by which time more than half the bookmakers in the UK had declared bankruptcy because of their huge Derby losses.

THE '250' QUIZ CHALLENGE

134. Where was the Derby run during the Second World War when Epsom was closed for racing?

WHY was the water jump omitted from the 1955 Grand National?

THE JUDGE: Torrential rain left the course waterlogged. The landing side of the water jump was flooded and considered unsafe. Quare Times, ridden by Pat Taaffe, won at 100-9.

WHO has been the oldest jockey to ride a Derby winner?

THE JUDGE: John Forth was in his sixties when he was first past the post on Frederick 1829.

WHICH was the last racehorse to complete the 2,000 Guineas/Derby double in the 20th Century?

THE JUDGE: Nashwan, ridden by Willie Carson, performed the rare double in 1989. In the same year he won the King George VI and Queen Elzabeth Stakes and the Eclipse Stakes to complete a unique quartet of victories.

WHO is the only jockey to have won both the Kentucky and Epsom Derbys?

THE JUDGE: This was, of course, the 'Kentucky Kid' Steve Cauthen who captured America's Triple Crown in 1977 and crossed the Atlantic to continue a career during which he twice won the Epsom Derby – on Slip Anchor (1985) and Reference Point (1987).

WERE Brigadier Gerard and Mill Reef ever beaten?

THE JUDGE: Brigadier Gerard, always ridden by Joe Mercer, lost just one of his 18 races – to Roberto in the Benson & Hedges Gold Cup at York. His most memorable victory was in the 1971 2,000 Guineas when he beat Mill Reef and My Swallow , overtaking his two rivals in the final furlong and winning by three lengths. Mill Reef, who won the 1971 Derby in Brigadier Gerard's absence, was beaten only twice in his 14 races, the first time by My Swallow. Brilliantly ridden by Geoff Lewis, he followed his Derby victory by capturing the Eclipse Stakes, King George VI and Queen Elizabeth Stakes (by six lengths) and the Prix de l'Arc de Triomphe in new record time.

WHEN did Bahram win the Triple Crown?

THE JUDGE: Owned and bred by the Aga Khan, Bahram won the 2,000 Guineas (7-2), the Derby (5-4f) and the St Leger (4-11f) in 1935.

THE '250' QUIZ CHALLENGE

135. Which jockey was on board Bahram for all three races when it completed the historic Triple Crown?

WHAT price was Nijinsky when it completed the Triple Crown in 1970?

THE JUDGE: Piloted bv Lester Piggott, Nijinsky started the St Leger at Doncaster at 11-2 on and won his 11th successive race easing up, a length ahead of 20-1 Meadowville. He had previously won the 2,000 Guineas at 7-4 on and the Epsom Derby at 11-8.

WAS Nijinsky ever beaten?

THE JUDGE: Nijinsky lost the last two races of his career. He was beaten by a head in the 1970 Prix de l'Arc de Triomphe by Sassafras (19-1). Then in his final race, the Champion Stakes at Newmarket, he started 4-11 favourite but finished one and a half lengths behind the five-year-old Lorenzaccio (100-7).

HOW many times did Sea Bird II race in Britain?

THE JUDGE: Bred and trained in France, Sea Bird II had only one of his eight races in Britain. He comfortably won the 1965 English Derby by two lengths from Meadowcourt. Pat Glennon was the jockey and he was 7-4 hot favourite.

WHAT is Aidan O'Brien's background and is he the son of that former great trainer Vincent O'Brien?

THE JUDGE: Aidan switched from riding to training at the age of 23 and in his first season finished as champion National Hunt trainer. In 1994 he took over from legendary Irish trainer Vincent O'Brien – no relation – at the famous Ballydoyle Stables in County Tipperary, and in that same year set an Irish record of 176 winners on the flat and over the jumps, a record he beat himself the following season. He had laid the foundation to what is already considered one of the greatest training careers in history, and he is still in his early thirties! Behind O'Brien's success lies the world-famous Coolmore Stud, a multi-million pound operation that provides him with a constant stream of potential equine talent.

HOW tall was Lester Piggott when winning everything in sight?

THE JUDGE: Lester was known as The Longfella because, at just a fraction under 5ft 8in tall, most of the other jockeys had to look up to him.

THE '250' QUIZ CHALLENGE

136. Which Vincent O'Brien-trained horse won the Arc de Triomphe in 1977 and again in 1978?

HOW old was that grand chaser Sabin du Loir when he ran his last race?

THE JUDGE: Sabin du Loir was 14 when finally put out to grass after winning his 41st and last race in the John Bull Chase at Wincanton on January 14 1993. It was his 21st victory.

WHAT was Shergar's record before he was kidnapped?

THE JUDGE: Shergar had a first and second as a two-year-old, and as a three-year-old won the 1981 Derby by a record 10 lengths, and finished first in the Irish Derby and King George VI and Queen Elizabeth Stakes. In his last race he finished fourth in the St Leger, and was retired to stud. He was kidnapped in February 1983 and has never been seen since.

WHO were the jockeys when Dawn Run completed the unique double of victories in the Champion Hurdle and Gold Cup at Cheltenham?

THE JUDGE: Jonjo O'Neill was on board for both the Champion Hurdle victory in 1984, and the Gold Cup win in 1986.

HAS a National Hunt rider ever won the Grand National in the same year that he was champion jump jockey?

THE JUDGE: Three jockeys have achieved this since the war: Fred Winter (Sundew 1957), Tommy Stack (Red Rum 1977) and Richard Dunwoody (Miinnehoma 1994).

WHAT was Hard Ridden's starting price when Charlie Smirke rode it to victory in the 1958 Derby?

THE JUDGE: Hard Ridden, 18-1, was the first Irish-trained winner of the Derby since 1907.

WHEN was the last racing appearance of that majestic steeplechaser Arkle?

THE JUDGE: Arkle's unforgettable career ended prematurely when he broke a pedal bone during the King George VI Chase in 1966. That was the year in which he completed a stunning hat-trick of Cheltenham Gold Cup victories. Of his 26 steeplechases, he won 22, was second twice and third twice. He won one of three races on the flat and four of six over hurdles.

THE '250' QUIZ CHALLENGE

137. Charlie Smirke won his second successive Epsom Derby in 1952 on which Aga Khan-owned horse?

UNDER what name did Lord Oaksey used to ride?

THE JUDGE: Lord Oaksey and John Lawrence are one and the same. He was a top amateur jump jockey before becoming a leading racing journalist and expert racing summariser for the Channel 4 team.

WHAT was the name of the horse that beat Sir Ivor in the 1968 Arc de Triomphe?

THE JUDGE: Vaguely Noble, the 5-2 favourite ridden by Bill Williamson. Lester Piggott was second three lengths away on the fast-finishing English Derby winner Sir Ivor.

WHO owned that great Cheltenham favourite Persian War?

THE JUDGE: Persian War was owned by West Ham United fanatic Henry Alper, and that is why he chose claret and blue colours. Ridden by Jimmy Uttley, he won the Champion Hurdle three times from 1968 to 1970 and was second in 1971.

WHAT were the prices of Nimbus when winning the 2,000 Guineas and Derby in 1949?

THE JUDGE: Nimbus, ridden by Charlie Elliott, won the 2,000 Guineas at 10-1 and the Derby by a head from Armour Drake at 7-1.

CONFIRM that Manny Mercer, as a 7lbs claiming apprentice, won the Lincoln Handicap on a 100-1 shot.

THE JUDGE: There were 46 starters in the 1947 Lincolnshire won by 100-1 Jockey Treble, carrying six stone and ridden by 17-year-old Manny Mercer. The older brother of Joe Mercer, Manny was tragically killed in a fall at Ascot in 1959, aged 30.

WHO were the jockeys and what were the betting odds when Red Rum won his three Grand Nationals?

THE JUDGE: 1973: Brian Fletcher (9-1), 1974: Brian Fletcher (11-1), 1977: Tommy Stack (9-1).

WHAT weights did Red Rum carry on the way to each of his three Grand National victories?

THE JUDGE: 1973: 10st 5lbs; 1974: 12st; 1977: 11st 8lbs.

THE '250' QUIZ CHALLENGE

138. Which horse did Red Rum pip at the post to win his first Grand National at Aintree in 1973?

WHO have been the trainers and jockeys of the last 20 Epsom Derby winners and what were the starting odds of each winner?

THE JUDGE: 2002: High Chaparral 7-2 (Aidan O'Brien, Johnny Murtagh); 2001: Galileo 11-4jf (Aidan O'Brien, Mick Kinane); 2000: Sinndar 7-1 (John Oxx, Johnny Murtagh); 1999: Oath 13-2 (Henry Cecil, Kieren Fallon); 1998: High Rise 20-1 (Luca Cumani, Olivier Peslier); 1997: Benny The Dip 11-1 (John Gosden, Willie Ryan); 1996: Shaamit 12-1 (William Haggas, Michael Hills); 1995: Lammtarra 14-1 (Saeed bin Suroor, Walter Swinburn); 1994: Erhaab 7-2f (John Dunlop, Willie Carson); 1993: Commander In Chief 15-2 (Henry Cecil, Michael Kinane); 1992: Dr Devious 8-1 (Peter Chapple-Hyam, John Reid); 1991: Generous 9-1 (Paul Cole, Alan Munro); 1990: Quest For Fame 7-1 (Roger Charlton, Pat Eddery); 1989 Nashwan 5-4f (Dick Hern, Willie Carson); 1988 Kahyasi 11-1 (Luca Cumani, Ray Cochrane); 1987: Reference Point 6-4f (Henry Cecil, Steve Cauthen); 1986 Shahrastani 11-2 (Michael Stoute, Walter Swinburn); 1985: Slip Anchor 9-4f (Henry Cecil, Steve Cauthen); 1984: Secreto 14-1 (David O'Brien, Christy Roche); 1983: Teenoso 9-2f (Geoff Wragg, Lester Piggott).

WHICH four horses were first home in the 2002 Grand National?

THE JUDGE: Cheltenham Gold Cup winner Jim Culloty completed a memorable double with victory in the 155th Grand National. Culloty brought 20-1 shot Bindaree home, just under two lengths ahead of What's Up Boys (Richard Johnson). Record-breaking jump jockey Tony McCoy, on 8-1 favourite Blowing Wind, was 27 lengths back in third. Kingsmark finished fourth. Culloty, who had never before managed to finish the world's greatest steeplechase, was handed the ride after Jamie Goldstein broke his leg earlier in the week.

WHY do the Americans claim that Man O'War was the greatest racehorse ever?

THE JUDGE: In his two-year career he lost just one of his 21 races (to Upset at Saratoga in 1919 after being stranded at the start). He started off odds-on in every race that he ran including three times at 100-1 on! A strong, fiery chestnut of 16.2 hands, he was nicknamed Big Red and sired 379 foals. Between them they won a total of 1,300 races.

THE '250' QUIZ CHALLENGE

139. Who trained 1995 Grand National winner Royal Athlete, which was ridden by Jason Titley?

 RUGBY

HOW many times did Will Carling captain England?

THE JUDGE: Carling led England 59 times, winning three Five Nations Grand Slams and four Triple Crowns in addition to contesting a World Cup final. He was first appointed captain in 1988 at the age of 22.

DID that outstanding commentator Bill McLaren play international rugby?

THE JUDGE: Born in the Borders town of Hawick in 1923, Billy McLaren developed into a talented flanker with the Hawick first XV in the late 1930s. He played in a Scotland trial in 1947 and was on the verge of a full international cap when he contracted tuberculosis which forced his early retirement. He made his first rugby commentary while recovering from TB, and the rest is history. McLaren studied Physical Education in Aberdeen, and went on to teach PE and coach schools rugby teams right through to 1987. He laid the foundation to the careers of several players who went on to play for Scotland, including Jim Renwick, Colin Deans and Tony Stanger.

WHAT did Clive Woodward achieve as a player, and what is his background?

THE JUDGE: Born the son of an RAF pilot in Cambridgeshire, Clive Woodward was educated at HMS Conway, the Naval college on Anglesey, where he first started to shine as a rugby centre. He spent four years studying sports science at Loughborough and after two seasons with Harlequins in London, he joined Leicester and was called up for the first of 21 international caps. He played in the Grand Slam team led by Bill Beaumont in 1980, and stood out as an elegant and thoughtful centre with a good tactical brain. At the age of 29, he went to Australia for two years, studying rugby methods while playing for Sydney suburbs side Manly. Clive became a coach on his return, with Henley and then with London Irish. He had briefly switched to Bath when England appointed him coach as rugby moved into the professional era.

THE '250' QUIZ CHALLENGE

140. Against which country did Will Carling skipper England in a rugby union World Cup final?

WHERE was that genius of a French full back Serge Blanco born?

THE JUDGE: Blanco, capped what was then a world record 93 times by France, was born in Caracas, Venezuela in 1958. He moved to France when a child, and throughout his rugby career played his club rugby with Biarritz Olympique. Since his retirement he has become a successful businessman and has launched his own range of fashion wear. He won 81 caps as a full back, 12 as a winger and his 38 international tries are a French record.

WHAT is Ben Cohen's link with former England international footballer George Cohen?

THE JUDGE: The England wing is the son of George's brother. 'Uncle' George was right-back in England's 1966 World Cup-winning team.

WHEN did England first play international rugby?

THE JUDGE: In 1871 when England and Scotland played the first rugby union international. Wales and Ireland started to challenge them in the 1880s, and the Home International Championships began. England and Scotland were the most successful teams in these formative years, but by the mid-1890s the Welsh had not only developed an impressive side but also a new system that would change the way the game was played. Wales brought in the "four three-quarter" system in 1893 and became champions for the first time, winning rugby's "invisible trophy", the Triple Crown - beating all three other home nations against opposition still playing with nine forwards and six backs.

WHY do Welsh rugby fans refer to the 1970s as their Golden Era?

THE JUDGE: This was the era of exceptional players like JPR Williams, Gareth Edwards, Gerald Davies and jinking fly-halves Barry John and Phil Bennett. From 1969 to 1979 Wales won the Triple Crown six times and only an outstanding French side prevented them from adding to the three Grand Slams achieved in this decade.

HOW many caps did Bill Beaumont win?

THE JUDGE: Bill won 34 England caps, and he was captain 21 times including during the 1980 Grand Slam season.

THE '250' QUIZ CHALLENGE

141. With which club side did former England skipper Bill Beaumont play throughout his career?

WHY does there appear to be less injury time in televised rugby matches than in soccer?

THE JUDGE: This is because referees often allow physiotherapists to come on to the pitch and treat injured players while play continues.

HOW many substitutes are allowed in international rugby union matches, and why do players sometimes go off and then return in place of their substitutes?

THE JUDGE: Up to seven substitutes are allowed fror each team. Players who are bleeding must go off for treatment and can be temporarily replaced while off the field.

WHAT is the rule for the kick-off to each half if the ball does not travel ten metres?

THE JUDGE: The kick must cross the opposition's 10-metre line, which the opponents are not allowed to move beyond until the ball is kicked. If the ball does not travel 10 metres, goes straight into touch, or goes over the dead ball line at the end of the pitch, the receiving team can opt for a scrum or a kick again.

FOR which club did Jonny Wilkinson play before joining Newcastle Falcons?

THE JUDGE: Jonny played for his local Farnham, Surrey, club before moving north to Newcastle where he developed his kicking technique under the tutelage of his former England hero Rob Andrew.

HOW much does Jonny Wilkinson weigh? He seems small compared with the giant forwards he is always tackling.

THE JUDGE: Jonny is not as small as he seems. He stands 5ft 10in and weighs just over fourteen stone.

WHO won most Welsh international caps out of Barry John and Phil Bennett?

THE JUDGE: 'King' John won 25 caps, 23 as fly-half partner to Gareth Edwards. Phil Bennett won 29 caps, 25 as fly-half partner to Gareth Edwards. Barry retired at the age of 27. Phil captained Wales eight times and also skippered the 1977 British Lions.

THE '250' QUIZ CHALLENGE

142. With which club side did both Barry John and Phil Bennett start their senior rugby careers?

WHAT has been the highest score posted in a World Cup finals match?

THE JUDGE: New Zealand 145 points against Japan in 1995. All Black Simon Culhane scored an individual record 45 points.

WHAT has been the highest score posted in a World Cup qualifying match?

THE JUDGE: Hong Kong amassed 164 points against Singapore in 1994, running in a record 26 tries.

WHAT have been the most points scored by a British player in a World Cup finals match?

THE JUDGE: Gavin Hastings piled up 44 of Scotland's 89 points against the Ivory Coast in 1995. He is the top World Cup scorer with 227 points.

WHO has scored most tries in World Cup finals matches?

THE JUDGE: Jonah Lomu, who has run in 15 tries for New Zealand.

WHO has scored most individual points in a World Cup finals tournament?

THE JUDGE: All Blacks fly-half Grant Fox, who scored 126 points in the 1987 finals, including ten conversions against Fiji.

WHO has been the most capped All Black?

THE JUDGE: Hooker and regular captain Sean Fitzpatrick, whose 93? caps included an unbroken sequence of 63 matches from 1987 to 1995. He first established himself with Auckland, and followed his father into the New Zealand team (Brian Fitzpatrick played 22 times for the All Blacks between 1951 and 1954).

WHICH All Black was voted the New Zealand Player of the Century in 1999?

THE JUDGE: Fittingly from the province of King Country, Colin Meads was the overwhelming choice. The man nicknamed Pinetree because of his enormous physical presence was a supreme lock forward who played in 55 Tests for the All Blacks. His brother Stan was his lock forward partner in several Tests.

THE '250' QUIZ CHALLENGE

143. How many tries did Jonah Lomu run in for New Zealand against England in their 1995 World Cup finals match in South Africa?

WHO was the All Blacks full back who could kick penalties in his bare feet?

THE JUDGE: This was the fabled Bob Scott, who during several tours of Great Britain in the immediate post-war years would give exhibitions of kicking bare-footed. He could land the ball between the posts from the halfway line. Only boot manufacturers were unimpressed!

WHEN did New Zealand introduce the haka into their pre-match ritual?

THE JUDGE: A Maori war cry used to be heard before matches as long ago as the 1880s, and it was heard in Britain for the first time in 1888 when a team of touring New Zeland 'Natives' or 'Originals' used it as a form of entertainment rather than a war cry. The haka became a permanent part of the pre-match ritual during the 1905-06 All Blacks tour of Great Britain. In response, in Cardiff, the Welsh players broke into their national anthem, 'Hen Mad fy Nhadau' (Land of my Fathers), which was taken up by the crowd and this too became a tradition.

HOW many tries did Australia concede on the way to winning the 1999 World Cup in Cardiff?

THE JUDGE: Astonishingly, just one! This was scored by Grobler for the United States on their way to a defeat by 55 points to 19. The Aussie mean machine flattened France 35-12 in the final in front of 72,000 spectators in the Millennium Stadium on November 4 1999.

WHO kicked England to defeat in the 1999 World Cup quarter-finals?

THE JUDGE: South Africa defeat England 44-21 in Paris thanks to a world record five dropped goals by Jannie de Beer. All his goals went between the England posts between the 43rd and 74th minutes.

WHERE and when were the first rugby union World Cup finals staged?

THE JUDGE: The first rugby World Cup was held in 1987, an invites only festival involving 16 nations. Australia and New Zealand were the joint hosts. The All Blacks beat France 29-9 in the final at Eden Park, Auckland. Wales survived longest of the Home nations, going down to a 49-6 defeat by the rampant All Blacks in the semi-final.

THE '250' QUIZ CHALLENGE

144. Who skippered the all-conquering Australian team that won the 1999 World Cup in such convincing fashion?

WHAT has been the biggest crowd for a rugby union match?

THE JUDGE: A world record crowd of 109,874 gathered in Sydney on July 15 2000 and witnessed one of the greatest rugby games of all time between Australia and New Zealand. The All Blacks quickly powered into a 24-0 lead and the match seemed over as a contest, but then the Aussies started a revival that saw them claw their way back to 24-24 at half-time. Australia grabbed command in the second-half and led by one point with two minutes to go. Then, enter stage right, Jonah Lomu! Jonah scored the winning try with a minute to go for a final scoreline of 35-39. It was Australia's highest score against New Zealand and the highest scoring game between the two nations ever.

WHO has scored most World Cup tries for England?

THE JUDGE: Rory Underwood, with eleven. David Campese leads the Australian list with ten and Gavin Hastings, of course, is top Scottish try scorer with nine.

WHO was the England wing who scored a hat-trick of tries in a match during the 1980 Grand Slam season?

THE JUDGE: John Carleton of Orrell, Lancashire, England and the British Lions, who was a permanent fixture in the number 14 shirt in the early to mid 1980s. Carleton scored four tries in that 1980 Grand Slam triumph. His first was in the away victory against France at Parc des Princes. Then, against Scotland in the Calcutta Cup match at Murrayfield and playing alongside young Clive Woodward, he crashed over for three memorable tries. It was the first hat-trick by an Englishman since Herbert Jacob against France in 1924.

WHAT was so special about the Prince Obolensky tries at Twickenham?

THE JUDGE: There are two that have gone down into rugby folklore, both scored against the previously unbeaten All Blacks at Twickenham on January 4 1936. Alexander Obolensky, who had fled the Russian revolution, was making his England debut. His first try was a conventional wing-threequarter's dash. The second, that clinched a 13-0 victory, started with a run down the right followed by a jinking journey across field and finishing with a dive eight yards in from the left corner flag.

THE '250' QUIZ CHALLENGE

145. With which club side was Rory Underwood registered when he played for England in the 1991 World Cup final?

RUGBY

WHAT is the Lance Todd Trophy, and which players have won it in the last 20 years?

THE JUDGE: The Lance Todd trophy is awarded to the Man of the Match in the rugby league Challenge Cup final and voted for by members of the Rugby League Writers Association. The trophy is named in memory of Lance Todd, a former New Zealand tourist who played for Wigan and was a renowned coach with Salford before his death in a road accident following a game at Oldham. The prestigious award, first presented to Wakefield Trinity's Billy Stott in 1945, is one of the highest individual honours in the game and has been won by the following players since 1980:

2002 Kris Radlinski (Wigan Warriors), 2001 Sean Long (St Helens), 2000 Henry Paul (Bradford Bulls), 1999 Leroy Rivett (Leeds Rhinos), 1998 Mark Aston (Sheffield Eagles), 1997 Tommy Martyn (St Helens), 1996 Robbie Paul (Bradford Bulls), 1995 Jason Robinson (Wigan), 1994 Martin Offiah (Wigan), 1993 Dean Bell (Wigan), 1992 Martin Offiah (Wigan), 1991 Denis Betts (Wigan), 1990 Andy Gregory (Wigan).

1989 Ellery Hanley (Wigan), 1988 Andy Gregory (Wigan), 1987 Graham Eadie (Halifax), 1986 Bob Beardmore (Castleford), 1985 Brett Kenny (Wigan), 1984 Joe Lydon (Widnes), 1983 David Hobbs (Featherstone), 1982 Eddie Cunningham (Widnes), 1981 Mick Burke (Widnes), 1980 Brian Lockwood (Hull KR).

WHICH two teams contested the inaugural Super League Grand Final in 1998?

THE JUDGE: Wigan Warriors and Leeds Rhinos, and it was the men from Central Park who emerged triumphant in a tight game. Jason Robinson's try and three Andy Farrell goals to a Richie Blackmore try lifted Warriors to a 10-4 win. Warriors had beaten the Rhinos 17-4 just 13 days earlier, but the final on October 24 1998 still attracted a crowd of 43,533 to Old Trafford.

WHICH clubs did Peter Gill represent before joining the London Broncos?

THE JUDGE: Gilly played for Toowoomba (1984-1986), Brothers (1986-1988), St George (1988-1991) and Gold Coast (1991-1995) before bringing his strength and skills to the Broncos in 1995.

THE '250' QUIZ CHALLENGE

146. Which team did Leeds Rhinos beat in the final eliminator to qualify for the 1998 Grand Final against Wigan Warriors?

WHAT were the teams for the rugby league World Cup final in 2000, and who was the referee?

THE JUDGE: Stuart Cummings, of the RFU, refereed the game at Old Trafford on November 25 2000 when Australia became world champions for the sixth successive time by crushing New Zealand 40-12. The jet-paced Wendell Sailor was man of the match with two typically sparkling tries, but it was the faultless boot of Mat Rogers that knocked the heart out of the New Zealanders as he consistently put the ball through the posts. The teams:

Australia: Lockyer, Rogers, MacDougall, Gidley, Sailor, Fittler, Kimmorley, Webcke, Johns, Kearns, Tallis, Fletcher, Hill. Replacements: Barrett, Hindmarsh, Britt, Stevens.

New Zealand: Barnett, N Vagana, Carroll, Talau, Vainikolo, H Paul, Jones, Smith, Swain, Pongia, Rua, Kearney, Wiki. Replacements: R Paul, J Vagana, Cayless, Swann.

FROM which club did Francis Cummins join Leeds, and did he score a hat-trick of tries in his Great Britain debut?

THE JUDGE: Francis joined Leeds from his local amateur Dewsbury club St John Fisher. He did not score a hat-trick in his debut for Great Britain, but he did go over for three tries in his first game for England against France at Gateshead in 1995.

WHO has been the youngest player to appear in a Challenge Cup final?

THE JUDGE: Leeds full back Francis Cummins, who played for Leeds against Wigan in the 1994 Challenge Cup final aged 17 years and 200 days.

WHO were the first Super League champions, and which club was first to be relegated?

THE JUDGE: The inaugural Super League champions were Shaun McRae's St Helens, who adapted so smoothly to the new competition that they did the Challenge Cup double in 1996. Workington Town were the first to be relegated from Super League, with Salford Reds moving into the top flight in their place.

THE '250' QUIZ CHALLENGE

147. Which British team played in Paris in the first ever Super League match in March 1996?

RUGBY

WHICH two teams contested the inaugural rugby league World Club Championship final?

THE JUDGE: Brisbane Broncos defeated the Hunter Mariners, with no European sides making the last four of the competition. Wigan put up the best show of the UK clubs, going down to the eventual runners-up at Central Park.

ON which three soccer grounds were Greast Britain's three rugby league internationals played against the New Zealanders in 1998?

THE JUDGE: The first was played at Huddersfield's McAlpine Stadium, the second at Bolton's Reebok Stadium and the third at the Vicarage Road ground where Watford play their home soccer matches.

HOW many tries did the legendary Billy Boston score?

THE JUDGE: Wing wonder Billy scored a career total of 560 tries, of which 482 were for his beloved Wigan. He played for Wigan in six Challenge Cup finals, and later wound down his spectacular career with Blackpool Borough. He later became a popular landlord of a hotel adjacent to the Central Park ground where he had scored so many of his stunning tries. Billy was capped 31 times by Great Britain, and on one tour of Australia the Wigan Express ran in a record 36 tries. It was said of Wigan's Billy that he had no peer!

WHAT was Ellery Hanley's transfer fee when he joined Wigan from Bradford Northern?

THE JUDGE: The1985 fee was a then record £150,000. Ellery quickly started to pay it back with 63 tries in his first season, a record haul for a non-winger. He scored 30 of the tries from loose forward, another record. One of the most versatile players ever to step foot on a rugby field, he was equally devastating whether at stand-off, centre, on the wing or at loose forward.

WHAT was Jim Sullivan's goal-kicking record?

THE JUDGE: Between 1921 and 1946, the man with the golden boot kicked 2,876 goals and amassed 6,192 points. He played 921 games for Wigan, a club he later coached. His most productive year was 1934 when he booted 204 goals.

THE '250' QUIZ CHALLENGE

148. To which club did man-for-all-seasons Ellery Hanley move from Wigan in 1991?

155

GOLF

WHAT is a 'Mulligan' in golf?

THE JUDGE: A 'Mulligan' is in essence a second chance after a muffed shot. It is a second ball played from the spot of an original shot that has gone astray, with no stroke penalty. A 'Mulligan' is frequently taken on the tee, particularly the first tee before a player has warmed up. It can be introduced by mutual consent anywhere on the course provided it has been agreed beforehand to allow 'Mulligans'. Of course, a 'Mulligan' violates the Rules of Golf, and would not be allowed in competition.

WHO has been the oldest golfer to have completed a full round of 18-hole golf?

THE JUDGE: There is no official record, but the oldest golfer ever to play a round was believed to have been Arthur Thompson of British Columbia. At the age of 103, he equalled his age on the 6,000-yards Uplands Golf Club in Victoria.

WHICH of Gene Sarazen's shots in the US Masters is referred to as The Miracle Shot?

THE JUDGE: It came at the par-5 fifteenth hole at Augusta in the final round of the 1935 US Masters and before the tournament had officially been given its famous title. Trailing Craig Wood by three strokes with four holes to go, Sarazen sent a 4-wood second shot over the pond fronting the marathon hole. The ball pitched forward on the green and rolled directly into the cup for an astonishing albatross two! Sarazen eventually won in a play-off.

WHY did the media start to call that outstanding golfer Billy Casper 'Buffalo Bill'?

THE JUDGE: Billy, US Open champion in 1959 and 1966 and Masters champion in 1970, went on a diet of buffalo meat to combat a recurring allergy problem. It must have worked because he became the second player to win more than a million dollars in prize money.

THE '250' QUIZ CHALLENGE

149. On which course did Gene Sarazen score a hole in one during the 1973 British Open at the age of 71?

GOLF

WHO was the first golfer to win four US Open titles?

THE JUDGE: Willie Anderson won in 1901, 1903, 1904 and 1905. He was born in Berwick in 1880 and emigrated to the United States with his parents at the age of five.

IS it true that the great Silver Scot Tommy Armour had only one eye?

THE JUDGE: Tommy Armour lost the sight of one eye during the First World War but went on to win every major championship. As an amateur, Edinburgh-born Armour played for Britain against the US and as a professional for the US against Britain. He was a meticulous player who would sometimes waggle his club more than 20 times before launching into a shot (shades of Sergio Garcia). He later became acknowledged as *the* leading golf teacher, and was a stickler for the rules. He once saw an opponent craftily teeing a ball up in the rough. Armour quietly walked over, trod the ball firmly into the ground with his spiked heel and said: 'That's where it landed and that's where you play it.'

WHY was Byron Nelson exempted from serving with the US forces during World War II?

THE JUDGE: A Texan who quickly established himself as one of the world's greatest golfers after turning professional in 1932, Byron was exempted from military service because he was a haemophiliac.

IS it fair to say that Byron Nelson was the Tiger Woods of his day in the way he dominated the golf tour?

THE JUDGE: Certainly during the 1945 season. Byron had one of the greatest winning streaks on record. He won eleven consecutive PGA Open tournaments, and in all that year won seventeen titles. He shot nineteen rounds in a row under 70 and compiled a stroke average of 68.33. In 113 consecutive tournaments he was never once out of the money.

WHAT made Ed Furgol develop such a unique swing?

THE JUDGE: Ed became 1954 US Open champion despite a childhood accident that left him with a withered left arm which was bent at the elbow and eight inches shorter than his right. He adapted his style to overcome this handicap.

THE '250' QUIZ CHALLENGE

150. Which fellow-Texan did Byron Nelson beat in the first ever eighteen-hole play-off in the US Masters in 1942?

WHAT was unusual about the way Roberto de Vicenzo lost the 1968 US Masters?

THE JUDGE: Roberto robbed himself of the chance of winning the US Masters. In the final round, US Ryder Cup player Tommy Aaron, with whom he was paired, marked a four on de Vicenzo's card after the seventeenth hole when millions of television viewers and the course spectators had seen him sink his putt for a three. His actual finishing score for the round was 65 which would have taken him into a play-off for the title with the American Bob Goalby. But de Vicenzo signed the card without double checking and as it showed a return of 66 that was the score that, according to the rules, had to be recorded. The big, amiable Argentinian shrugged at the presentation ceremony and said in fractured English: 'What a stupid I am.'

WHY did Brian Huggett have to forfeit a hole in a champion match with Dai Rees?

THE JUDGE: There was a sensational climax to the *News of the World* match play championship semi-final between defending champion Brian Huggett and his fellow Welshman Dai Rees. Huggett was one-up standing on the eighteenth tee but lost the hole without playing a stroke. A wildly hooked drive by Rees struck a post and rebounded against Huggett's golf bag. The law states that 'If a player's ball be stopped or deflected by his opponent, his caddie or equipment, the opponent's side shall lose the hole'. So Huggett had to forfeit the hole and, to rub it in, Rees then went on to win the nineteenth hole and the match.

WHAT what amazing about the play-off for the US Open title between Lloyd Mangrum and Ben Hogan?

THE JUDGE: Mangrum, US Open champion in 1946, was penalised two strokes for blowing an insect off his ball during the play-off, and Hogan went on to win the 1950 US Open at Merion.

WHICH is the longest golf hole in the world?

THE JUDGE: Among several claimants is the seventh at the Sano Course, Satsuki, in Japan. It runs 831 metres (909 yards) from tee to green and is a par seven. The sixth hole at Koolan Island Golf Course, Western Australia, measures 782 metres (860) yards and is also a par seven.

THE '250' QUIZ CHALLENGE

151. Who was runner-up to Roberto de Vicenzo when he won the British Open golf title at his 20th attempt in 1967?

HOW did Mike Austin get himself into the golf news headlines?

THE JUDGE: Spectators gathered round the fifth green at the US National Seniors' Open at the Winterwood Course, Las Vegas, wondered who had hit his second shot through the green on the 450-yard hole. They could not see anybody on the fairway. The ball had been driven from the tee by sixty-four-year-old Los Angeles professional Mike Austin. Aided by a 35mph tailwind, the ball had travelled sixty-five yards past the flag for a drive of 515 yards.

WHAT has been the longest drive on the official golf tour?

THE JUDGE: The longest officially recorded drive on the US tournament circuit is 426 yards by George Bayer in the 1955 Tucson Open. Bayer was famed for his big hitting and once cleared 500 yards with a drive that put him within chipping distance of a 589-yard hole in Australia.

WHAT has been the longest drive in the British Open?

THE JUDGE: Craig Wood, US Masters champion in 1941, hit an extraordinary drive in his play-off for the 1933 British Open with fellow-American Densmore Shute. Playing the 530-yard fifth at St Andrews, he drove into a bunker guarding the green. His wind-assisted shot was measured at 430 yards. Wood was beaten by five strokes in the thirty-six-hole play-off.

HAS anybody ever won a big tournament with a final hole eagle?

THE JUDGE: Lew Worsham, 1947 US Open champion, holed a 135-yard wedge shot for an eagle two at the 410-yard final hole of the Tam O'Shanter World Championship at Chicago in 1953. It gave him victory by one stroke and a $25,000 first prize.

WHICH golfer scored an albatross in the British Open some time in the 1970s?

THE JUDGE: Johnny Miller holed out his second shot with a three-wood on the 558-yard fifth hole in the 1972 Open at Muirfield. He produced this spectacular three-under-par albatross on his way to a round of 66. Lee Trevino won the title that year.

THE '250' QUIZ CHALLENGE

152. In which year did Johnny Miller win the British Open at the Royal Birkdale course?

WHEN did a broken beer bottle cost a player the British Open title?

THE JUDGE: Harry Bradshaw drove into the rough at the fifth hole in the second round of the 1949 Open at Sandwich. He found his ball lodged against the neck of a broken beer bottle. The Irishman risked disqualification if he claimed the ball was unplayable and so elected to play it as it lay. He took out his sandblaster and smashed through the glass to send the ball thirty yards towards the hole. Bradshaw got down in six on the par-four hole and at the end of the final round was tied for the lead with eventual champion Bobby Locke.

WHY is there a plaque commemorating Bobby Jones at the seventeenth hole at Royal Lytham?

THE JUDGE: Uncharacteristically, Bobby Jones drew his drive at the seventeenth in the final round of the 1926 Open at Royal Lytham and the ball came to rest in a shallow bunker 170 yards from the green. His fellow-American Al Watrous, with whom he was locked in a neck-and-neck duel for the championship, was on the green in two. Jones took his mashie iron (equivalent of a 4-iron) and struck a glorious shot to the heart of the green. He got down in four while Watrous three-putted for a five. Jones went on to win his first British Open and that remarkable shot from the bunker has been commemorated by a bronze plaque at the spot where he played the ball.

WHAT was the length of the famous putt Bobby Jones holed at St Andrews?

THE JUDGE: Bobby Jones, the Amazin' Amateur, holed a monster putt of around 100 feet (30 metres) for a birdie three on the Hole o'Cross fifth at St Andrews in 1927 on his way to a first round 68 that set him up for his second Open championship.

WHO has put down the longest post-war putt to win a major tournament?

THE JUDGE: There are many contenders, but the two that stand out were both in the US Masters: Cary Middlecoff's effort of 86 feet (26 metres) on the thirteenth green in the US Masters at Augusta in 1955, and Nick Faldo's 100-foot eagle putt at the second when he won the US Masters for the first time in 1989.

THE '250' QUIZ CHALLENGE

153. How many times did the great Bobby Jones win the British Open golf championship?

IS is right that Peter Alliss once won three open golf titles in less than a month?

THE JUDGE: Peter Alliss, one of the most gifted British golfers of all time and now the respected 'Voice of Golf' on television, worked hard as captain of the Professional Golfers' Association in 1962 to remove the cloth-cap image of club professionals. He illustrated the point with a story about his purple patch in 1958 when he won the Spanish, Portuguese and Italian Open titles within a month. Peter returned triumphant to his Parkstone Club, Dorset, only to be greeted by an irate member who growled: 'Where have you been? I've been waiting three weeks for a lesson.'

WAS Peter Alliss born in Germany?

THE JUDGE: Yes, in 1931 in Berlin where his father, Percy, was a club golf pro. He perfected his golf on the beautiful Ferndown, Dorset, course.

DID Arnold Palmer once uproot a bush with a shot in a British Open championship?

THE JUDGE: Arnold Palmer removed a bush – roots and all – from the ground with a mighty six-iron shot at the sixteenth in the final round of the 1961 Open at Royal Birkdale. He had pushed his drive into heavy rough and found his ball in an almost unplayable position beneath the small bush. To most golfers it would have been a case of trying to play the ball out on to the fairway, but the one and only Palmer decided to go for the green 140 yards away. He dug out the ball – and the bush – with a prodigious shot. The ball landed on the green and he two-putted for his par on the way to the first of his two successive Open championships. The bush was never replanted and in it's place there is a plaque that reads simply: ARNOLD PALMER, THE OPEN CHAMPIONSHIP 1961.

DID Arnold Palmer once climb a tree on his way to a tournament victory?

THE JUDGE: Arnie was playing in the Australian Wills Masters tournament in Melbourne in 1964, when he hooked his second shot at the ninth hole high into the fork of a gum tree. The enterprising Palmer clambered up the 20 feet to where his ball lay and, using his No. 1 iron hammer-style, knocked it forward thirty yards from where he chipped on to the green and one-putted.

THE '250' QUIZ CHALLENGE

154. On which course did Arnold Palmer win the first of his British Open golf championships?

THE JUDGE

WHAT was Eric Brown's Ryder Cup record?

THE JUDGE: Scottish golfer Eric Brown had a peerless record in the Ryder Cup. On each of the four occasions he played he won his singles match and, in 1969, he was non-playing captain of the British side that figured in the first tie in the history of the competition. His American 'victims' in the Ryder Cup singles were Lloyd Mangrum (1953, victory by two holes), Jerry Barber (1955, three and two), Tommy Bolt (1957, four and three) and Cary Middlecoff (1959, four and three).

IS it true that a competitor in the British Open once failed to break the 100 total for a round?

THE JUDGE: Walter Danecki, a forty-three-year-old self-described 'golf professional' from Milwaukee, astonished everybody in the second qualifying round for the 1965 Open at Royal Birkdale when he recorded an amazing score of 58. What made it so amazing was that it was his total for the first nine holes! He came back in 55 for an aggregate 113. His first round total was 108, and he missed the qualifying total of 151 by a mere 70 strokes. Walter, who got into the draw on false qualifications, later confessed that he was not really a professional – 'I just wanted to try to win that crock of gold.'

WHO was the rabbit golfer who twice tricked his way into the British Open qualifying rounds in the 1970s?

THE JUDGE: In the Open qualifying round of 1976, Maurice Flitcroft recorded an eighteen-hole total of 121. Six years later – describing himself as 'Gerald Hoppy, a full-time club professional golfer from Switzerland' – Maurice tried again but was persuaded to retire from the qualifying round after amassing 63 shots to the ninth hole. It later emerged that joker Maurice was, in fact, a crane-driver from Barrow-in-Furness who was just a weekend hacker.

WHICH has been the golf shot watched by the biggest television audience?

THE JUDGE: If you're trying to think of a shot by Nicklaus, Watson or Ballesteros you're not aiming high enough. It was actually a six-iron shot struck by astronaut Alan Shephard while on the moon during the Apollo 14 expedition of 1971. The club used by golf-crazy Shephard is now a prized exhibit in the US PGA Museum.

THE '250' QUIZ CHALLENGE

155. What was the first name of the seed merchant who founded the Ryder Cup?

WHAT was known as Gary Player's Miracle Comeback?

THE JUDGE: Gary Player's great fighting spirit was never more in evidence than when he beat Tony Lema in the Piccadilly World Match Play championship at Wentworth in 1965 after being seven down with seventeen to play. Player overheard two spectators chatting as he walked towards the 20th tee. One said to his companion that they should wait for the next match because this one would soon be over. Gary paused and said: 'Sir, you are obviously not a golfer or you would know that a game is never over until it's over. Stick around and you might see something.' He then proceeded to unwrap one of the greatest comebacks in golfing history. He squared the match on the thirty-sixth and won it on the thirty-seventh. He went on to beat Peter Thomson in the final.

HAS any golfer ever achieved two holes-in-one in the British Open golf championship?

THE JUDGE: Charles Ward, a golf professional from Little Aston, Birmingham, is the only golfer who has achieved two aces. He holed out at the eighth in the Open at St Andrews in 1946 on his way to finishing in fourth place. Two years later at Muirfield he holed-in-one at the thirteenth and finally tied for third place.

WHO registered the first hole-in-one in a major championship?

THE JUDGE: Tom Morris Jnr, who followed his father Tom Snr as Open champion in the 1860s, holed out at the 145-yard eighth at Prestwick in the 1868 Open.

DID a golfer once win a house with a hole-in-one?

THE JUDGE: Isao Aoki holed-in-one at the second against David Graham in the 1979 Suntory World Match Play championship at Wentworth and was rewarded with a Bovis home at Gleneagles valued at £55,000. It became known as the 'home-in-one' shot.

WHAT is the longest recorded hole-in-one?

THE JUDGE: Robert Mitra achieved an astonishing hole-in-one at the tenth hole on the Miracle Hills golf course in Nebraska on October 7 1965. From tee to green the hole is 408 metres (447 yards) and Mitra's ball was carried by a sudden gust of wind and straight down the hole!

THE '250' QUIZ CHALLENGE

156. Which British golfer was runner-up to Gary Player when he won his third Open championship at Royal Lytham in 1974?

WHO performed the first hole-in-one live on television?

THE JUDGE: Tony Jacklin, when he aced at the sixteenth at Royal St George's, Sandwich, on his way to a round of 64 and victory in the 1967 Dunlop Masters. Jacklin was bang on target again in the 1978 German Open when his hole-in-one won him a Mercedes sports car.

WAS there once a British Open when there were a hat-trick of holes-in-one at the same hole?

THE JUDGE: There were a record three holes-in-one at the 1981 Open at Sandwich, all at the short 165-yard sixth. Gordon Brand was first to ace in the second round, using a five-iron. The next day amateur Roger Chapman took a nine-iron and was down in one. Then on the final day, Sam Torrance holed out with his tee-shot, using a six-iron.

WHAT exactly is a golden ferret in golf?

THE JUDGE: A golden ferret is when a golfer holes a bunker shot. It's a sandy ferret if the player is up and down from a bunker.

WAS Henry Cotton knighted and what was his record in the British Open?

THE JUDGE: Henry Cotton was knighted in 1986, shortly before his death at the age of 80. He won the British Open three times – in 1934, 1937 and 1948. His victory at Carnoustie in 1937 was particularly outstanding because the chasing field included the entire USA Ryder Cup team. His round of 65 on his way to winning his first Open in 1934 inspired the development of the popular 'Dunlop 65' ball.

WHAT is the full name of Tiger Woods and what is his ehtnic background?

THE JUDGE: Eldrick Tiger Woods was born on December 30, 1975, and grew up in Cypress, California. He is the son of Earl Woods, a retired lieutenant colonel in the US army, and his wife, Kultida, a native of Thailand. His father is half black, a quarter American Indian and a quarter Chinese, and his mother half Thai and half Chinese. Earl decided to call his son Tiger after a Vietnamese soldier called Nguyen 'Tiger' Phong who saved Woods Snr's life twice while he was on military duties in Vietnam (Judge note: I get more questions about Tiger Woods than any other ten players put together!).

THE '250' QUIZ CHALLENGE

157. On which course did Henry Cotton win his third and final British Open golf championship?

WHERE did Tiger Woods finish in his first tournament in Great Britain?

THE JUDGE: Tiger finished in a tie for 47th place at the 1995 Scottish Open at Carnoustie. Later that summer, he was a member of the vanquished US Walker Cup team at Royal Porthcawl, losing to Gary Wolstenholme by 1 hole in the opening singles but then reversing that result 24 hours later, winning 4 & 3. Playing in the 1996 Open at Royal Lytham he won the Silver Medal as highest placed amateur.

WHAT did Tiger Woods achieve in golf while at university?

THE JUDGE: In two years at Stanford University, Tiger won 10 collegiate events, including seven of his last nine tournaments, culminating with the NCAA crown which featured a course record 67 at the Honers Club in Chattanooga, Tennessee. His other amateur titles included the 1994 Western Amateur. He won the US Amateur three times in succession.

HOW old was Tiger Woods when he won his first US amateur championship?

THE JUDGE: At 18, in 1994, Tiger became the youngest ever winner of the US Amateur, coming from six holes behind to beat Trip Kuehne by 2 holes in the final at the TPC of Sawgrass. He was 4-under par for his last 12 holes, and still three behind with nine holes remaining.

IN which position did Tiger Woods finish in his professional debut?

THE JUDGE: This was in the Greater Milwaukee event in 1996. Tiger finished in joint 60th place after rounds of 67-69-73-68. Shortly afterwards he had his first US PGA Tour victory at the Las Vegas Invitational at Las Vegas CC. During that first 1996 season, Tiger competed in a total of eight US PGA events, won twice, and became the first player since Curtis Strange in 1982 to record five consecutive top-5 finishes.

HOW old was Tiger Woods when he won his first US Masters title at Augusta?

THE JUDGE: At 21 years, 3 months and 15 days, Tiger was the youngest ever winner of the Masters in 1997. He set two other records – the lowest ever score (270) and a record margin of victory by 12 shots.

THE '250' QUIZ CHALLENGE

158. Which European golfer did Tiger Woods pip by one shot to win the 1999 US PGA golf championship in Chicago?

WHERE was Fred Perry born and what was his background?

THE JUDGE: Fred Perry was born on May 18 1909, in Stockport, Cheshire. The son of a Labour MP, he did not take up tennis until he was 18. His early love was table tennis and he was world champion in 1929. The last British man to win the Wimbledon singles title, he captured eight Grand Slam crowns (three Wimbledon, three US, one French and one Australian). He turned professional in 1936 after winning his third successive Wimbledon title, and moved to the United States where he became an American citizen and served with the US Forces during the Second World War. In his later years he spent more time in his homeland as a broadcaster, and his Centre Court feats are commemorated by a striking statue at Wimbledon. He died on February 2 1992 in Melbourne while on a tennis-watching trip.

HOW many titles did Billie Jean King win at Wimbledon?

THE JUDGE: Billie Jean, who first competed at Wimbledon as 17-year-old Miss Moffitt in 1961, won 20 championships in all – 10 doubles and four mixed doubles to go with her six singles titles. She competed at Wimbledon 22 times in 23 years and played a record 265 matches there, losing just 41 of them.

WHAT were the two records Boris Becker set in his first Wimbledon championship?

THE JUDGE: At seventeen years 227 days, Boris Becker was the youngest men's Wimbledon champion and also the first unseeded player to win the title. He was also the first German to be hailed as champion on the Centre Court when he beat South African Kevin Curren 6-3, 6-7 (4-7), 7-6 (7-3), 6-4 in the 1985 final. Nicknamed 'Boom-Boom' because of his power on court, Boris retained the title in 1986 by beating Ivan Lendl in straight sets, and captured it for a third time in 1989.

THE '250' QUIZ CHALLENGE

159. Who did Boris Becker beat in straight sets when winning his third Wimbledon singles title in 1989?

HOW many titles did Jimmy Connors win during his career?

THE JUDGE: Battling Jimmy, the Streetfighter of the courts, won a world record 109 titles and spent a record consecutive 268 weeks as world number one. His first title at Wimbledon came at the age of 21 when he conquered the 39-year-old Ken Rosewall. He triumphed at Wimbledon again when he beat his old rival John McEnroe in a five setter that lasted over four hours. Jimbo came into his own in the competitive atmosphere of New York, where he won the US Open five times.

WHAT was the head-to-head record of Martina Navratilova and Chris Evert?

THE JUDGE: Two of the greatest women tennis players of all-time, they met each other 80 times. Chris won 11 of the first 12 matches, but Martina eventually overtook her and finished with a record of 43 wins to 37 losses. They faced each other in the Wimbledon final five times, Navratilova winning all of them.

HOW many Grand Slam titles did Steffi Graf win in all, and is it a record?

THE JUDG: Steffi – now Mrs Agassi – won 22 Grand Slam singles titles in all, including seven at Wimbledon. Only Margaret Court has more, with 24, but 11 of hers came in Australia, where few northern hemisphere players ventured in the 1960s. Steffi had an incredible run of 374 weeks as number one in the world, ahead of Martina Navratilova's previous record of 332 weeks. She became the second woman in the history of Open tennis to win the Grand Slam of all four majors, in 1988, a year she also added the Olympic title to her collecxtion. She is the only player ever to have won each of the majors at least four times.

WHERE was Martina Navratilova born, and what does she consider her nationality to be today?

THE JUDGE: Martina was born in Prague, Czechoslovakia, on October 18 1956, under the repressive Communist regime. She became an American citizen in 1975. Martina won 18 Grand Slam singles titles, including a record nine singles championships at Wimbledon where her reign included six successive Centre Court triumphs between 1982 and 1987. She continues to play doubles events at Wimbledon.

THE '250' QUIZ CHALLENGE

160. Who was Martina Navratilova's partner when they won four successive women's doubles titles at Wimbledon?

WHAT was the final score in the professional series between Pancho Gonzales and Lew Hoad?

THE JUDGE: They started their world-wide series of matches when Lew Hoad turned professional after winning his second successive Wimbledon crown in 1957. The great Pancho Gonzales was leading in their head-to-head duels 51-36 when Lew's troublesome back started to handicap him in the early 1960s. 'When Lew's game was at its peak nobody could touch him,' said Gonzales, who picked out Hoad as his toughest opponent during his 25 years of one-night-stand pro tours.

WHO was the eldest out of Lew Hoad and Ken Rosewall?

THE JUDGE: Lew was born on November 23, 1934, 21 days after Ken Rosewall, in the same city, Sydney. Although entirely different in stature, style and attitudes, the two were called Australia's tennis twins, and together helped to make Australia virtually unbeatable in the Davis Cup in the mid-1950s.

WHAT was Ken Rosewall's nickname, and how many times was he runner-up at Wimbledon?

THE JUDGE: Jokingly nicknamed Muscles, the small (5ft 7in), slim (9st 10lbs), wonderfully stylish Rosewall collected his first major titles in Australia and France at the age of 19 in 1953 and continued winning right up into his early 40s ... but the one championship that always eluded him was the Wimbledon crown. He reached and lost four Centre Court finals, going down to Jaroslav Drobny (1954), Lew Hoad (1956), John Newcombe (1970) and Jimmy Connors (1974).

IS it true that Ken Rosewall was a natural left-hander?

THE JUDGE: Correct. Ken did everything left handed, but his father coached him to play tennis right handed, which helped explain one of the most explosive backhands in the game. For much of his career, he had to play second fiddle to first Lew Hoad and then on the professional circuit to Pancho Gonzales and later, Rod Laver. Yet he outlasted them all, and was still winning titles in the 1970s. In all, Rosewall won 18 major titles in singles, doubles and mixed – the sixth-highest male total. His last pro triumph, Hong Kong in 1977 over Tom Gorman, was recorded two weeks after his 43rd birthday, making him the second oldest after Gonzales to win an open-era title.

THE '250' QUIZ CHALLENGE

161. Which fellow-Australian took just five games off Lew Hoad in the 1957 Wimbledon final?

HOW many Grand Slams did Rod Laver complete?

THE JUDGE: Born on August 9, 1938, the 'Rockhampton Rocket' from Queensland, was arguably the greatest tennis player ever. In 1962, he became the first player to complete the Grand Slam since the pre-war Donald Budge (beating fellow Aussies Martin Mulligan and in three of the finals Roy Emerson), and he added an historic second Grand Slam in 1969 (beating John Newcombe, Tony Roche, Andres Gimeno and Ken Rosewall in the four finals).

WHO was the first professional to win a tournament at Wimbledon?

THE JUDGE: Rod Laver, who conquered Ken Rosewall in the final of a special showcase eight-man competition in 1967. The following year, Laver became the first professional to win the Wimbledon title when he beat Tony Roche in the final on the Centre Court where he had first triumphed as an amateur in 1961. During a 23-year career that spanned the amateur and open eras, Laver won 47 pro titles in singles and was runner-up 21 times.

IS John McEnroe German by birth?

THE JUDGE: John was born in Wiesbaden, Germany, on February 16 1959, where his father was serving with the US Air Force, but there is no doubt that he is all American. He grew up and learned to play his tennis in the Long Island suburb of Douglastown, New York, where his father was a lawyer.

WAS John McEnroe ever disqualified from a major tournament?

THE JUDGE: Yes, in the Australian Open in 1990 when he was thrown out for an outburst of abusive language against the umpire and court officials while leading against Mikael Pernfors.

WHAT was the final tally in the head-to-head wars between John McEnroe and his leading rivals Borg, Connors and Lendl in proper competitions?

THE JUDGE: McEnroe and Borg finished level on seven victories each. Supermac beat Jimmy Connors 31 times in their 51 head-to-head battles, and came out second best to Ivan Lendl, who won 21 of their 36 matches.

THE '250' QUIZ CHALLENGE

162. What was the name of the Peruvian-born American who beat Rod Laver in his first Wimbledon final in 1959?

WHAT were the scores when John McEnroe met Bjorn Borg in their epic back-to-back Wimbledon finals?

THE JUDGE: McEnroe lost the first battle in 1980 1-6, 7-5, 6-3, 6-7 (16-18), 8-6, bravely and brilliantly staving off seven match points during the unforgettable fourth-set. The tie break lasted 20 breath-taking minutes. He got his revenge a year later when he mastered Borg on Centre Court 4-6, 7-6 (7-1), 7-6 (7-4), 6-4, ending Bjorn's incredible six year, 41-match unbeaten Wimbledon run.

WHO was the opponent when John McEnroe made his famous 'Pits of the world' outburst?

THE JUDGE: This was the year of McEnroe's first triumph at Wimbledon in 1981. Already nicknamed Superbrat, he risked being thrown out during an explosive second round loss of temper while beating Tom Gullikson. At one stage, he yelled at umpire Ted James: 'You're the pits of the world, man.' He survived the wrath of the committee to go on to famously beat Bjorn Borg in the final, and in the following year lost in the final to Jimmy Connors in five sets.

DID John McEnroe and his brother Patrick ever meet in a major final?

THE JUDGE: They faced each other in the final of the Chicago Open in 1991. John, older than Patrick by seven years, won 3-6, 6-2, 6-4.

HOW old was Bjorn Borg when he retired?

THE JUDGE: Not counting a couple of abortive comeback attempts, Bjorn was 25 and at his peak when he suddenly quit the game in which he had set new standards on the way to winning 11 Grand Slam singles titles. He earned nearly $4-million in prize money and trebled that with his sponsorship and endorsement deals. Between losing to the eventual champion Arthur Ashe in 1975 and John McEnroe in the 1981 final, "Ice Borg" won a record 41 consecutive matches at Wimbledon.

WHO was the first black Wimbledon singles champion?

THE JUDGE: Althea Gibson, who became the first black champion when beating Darlene Hard in the 1957 women's final. She retained the title the following year. Arthur Ashe was the first black men's singles champion on the Centre Court, defeating Jimmy Connors in the 1975 final.

THE '250' QUIZ CHALLENGE

163. Against which European opponent did Bjorn Borg win the first of his Wimbledon singles titles?

WHO presented the men's trophy to Boris Becker when he won his second singles title in 1986?

THE JUDGE: French Davis Cup legend Jean Borotra, one of the famous French Musketeers. It was the one and only time since the war that Royalty has not presented the trophy.

WHO is the eldest of the Williams sisters?

THE JUDGE: Venus was born in Lynwood, California, on June 17 1980. Serena was born in Saginaw, Michigan, on September 26 1981.

HAS Anna Kournikova ever won a Grand Slam title?

THE JUDGE: Not in singles competition, but she shared a doubles triumph with Martina Hingis when they beat Lindsay Davenport and Natasha Zvereva 7-5, 6-3 in the final of the 1999 Australian Open. It was the first tournament in which they had been paired together.

WHO was the Olympic singles gold medallist in Barcelona in 1992?

THE JUDGE: Jennifer Capriati, beating the defending champion Steffi Graf in the final 3-6, 6-3, 6-4.

HOW old was Pete Sampras when he won his first Grand Slam title?

THE JUDGE: Pistol Pete was 19 years 28 days when he became the youngest ever winner of the men's singles title at the US Open in 1990, beating Ivan Lendl, John McEnroe and Andre Agassi in the last three rounds. Three years later he won the first of his record seven Wimbledon championships.

WHY didn't Goran Ivanisevic defend his Wimbledon singles title in 2002?

THE JUDGE: Goran, the first ever wild card to win a Grand Slam event at Wimbledon in 2001, was out of action a year later because of surgery to a recurring shoulder injury.

WHEN did Lleyton Hewitt win his first Grand Slam title?

THE JUDGE: Lleyton collected his first major when defeating Pete Sampras 7-6 (7-4), 6-1, 6-1 in the 2001 US Open final in New York.

THE '250' QUIZ CHALLENGE

164. Who was the last Australian before Lleyton Hewitt to win the men's singles championship at Wimbledon?

HOW tall is Tim Henman and where was he born?

THE JUDGE: Tim, born in Oxford on September 6 1974, is 6ft 1in.

WHO partnered Tim Henman when he won an Olympic medal?

THE JUDGE: Tim's partner in the 1996 Olympic final in Atlanta was Neil Broad. They won the silver medal, losing in straight sets to the all-conquering Woodies – Todd Woodbridge and Mark Woodforde, of Australia.

WHERE was Andre Agassi born, and was his father a famous sportsman?

THE JUDGE: Andre was born in Las Vegas on April 29 1970. His father, Emmanuel Agassian, was an Armenian who emigrated to the United States from Iran in 1952. He boxed in the Olympics for Iran and had a brief professional career before becoming a tennis coach, with his son as his most famous pupil.

WHAT is the capacity of the main courts at Wimbledon?

THE JUDGE: The Centre Court seats 13,812, No. 1 Court 11,428 and No. 2 Court 2,220, with standing room for a further 770 spectators.

HOW many courts are there at Wimbledon?

THE JUDGE: Eighteen, and there are 130 court coverers employed each year. When it rains, every court can be covered within five minutes of the first downpour.

WHEN were the first Wimbledon championships held?

THE JUDGE: In 1877 at the original Worple Road venue. The first championships at Church Road were held in 1922. The first finals were watched by just over 200 spectators. In 2002, they were beamed to 174 countries, with an estimated global audience of one billion viewers.

WHAT is the quotation the players see on the wall before coming out on to the Centre Court at Wimbledon?

THE JUDGE: The quotation is an extract from Rudyard Kipling's motivational 'If' poem: 'If you can meet with triumph and disaster and treat those two impostors just the same...'

THE '250' QUIZ CHALLENGE

165. Which future Wimbledon champion did Andre Agassi beat in the final when winning the title on the Centre Court in 1992?

TENNIS

WHAT are the Grand Slam tennis tournaments?

THE JUDGE: The Australian Open, The French Open (Roland Garros), Wimbledon and the United States Open.

WHO was the last British player to appear in the men's Wimbledon singles final?

THE JUDGE: Henry 'Bunny' Austin, who was beaten in straght sets by Don Budge in the 1938 final. Budge The valiant Austin also lost in straight sets to Ellsworth Vines in the 1932 final.

WHICH players have completed the Grand Slam, winning all four titles in the same calendar year?

THE JUDGE: Don Budge (USA) in 1938 and Rod Laver (Aus) in 1962 and 1969. Three Ladies have won the Grand Slam singles – Maureen Connolly (USA) in 1953, Margaret Smith Court (Aus) in 1970 and Steffi Graf (Ger) in 1988 - Steffi Graf also won a gold medal at the Seoul Olympics in 1988 giving her what was dubbed a Golden Grand Slam.

HAS a rugby union international won a Wimbledon championship?

THE JUDGE: JPR Williams, legendary Wales full back, won the Junior championship of Great Britain at Wimbledon in 1966, beating David Lloyd in the final.

IS it true that Tim Henman was once disqualified at Wimbledon?

THE JUDGE: Tim was disqualified in 1995 after he angrily hit a ball that struck a ball girl during his first round doubles. He was also fined $2,000.

HOW many balls are used during the Wimbledon championships?

THE JUDGE: Around 15,000 balls are used on average during the championships and approximately 6,000 balls for the qualifying tournaments. Another 22,000 balls are used for practice. New balls are supplied after seven games (to allow for the preliminary warm-up) and then after every nine games. Yellow balls were used for the first time in 1986. Slazenger has provided every tennis ball for the championships at Wimbledon since 1902.

THE '250' QUIZ CHALLENGE

166. Which Argentinian opponent did Steffi Graf beat in the 1988 Olympic singles final in Seoul?

WHAT happens to all the balls used at Wimbledon?

THE JUDGE: Many are sold cheaply to clubs affiliated to the Lawn Tennis Association. Others are sold daily from a kiosk positioned near No. 14 Court. The proceeds are given to British Schools LTA 'Wimbledon Balls for Schools Scheme.'

DO the champions get to keep the Wimbledon trophies for a year?

THE JUDGE: No, they have to be handed back for security reasons. Each champion receives a miniature version of the trophies.

WHAT has been the record number of games played in a Wimbledon doubles final?

THE JUDGE: The record was set in 1992 when John McEnroe and Michael Stich beat James Grabb and Richard Reneberg after 83 games – 5-7, 7-6 (7-5), 3-6, 7-6 (7-5), 19-17.

WHO has the official fastest serve?

THE JUDGE: Greg Rusedski has the world's fastest serve on record in an official event. He was clocked at an explosive 149 mph.

WHO was the first left-handed Wimbledon champion?

THE JUDGE: Australian Norman Brookes, who also became the first overseas champion when he beat Arthur Gore in the 1907 final. Britain's Ann Jones became the first left-handed women's champion when she beat Billie-Jean King in the 1969 final.

WHAT was so special about Maureen Connolly?

THE JUDGE: I need a book to answer that one properly. 'Little Mo' was the first woman to win the Grand Slam and in the space of four years captured six major titles – and her career was all over by the time she was 19! She was never beaten in her three Wimbledon tournaments, winning the title each time from 1952 through to 1954. She looked a certainty to win her fourth successive US singles title, but her leg was badly damaged in a riding fall and her career was finished. Maureen was born in San Diego, California, on September 17 1934. In 195, she married US Olympic equestrian rider Norman Brinker. She died tragically young from cancer at the age of 34 on June 21 1969. Without doubt, one of the greatest women tennis players ever to swing a racket.

THE '250' QUIZ CHALLENGE

167. In which other sport was Ann Jones a world champion in the days when she was known as Ann Haydon?

OLYMPICS

WERE the London Olympics of 1948 televised?

THE JUDGE: The 1948 London Games were the first to be shown on home television, but so few people owned sets that the viewing audience was less than 20,000. There was an experiment with televised events during the 1936 Olympics in Berlin, but this was restricted to closed-circuit theatres. The 2000 Sydney Olympics were watched by a world-wide audience of more than a billion viewers.

WHICH have been the host cities for each Olympics?

THE JUDGE: Summer Games – Athens 1896, Paris 1900, St Louis 1904, London 1908, Stockholm 1912, Antwerp 1920, Paris 1924, Amsterdam 1928, Los Angeles 1932, Berlin 1936, London 1948, Helsinki 1952, Melbourne 1956, Rome 1960, Tokyo 1964, Mexico City 1968, Munich 1972, Montreal 1976, Moscow 1980, Los Angeles 1984, Seoul 1988, Barcelona 1992, Atlanta 1996, Sydney 2000.

Winter Games: Chamonix 1924, St Moritz 1928, Lake Placid 1932, Garmisch-Partenkirchen 1936, St Moritz 1948, Oslo 1952, Cortina d'Ampezzo 1956, Squaw Valley 1960, Innsbruck 1964, Grenoble 1968, Sapporo 1972, Innsbruck 1976, Lake Placid 1980, Sarajevo 1984, Calgary 1988, Albertville 1992, Lillehammer 1994, Nagano 1998, Salt Lake City 2002.

DID Jesse Owens anchor the sprint relay team to clinch his fourth gold medal in the 1936 Berlin Olympics?

THE JUDGE: No, he ran the first leg to set the US quartet on the way to a world record of 39.8secs that would last for 20 years. Frank Wykoff ran the last leg and won his third successive sprint relay gold medal, the team setting a world record each time. Jesse Owens, of course, also won the individual 100 metres, 200 metres and long jump, and was so supreme that he was snubbed by Adolf Hitler, who did not want to be seen congratulating somebody from what he considered an inferior race.

THE '250' QUIZ CHALLENGE

168. In which event did Jesse Owens set an individual world record that lasted for more than 25 years?

WHO was the first athlete to win gold medals at four successive Olympic Games?

THE JUDGE: American discus thrower Al Oerter, a feat since equalled only by Carl Lewis in the long jump. Oerter took the gold medal in the discus in 1956, 1960, 1964 and 1968, setting a new Olympic record on each occasion. His third victory in 1964 was remarkable because he had to wear a brace because of neck and rib injuries. Yet he still managed to set a career best.

DID Steve Ovett run in an Olympic final before his 800 metres gold medal victory in the 1980 Moscow Games?

THE JUDGE: Steve finished fifth in the 1976 final in Montreal. He went into the Moscow Games second favourite to Sebastian Coe in the 800 metres but a hot favourite for his specialist race, the 1500 metres. He won the 800 metres gold medal, with Coe in second place. Coe got his revenge by winning the 1500 metres, with a shocked Ovett back in the bronze medal position.

WHO took the silver medal behind Sebastian Coe in the 1500 metres in the 1984 Olympics, and what happened to Steve Ovett?

THE JUDGE: Steve Cram took second place as Coe retained his title in an Olympic record 3mins 32.53secs. Ovett suddenly stepped off the track while running in fourth place, and was taken away on a stretcher suffering the after-effects of a chest problem that affected him throughout the Games. As in Moscow, Coe had earlier taken a silver in the 800 metres.

WHO was known as the Flying Dutchwoman of the Olympics?

THE JUDGE: The one and only Fanny Blankers-Koen, who at the age of 30 – and a mother of two – won four gold medals in the 1948 London Olympics, winning the 100m, 200m, 80m hurdles and anchoring the Dutch team to victory in the sprint relay. She was deprived of more championships by a rule limiting women to three individual events. At the time, Fanny was also the world record holder in the high jump and long jump. She later revealed that she was in the early stages of pregnancy when on the way to her four gold medals.

THE '250' QUIZ CHALLENGE

169. Who was the Brazilian who beat Sebastian Coe to the gold medal in the 800 metres final in the 1984 LA Games?

HOW many Olympic gold medals did the great pole vaulter Sergey Bubka win?

THE JUDGE: Despite being the master of his event for a stretch of ten years, he managed only one gold medal. He missed the Los Angeles Olympics because of the Soviet Union boycott, and then won comfortably in Seoul. He was the hottest of hot favourites for gold in the Barcelona Games, but incredibly failed to register a single vault. But he remains a legendary figure in his event having set no fewer than 30 world records – 14 outdoors and 16 indoors.

IS it right that a bare-footed runner won an Olympic marathon?

THE JUDGE: This was Abebe Bikila, who padded to his first gold medal on bare feet in the 1960 Rome Olympics. He became the first man to win two Olympic marathons in Tokyo four years later, this time wearing conventional running shoes. His winning time in Tokyo was then a world best of 2 hrs 12 mins 11.2 secs, and he managed it just 40 days after an appendix operation. A member of the Ethiopian Imperial Guard, he was paralysed in a car accident in 1969 and died four years later.

WHO is the athlete who won ten Olympic gold medals?

THE JUDGE: Ray Ewry, an American who took up jumping to help strengthen his legs after being crippled by polio as a child. He was a master at the now defunct standing events. Two of his golds came in the unofficial Olympics of 1906. He finished first in every Olympic event he ever entered, winning the standing high jump and standing long jump four times (1900, 1904, 1906, 1908), and the standing triple jump twice (1900, 1904). His ten individual gold medals remain an Olympic record for any sport.

HOW many men have won more than one gold medal in the 400 metres on the Olympic track?

THE JUDGE: Just Michael Johnson, who retained the championship he had won in Atlanta with a storming run in the Sydney Olympics. Supreme at the one lap event for seven years, he produced his greatest Olympic performance in the 200 metres in Atlanta when he blitzed to victory in a world record 19.32secs. He took his haul to five Olympic golds by twice anchoring the USA 4 x 400m relay team to victory.

THE '250' QUIZ CHALLENGE

170. Which sprinter from Namibia was second behind Michael Johnson when he broke the world 200m record in the 1996 Games?

HOW many medals did Marion Jones win in Sydney?

THE JUDGE: Marion competed in five events and won five medals, but not the all-gold collection she had set her heart on. She began with an impressive victory in the 100m. Five days later she imperiously won the 200 metres. Her big disappointment came in the long jump when she had to settle for third place. On the final day of the Games , she anchored the US 4 x 100m relay team to third-place, and then ran the third leg for the winning 4 x 400m relay squad. She was the first woman to win five medals in athletics in the same Olympics.

WHO was known as White Lightning?

THE JUDGE: Cuban Alberto Juantorena, who made Olympic history in the 1976 Montreal Olympics by becoming the first man to win both the 400 metres and 800 metres. He was a novice at 800 metres, but had the strength and speed to lead for virtually the whole race. Three days later he powered to victory in the 400m, using his three metre stride that earned him another nickname – El Cabello (The Horse). He was the first runner from a non-English-speaking country to win either event.

IS it right that the legendary Kip Keino was once disqualified in an Olympics race?

THE JUDGE: Kip – an uncoached Nandi tribesman from Kenya – was making his Olympic debut in the 10,000 metres at the 1968 Mexico Olympics when he got a violent attack of stomach pain. With two laps to go, he stumbled and fell off the track and on to the infield. Bravely, he got up and finished the race but was disqualified for leaving the track. Four days later, he took the silver in the 5,000 metres and then, on the final day, ran away with the 1,500 metres – beating the favourite Jim Ryun by a record margin of more than 20 metres. Elevated to police inspector in Nairobi, Kip won the 3,000 metres steeplechase in the Munich Games and a silver in the 1,500 metres. Known as the 'Father' of African middle-distance running, he has added to his legend by setting up a famous children's home and school for African orphans.

WHICH Olympic champion sprinter became a top American footballer?

THE JUDGE: Bob Hayes, 1964 100 metres gold medallist, who later established himself as an exceptional wide receiver with Dallas Cowboys.

THE '250' QUIZ CHALLENGE

171. What was the nationality of Pekka Vasala, who beat Kip Keino to the gold medal in the 1972 Olympic 1500 metres final?

HAS any athlete won more than two gold medals in the men's javelin?

THE JUDGE: Jan Zelezny completed the hat-trick in Sydney in 2000. The Man with the Golden Arm won the championship in the 1992 Barcelona Games with his first throw, and in the Games of 1996 and 2000 edged Britain's Steve Backley into second place. In each year Jan – at around 13 stone – was the lightest competitor in the field. In his Olympic debut in 1988, the Czech had to be content with a silver after throwing six feet farther than the eventual champion, Finn Tapio Korjus, in the qualifying round, an effort that did not count in the final.

WHICH Olympic champion was known as The Shifter?

THE JUDGE: Miruts Yifter, an Ethiopian who could have been anywhere between 33 and 42 when winning both the 5,000 and 10,000 metres in the 1980 Moscow Games. Eight years earlier, he had missed the start of an Olympic 5,000 metres heat because he was in the toilet as the gun went to start the race. His consolation was a bronze in the 10,000 metres. Ethiopia joined the African boycott of the Montreal Games, but Yifter the Shifter made up for his frustration in Moscow. Asked how old he was, Miruts replied, 'Men may steal my chickens; men may steal my sheep. But no man can steal my age.'

WAS Daley Thompson ever beaten in an Olympic decathlon?

THE JUDGE: Daley first competed in the Olympics at the age of 18 in 1976, finishing 18th in the decathlon. He won back to back decathlons in 1980 and 1984, and finished fourth in the 1988 Seoul Games when handicapped by a groin injury. Daley won 19 decathlons in all, yet strangely never ever competed in a decathlon in England.

DID Mary Peters break the world record when winning the pentathlon gold medal in the 1972 Games?

THE JUDGE: Mary – now Dame Mary – needed a personal best in her final event, the 200 metres, to clinch victory. She managed it by a fraction to lift her points haul to a world record 4,801 points, just ten ahead of the favourite Heide Rosendahl, which in pentathlon terms is a photo-finish. For all those readers who ask the question as to whether Mary is Irish, the answer is she was born in Halewood, Lancashire.

THE '250' QUIZ CHALLENGE

172. In which of his decathlon events did Daley Thompson twice win individual national titles?

IS it true that a Red Indian won an Olympic gold medal and was then forced to give it back?

THE JUDGE: Jim Thorpe, who would now be known as a Native American, won the 1912 Olympic pentathlon and decathlon in Stockholm by huge margins, setting world records in both events. At the awards ceremony, the King of Sweden told Thorpe, 'Sir, you are the greatest athlete in the world.' Jim replied, 'Thanks King.' A year later, Thorpe's name was struck from the roll of Olympic champions after it was alleged that he had earlier been paid expenses for playing minor league baseball. Not until 1982 did the IOC reverse its decision and, after an interval of 70 years, the medals were returned, posthumously, to the Thorpe family. Part French and part Sac-and-Fox Indian, he attended Carlisle Indian School where he was known as né Wa-tho-huck, meaning 'Bright Path'. He once represented the school on his own against two college teams, and won the meeting! He later played professional football for the Canton Bulldogs and was a figurehead first President of the National Football League. Thorpe also played major league baseball for the New York Giants, Boston Braves and Cincinnati Reds. He died in relative poverty in 1953, a forgotten hero. More than 20 years later, a statue was put up by Native Americans to honour a legendary man of the Olympics. Burt Lancaster portrayed him in a 1950s film, Jim Thorpe – All American (released in Europe as Man of Bronze). Even with this, Jim was ripped off. He sold the rights to his story back in the 1930s for $1500, and was not paid another nickel.

WHY was Olympic sprint champion Wilma Rudolph known as Wonder Woman?

THE JUDGE: Born with polio, Tennessee Tigerbelle Wilma Rudolph, the 20th of 22 children, overcame her handicap to become one of the greatest women sprinters of all time. As a 16-year-old, she won a bronze medal in the relay at the 1956 Olympics and four years later she was the heroine of the Rome Olympics, finishing first in the 100m, 200m and running the winning anchor leg in the 4x100 relay. Wilma, a mother of four, tragically died from a brain tumor in 1994 at the age of 54.

WHO was the first modern Olympic track champion?

THE JUDGE: American sprinter Thomas Burke, winner of the 100 metres in Athens in 1896 in a time of 12.00secs.

THE '250' QUIZ CHALLENGE

173. Which British sprinter from Yorkshire won a silver medal behind Wilma Rudolph in the Olympic 100 metres final in Rome?

WHO was the British athlete who finished his race in the Barcelona Olympics despite being injured?

THE JUDGE: Derek Redmond, who tore a hamstring muscle coming off the first bend in the 400 metres semi-final. He fell to the track in agony, but as the stretcher-bearers approached him, he waved them away. He was determined to finish the race. As Derek got up and started to hobble forward his father, Jim, ran out of the stands and joined him on the track. Hand in hand, with Derek sobbing, they continued. Just before the finish, Jim let go of his son and Derek completed the course on his own, with the crowd of 65,000 giving him a standing ovation. He had set the fastest time in his heat and had won his quarter-final.

IS it true that Emil Zatopek won an Olympic gold medal in his first ever marathon?

THE JUDGE: The galloping Czech had already won the 5,000 and 10,000 metres in the 1952 Helsinki Olympics and decided to run in his first ever marathon just for the hell of it. He was running alongside British favourite Jim Peters and said, 'Should we not be going faster?' He then ran away from Peters and on to his third gold medal. Between 1949 and 1954, he set 18 world records at every distance from 5,000m to 30,000m. His wife, Dana (né Ingrova), was winning the gold medal in the 1952 Olympic javelin while he was on the way to victory in the 5,000 metres.

WHAT did the great Lasse Viren do for a living?

THE JUDGE: Lasse was a 23-year-old village policeman in Finland when he astonished the world by winning both the 5,000 and 10,000 metres in the 1972 Olympics. His 10,000 metres victory was particularly amazing because he fell over in the final and was stranded at the back of the field before galloping through to win. He retained both titles in the 1976 Olympics and then broke down attempting a Zatopek-style hat-trick in the marathon. His career was cloaked with controversy because of allegations that he was involved in blood-boosting experiments.

WHAT is the slowest time ever recorded in an Olympic 10,000 metres race?

THE JUDGE: Olmeus Charles, of Haiti, clocked 42m 11s in a heat in 1976. He was lapped ten times by the rest of the field. It was his first attempt at the distance!

THE '250' QUIZ CHALLENGE

174. Which British runner took the bronze medal in the 1976 Olympic 10,000 metres final won by Lasse Viren?

WHICH marathon runner was presented with a special gold cup by British Royalty?

THE JUDGE: Dorando Pietri, a candymaker from Capri who famously collapsed coming into the White City stadium when leading at the end of the 1908 Olympic marathon. Officials helped him over the line as he staggered from one side of the track to the other. He was later disqualified for being given illegal assistance. Queen Alexandra presented him with a gold cup as consolation.

HAS a British runner ever won an Olympic marathon?

THE JUDGE: Thomas Hicks, winner of the 1904 Olympic marathon, was born in Birmingham but was representing the United States. Britain has produced four silver medallists – Sam Ferris (1932), Ernest Harper (1936), Tom Richards (1948) and Basil Heatley (1964). Charlie Spedding got a bronze medal in 1984.

WHICH athlete has won most Olympic gold medals?

THE JUDGE: Paavo Nurmi, the famous Flying Finn, won a record nine Olympic gold medals (seven individual; two team) and three individual silver medals. His medals came in a wide range of events: 1,500m, 3,000m (team), 5,000m, 10,000m, steeplechase and cross-country. In 1932, he was banned for alleged professionalism and missed the chance to add the 1932 marathon to his list of Olympic successes. He returned to the Olympic arena in 1952 when he carried the torch into the Helsinki stadium. Nurmi set 22 official and 13 unofficial world records.

DID that magnificent hurdler Ed Moses set a world record when winning an Olympic title?

THE JUDGE: Moses, who graduated from the same Atlanta Morehouse college as Martin Luther King, set a new world record of 47.63 seconds when taking the 400 metres hurdles gold medal in 1976. He was at his peak when the USA boycotted the Moscow Games, but was still good enough four years later to win his second gold medal in the LA Games. He was undefeated from 1977 to 1986, hurdling to 107 consecutive victories. He had to settle for a bronze in the 1988 Seoul Games at the close of his career. An outstanding humanitarian, Edwin now gives a lot back with unceasing work for children's charities, and he is the Chairman of the distinguished Laureus World Sports Academy.

THE '250' QUIZ CHALLENGE

175. Who was the American who succeeded Ed Moses as Olympic 400 metres hurdles champion in Seoul in 1988?

IS it right that a schoolboy won an Olympic gold medal in the decathlon?

THE JUDGE: Bob Mathias was a 17-year-old Californian high school pupil when he won the decathlon in London in 1948. It was only the second time he had attempted the event. Four years later, he retained the title before becoming a film actor. He later went into politics and was a Congressman. Bob remains the youngest person to have won an Olympic gold medal in track and field athletics.

WHO won the first ever marathon in the modern Olympics?

THE JUDGE: Spiridon Louis, a 24-year-old shepherd, was hailed as a Greek hero when he won the marathon at Athens in 1896. The race had been created to honour the legend of Philippides, who carried the news of the Greek victory at the Battle of Marathon in 490 BC by running the 26 miles from Marathon to Athens. Louis, who won by a margin of seven minutes over his nearest competitor, was timed at 2hr 58min 50secs. He returned to the spotlight 40 years later when he was a guest of honour alongside Hitler at the opening of the Berlin Games.

HOW many Olympic medals did Carl Lewis win?

THE JUDGE: Carl Lewis is one of only four Olympic athletes to have won nine gold medals, and one of only three to win the same individual event four times. In 1984, Lewis matched Jesse Owens' feat of winning four gold medals with victories in the 100m, the 200m, the long jump and the 4x100m relay. At the 1988 Seoul Games, he gained a second gold medal in the 100m after drug cheat Ben Johnson was disqualified. He also defended his long jump title and finished second in the 200m. At the 1992 Barcelona Games, Lewis won a third gold medal in the long jump, defeating world record holder Mike Powell by three centimetres. He also anchored the world record-setting US relay team. In 1996, he won his fourth long jump gold medal 12 years after his first triumph.

WHY is the high jump style known as the Fosbury Flop?

THE JUDGE: It is named after the 1968 gold medallist Dick Fosbury, who revolutionised high jumping by going over the bar backwards. Until then, the western roll or straddle were the most popular styles. Fosbury was virtually unknown until his startling 1968 victory.

THE '250' QUIZ CHALLENGE

176. Who set the Olympic long jump record that neither Carl Lewis nor Mike Powell could beat in their 1988 duel in Seoul?

THE JUDGE

HOW many perfect sixes did Torvill and Dean score in the 1984 Winter Olympics?

THE JUDGE: Jayne Torvill and Christopher Dean, ice dance partners from Nottingham, mesmerized the audience with their interpretation of Maurice Ravel's Bolero. The judges awarded them 12 scores of 6.0 out of 18 marks, including across-the-board perfect scores for artistic impression. They got an ovation from the crowd that lasted five minutes. In 1994, they returned to the Olympics and placed third, although most neutral observers thought they were the best of the couples.

WHAT was controversial about John Curry's skating style in the 1976 Olympics?

THE JUDGE: Some blinkered judges did not approve of John's figure skating style because he emphasised balletic grace and artistic expression over athleticism. The gentle yet strong-willed man from Birmingham defended his skating as being in the tradition of Olympic figure skating pioneer Gillis Grafström. He compromised for the 1976 Olympics, supplementing his natural elegance with dynamic jumps. He performed his freestyle long programme to Ludwig Minkus' ballet Don Quixote, and brought a standing ovation from the crowd. Although the Soviet and Canadian judges awarded first place to their own skaters, overall the nine judges gave Curry 105.9 points out a possible 108 points. This remains the highest point total in the history of men's figure skating and Curry won a clear victory.

WHO was known as the Ice Queen?

THE JUDGE: This was Sonja Henie, who was the first superstar of women's figure skating after winning three Olympic gold medals in 1928, 1932, and 1936. She made her Olympic debut in 1924 when just eleven. Sonja turned professional in 1936, amassing a fortune in a sequence of ten Hollywood films and touring the world with her own ice-dance show.. She became one of the world's wealthiest women.

HOW many Olympic gold medals did French skier Jean-Claude Killy win?

THE JUDGE: Jean-Claude matched Austrian Toni Sailer's record by winning all three Alpine skiing gold medals at the 1968 Olympics in Grenoble, close to his home in Val d'Isere.

THE '250' QUIZ CHALLENGE

177. What nationality was the three times Olympic figure skating champion Sonja Henie?

DID a British rower win five Olympic gold medals before Steve Redgrave?

THE JUDGE: Jack Beresford was the Steve Redgrave of his time, winning what was then a record five Olympic medals. But they were not all gold. Jack, who rowed for the Thames, Leander and Kingston clubs, won gold medals in the single sculls (1924), coxless fours (1932) and double sculls (1936), and added silver in the single sculls (1920) and the eights (1928). His remarkable career spanned five Olympic Games and it was almost certainly only the cancellation of the 1940 Games that prevented a sixth Olympic appearance. He was awarded the Olympic Diploma of Merit in 1949. At Henley, he won the Diamond Sculls four times (1920 and 1924-1926), the Nickalls Challenge Cup in 1928 and 1929 (coxless pairs with Gordon Killick), and the Double Sculls Challenge Cup in 1939 with Dick Southwood. He also won the Wingfield Sculls for seven consecutive years from 1920. He later managed the British rowing team at the 1952 Olympics. His father, Julius Beresford, won an Olympic silver medal in the eights in 1912.

GIVE a breakdown of Steve Redgrave's Olympic achievements.

THE JUDGE: Sir Steven is the only Olympian to win gold medals in five consecutive Olympics. He began his golden reign at the 1984 Los Angeles Games as a member of the British coxed fours crew. In Seoul in 1988, Steve teamed with Andrew Holmes to win the coxless pairs, and they also got a broze in the coxed pairs (with Patrick Sweeney as cox). Teaming up with new partner Matthew Pinsent, they won the coxless pairs at the 1992 Barcelona Games. In 1996, in their 100th race together, Redgrave and Pinsent successfully defended their title. At the age of 38, Redgrave returned to the Olympics in 2000 and earned a fifth gold medal, this time as a member of the British coxless fours team that included Pinsent in the crew. Sir Steven, knighted for his services to rowing, achieved all this despite being a chronic diabetic.

HAVE Great Britain ever won the Olympic football championship?

THE JUDGE: Three times, in 1900, 1908 and 1912. When football was first introduced in the 1900 Games in Paris, Britain won with a team from Upton Park (West Ham) representing their country.

THE '250' QUIZ CHALLENGE

178. Which country won the men's soccer gold medal in the 2000 Olympics in Sydney?

WHO was the gymnast who performed to the music of the Mexcian hat dance?

THE JUDGE: Vera Caslavska of Czechoslovakia, who was the outstanding gymnast at the 1964 and 1968 Games. In Tokyo, she won three gold medals and a silver, winning the all-round, balance beam and horse vault, and finishing second in the team event. In 1968, in Mexico City, she dominated, winning four golds (one shared) and two silvers. Her 1968 golds came in the individual all-round, floor exercises, horse vault, and asymmetrical bars. She also won a silver medal in the team event in 1960, giving her a total of 11 Olympic medals which has only been bettered by Russia's Larisa Latynina. After winning her final gold medal in 1968, she married Czech Olympic 1,500m silver medallist Josef Odlozil, in Mexico. Her victories in Mexico City were achieved against the backdrop of Russian tanks invading her homeland and she had all neutrals on her side when performing her floor exercises to the Mexican hat dance. In 1989, Vera – still vivacious – was appointed President of the Czech Olympic Committee, and in 1995 she was elected as a member of the International Olympic Committee.

HOW old was Olga Korbut when she captured the world's imagination in the 1972 Olympics?

THE JUDGE: Olga was seventeen but looked more like a twelve-year-old. She earned gold medals on the balance beam and for the floor exercise and a silver medal on the asymmetrical bars. Back home in Grodno, Belarus, Olga received so much fan mail – more than 20,000 letters – that the post office had to assign a special clerk to sort her mail. In 1976, the still smiling and elfin-like Olga won a gold medal in the team competition and a silver on the balance beam.

WHO was the first gymnast to score a perfect 10 in an Olympic event?

THE JUDGE: Romania's Nadia Comaneci. She was the sensation of the 1976 Olympics in Montreal, and earned her first perfect 10 on the asymmetrical bars. Before the Games were over, she had earned another six maximum marks. In the 1976 and 1980 Games she won a total of nine Olympic medals. In 1989, she defected from Romania and settled in the United States where she married American Olympic gymnastic medallist Bart Conner.

THE '250' QUIZ CHALLENGE

179. In which other discipline did Nadia Comaneci score a 10?
180. Which Russian girl won the floor exercises gold in Montreal?

WHO was the first woman swimmer to win three gold medals in the 100 metres freestyle?

THE JUDGE: The wonderful Dawn Fraser, of Australia. 'Dazzling Dawn' won four gold and four silver medals at the Games of 1956, 1960 and 1964, including three successive golds in the 100m freestyle, a record for any Olympic swimming event (since equalled by Hungary's Krisztina Egerszegi). She was the first of only three women swimmers to win a total of eight Olympic medals, later followed by Kornelia Ender and Shirley Babashoff. Dawn might have added to her collection but for the stupidity of officialdom. In a midnight prank, she and some other high-spirited Aussies stole a flag from the Emperor's palace in Tokyo during the 1964 Olympics. It was harmless fun that deserved a smack on the wrist. The Australian IOC reacted by banning her from international events for ten years! Before this heavy-handed treament, fun-loving Dawn set 27 individual and 12 relay world records, including becoming the first woman swimmer to break the 60-seconds barrier over 100 metres. She was later elected Australia's female athlete of the twentieth century, and – while running a pub – was elected to the New South Wales Parliament where she represented the seat of Balmain until 1991. Incidentally, the Emperor of Japan sent her a special souvenir flag. At least he had a sense of humour, unlike the daft officials who banned her.

WHICH Olympic swimming champion was known as Tarzan?

THE JUDGE: Johnny Weissmuller, who was the winner of the 100m freestyle in 1924 and 1928, the 400m freestyle in 1924 and a member of the winning United States relay team in both years. Weissmuller set 28 world records, and his 1927 world record for the 100 yards freestyle was unbeaten for 17 years. Invited for a screen test for the role of Tarzan, Weissmuller was preferred to 150 other applicants and went on to become the most famous screen Tarzan of all, playing the role in 19 movies between 1932 and 1948.

IN which event did Anita Lonsbrough strike gold?

THE JUDGE: Anita, from Huddersfield, won the 200 metres breaststroke in a world record 2m 49.5s. She was simultaneously Olympic, European and Commonwealth champion.

THE '250' QUIZ CHALLENGE

181. At which Olympics did Anita Lonsbrough win a gold medal?
182. In which team sport did Weissmuller win an Olympic medal?

HOW many days did it take Mark Spitz to complete his historic haul of seven gold medals?

THE JUDGE: The Mark Spitz Blitz lasted a period of eight days. He entered seven events, won all seven and set a world record in every one. Spitz remains the only person to win seven gold medals at one Olympics. He started his golden splash by winning the 200m butterfly, the event in which he had finished last in the 1968 final when he collected 'only' two relay golds. It was this comparitive failure that motivated the Californian student in Munich, and he won the event in a new world record. Later that evening, he anchored the US 4x100m freestyle relay team to earn his second gold medal of the Games and his second world record. The next day, Spitz won the 200m freestyle with another world record. Two days later, he added the 100m butterfly and the 4x200m freestyle relay to his collection. Next, in what he considered his weakest event, he won the 100m freestyle, setting another world record. Finally, Spitz swam the butterfly leg for the US medley relay team: gold medal and world record. It was a swimming spree beyond belief.

WHO was known as The Albatross?

THE JUDGE: Michael Gross, a West German butterfly specialist who stood 6ft 7in and had a 'wing span' of more than eight feet. He won the 100m butterfly and 200m freestyle in world record times at the 1984 LA Olympics, but was surprisngly beaten by Australian Jon Sieben in his main event, the 200m butterfly. Four years later, he picked up the gold medal that had eluded him in 1984. He also won 13 medals at three world championships, and only Germany's boycott of the 1980 Games stopped him making an even bigger splash in the Olympic pool.

WHO was the first boxer to win three gold medals?

THE JUDGE: Hungarian southpaw Laszlo Papp, who won the middleweight title in 1948 and the light-middleweight gold medals in 1952 and 1956. In the Melbourne Games, he mastered Jose Torres, who went on to become world professional light-heavyweight champion. Papp was the first 'Iron Curtain' boxer to be allowed to box for pay. He had just established himself as European champion, and he was on the brink of a world title challenge when the Hungarian authorities banned him from continuing his professional career. Laszlo coached the Hungarian national team for 20 years.

THE '250' QUIZ CHALLENGE

183. In which profession did Mark Spitz become qualified?
184. Which Scot took a bronze in Laszlo Papp's division in 1956?

AT which Olympics did Cuban Teofilo Stevenson win his gold medals?

THE JUDGE: The giant Cuban was champion in 1972, 1976 and 1980, and might easily have added an historic fourth gold medal but for Cuba joining the boycott of the 1984 LA Games. He was beaten just 14 times in 170 contests and only once in a major championship. On his way to winning his first title in Munich, he beat highly-touted American Duane Bobick, who the previous year had inflicted one of his rare defeats. American promoters offered him fortunes to turn professional and to fight Muhammad Ali, but the Cuban authorities persuaded him to continue to box just for the honour of his country.

WHY did Felix Savon miss the 1988 Olympics when he was world amateur heavyweight champion?

THE JUDGE: Felix, who followed his hero and countryman Teofilo Stevenson as a three-time Olympic heavyweight champion, would have been favourite for the gold medal in the Seoul Olympics but Cuba boycotted the Games.The politicians could not stop Savon winning in 1992, 1996 and and 2000.

DID the basketball genius Michael Jordan compete in the Olympics as an amateur?

THE JUDGE: Michael Jordan represented the United States at the 1984 Los Angeles Games, leading the US team in scoring with an average 17.1 points per game on the way to a gold medal. Eight years later, and established with the Chicago Bulls as the greatest basketball player of all time, Michael was in the US 'Dream Team' of professionals who were allowed to compete in the 1992 Barcelona Olympics. He was the team's second highest scorer with 14.9 points per game and he had a tournament high 37 steals. When the US coasted to a 117-85 victory in the final, 'Air' Jordan picked up his second Olympic gold medal.

HOW many Olympic medals did Reg Harris win?

THE JUDGE: Two, both silver at the 1948 London Olympics – in the individual sprint and the tandem, partnered by Alan Bannister. The Nottingham racer was world amateur sprint cycling champion at the time, but his training for the Games was interrupted by a broken arm. He turned professional and won four world sprint titles.

THE '250' QUIZ CHALLENGE

185. Who did the USA beat in the 1992 Olympic basketball final?
186. Who was Olympic heavyweight boxing champion in 1968?

OTHER SPORTS

WHO achieved the first nine dart finish and in which tournament?

THE JUDGE: John Lowe won £102,000 for completing the first 501 scored with the minimum nine darts in a major televised event on 13 October 1984. He performed the feat at Slough in the quarter-finals of the World Match-play Championships. His darts sequence: six successive treble 20s, treble 17, treble 18 and double 18.

WHICH snooker player scored the first televised maximum 147 and at which venue?

THE JUDGE: Steve Davis scored the first 147 in front of the Granada cameras in the Lada Classic at Oldham in 1982. It featured on ITV's Midweek Sports Special. John Spencer was the opponent.

WHO scored the first televised 147 snooker break in a world championship match?

THE JUDGE: Canadian Cliff Thorburn was first with a televised 147 in the world championships, scoring the maximum against Terry Griffiths in the second round of the 1983 finals.

WHAT is the highest maximum break possible in snooker?

THE JUDGE: It is possible to score a 155 when the break includes a free ball as an 'extra' red. Malta's Tony Drago once scored 149 in this freak situation, but not in an official tournament. There have been various reports from around the world of 155 scores, but none witnessed for official record purposes.

HOW old is the Greyhound Derby and on which track was it first run?

THE JUDGE: It was first run at London's White City Stadium over 500 yards in 1927 and was won by 4-1 on favourite Entry Badge.

THE '250' QUIZ CHALLENGE

187. Which Welshman did John Lowe beat in the 1979 world final?
188. Which Welshman did Steve Davis beat in the 1981 world final?

WHERE and when was the hare introduced to greyhound racing?

THE JUDGE: The mechanical hare was invented by Owen Smith in the United States in the early 1920s and was first used in the UK at Belle Vue, Manchester, in 1926.

IN which sport do you use a chistera?

THE JUDGE: It is a type of wicker basket used in some variations of the Basque game Pelota.

WHO were the pacemakers when Roger Bannister first broke the four-minute mile barrier?

THE JUDGE: Chris Brasher led through the first two laps, reaching halfway in 1 min 58 sec. Chris Chataway took over on lap three and reached the bell in 3 min 0.4 sec. Bannister, a stride behind, hit the front with 230 yards to go and fell exhausted through the tape at 3 min 59.4 sec. The date was May 6 1954, and the race was staged on the cinder track at Iffley Road, Oxford. The record attempt was almost called off because of a buffeting wind. The clock on the nearby church tower was chiming six o'clock as the race reached its climax.

WAS Tommy Simpson the first English cyclist to win a stage in the Tour de France?

THE JUDGE: No. This was Brian Robinson, who was a stage winner in the 1958 Tour. Yorkshireman Tommy Simpson wore the yellow jersey in 1962.

IS it true that Great Britain were once Olympic ice hockey champions?

THE JUDGE: Great Britain were the shock winners of the Olympic ice hockey title at Garmisch in 1936. They included two Canadian-born players in Alex Archer and goalminder James Foster, despite protests from the Americans. Canada's 20-match unbeaten run in the Olympics was ended by Britain in the semi-final, and the British team survived a 0-0 triple overtime tie with the United States in their final match.

IN which sports event is there a Rudolph and a Randolph?

THE JUDGE: They are twisting front somersaults in trampolining.

THE '250' QUIZ CHALLENGE

189. Who was the second man to break the four-minute mile barrier?
190. Which Irishman won the Tour de France in 1987?

HOW many world speedway titles did Ivan Mauger win, and was he born in England?

THE JUDGE: Mauger, born in Christchurch, New Zealand, won 15 world titles, including a record six individual championships between 1968 and 1979.

WHICH sportsman had the nickname The Cannibal?

THE JUDGE: This was Belgian master cyclist Eddie Merckx. As well as his five victories in the Tour de France, Merckx won 525 of the 1,800 races he entered in a 13-year professional career. He was called The Cannibal because of the way he used to eat up the miles.

WHERE and when did John Surtees win his first Grand Prix as a motor racing driver?

THE JUDGE: Surtees, the only man to win world titles on two wheels and four, registered his first F1 victory in the German GP at Nurburgring in 1963, three years after switching from motor cycles. He won six of his 111 GP races, and was world champion in 1964 when driving for Ferrari.

WHO had the fastest mile and 1500 metres times out of Steve Ovett, Sebastian Coe and Steve Cram?

THE JUDGE: Steve Cram wins this battle of the clock. His fastest times: mile (3m 46.32s), 1500m (3m 29.67s). Coe: mile (3m 47.33s), 1500m (3m 29.77s). Ovett: mile (3m 48.40s), 1500m (3m 31.36s).

HOW many times was the Australian Herb Elliott beaten in a mile or 1,500 metres event?

THE JUDGE: Never in a senior race. Considered by many to have been the greatest miler of all time, he retired at the age of 23 after winning the Olympic 1,500m in the Rome Olympics in majestic style. He set a new world record and left silver medallist Michel Jazy trailing by 20 metres. Elliott, coached by the fanatical Percy Cerruty, won the half mile and mile double in the 1958 Commonwealth Games. He went to Cambridge to study in 1961 and refused all overtures to resume his running career.

HOW many Grand Prix races did the great Fangio win?

THE JUDGE: Juan Manuel Fangio won 24 of his 51 Grand Prix races on his way to capturing the world championship in 1951 and each year from 1954 to 1957.

THE '250' QUIZ CHALLENGE

191. Which Scot was F1 world champion in 1963 and 1965?
192. In which city did Herb Elliott set a world mile record in 1958?

IN how many successive Embassy world snooker championship finals did Steve Davis appear?

THE JUDGE: Seven, from 1983 to 1989. He won five of them to add to the title he first captured in 1981.

FOR what was an athlete called Arthur Newton famous?

THE JUDGE: English-born Newton emigrated to South Africa, and to draw attention to racism took up long-distance running at the age of 39. He averaged 20-mile runs every day from 1922 to 1935, and his feats included a world best for 100 miles (14 hours 6 mins at the age of 51) and a track distance record of 152 miles during a 24-hour indoor race. In each after-race interview he would make a point of talking about the way black South Africans were being exploited.

WHO was the first Welshman to win an Olympic athletics gold medal?

THE JUDGE: Lynn 'The Leap' Davies, winning the long jump in the 1964 Olympics in Tokyo.

DID Linford Christie ever hold the world record for the 100 or 150 metres?

THE JUDGE: Christie's fastest time for 100m was 9.87s when winning the world championship in Stuttgart on August 15 1993, a stride away from Carl Lewis's then world record of 9.86s. He set a national 150m record at 14.97 in 1994, just outside Pietro Mennea's world best of 14.8s.

IN which sport is the Sterling Cup contested?

THE JUDGE: It is a shooting trophy, and was competed for annually at Bisley by military marksmen.

HAS American football ever been played with 15 players a side on the pitch?

THE JUDGE: The game evolved in the late 19th century from a mix of the British games of soccer and rugby. Under the original rules drawn up at Harvard University, there were 15 players a side, but this was soon reduced to the present 11-a-side as featured in the game today, and with coaches sending on offensive, defensive and special teams depending on the state of the game.

THE '250' QUIZ CHALLENGE

193. On which West Indian island was Linford Christie born?
194. What are attacking wing men called in American football?

WHO was the British runner who collapsed just yards from the finish when leading in a major marathon?

THE JUDGE: Jim Peters, one of the all-time great British marathon runners. He entered the stadium in the 1954 Empire Games marathon in Vancouver an astonishing 20 minutes ahead of his nearest rival. He had become badly dehydrated in the 90 degree heat and started to stagger across the track. His team-mates, including Roger Bannister, looked on anxiously from the track side, and did not attempt to assist him because they recalled Dorando Pietri's disqualification in the 1908 Olympic marathon after being helped across the line. Peters, an Essex man with a long sequence of marathon victories behind him, stumbled and fell and then got up and was reeling like a drunken man. Eventually, caring officials put a blanket around him and led him off the track for emergency medical treatment. Scotland's Joe McGhee, who had been more than three miles behind, was the eventual winner, by which time Peters was in hospital, recovering with the help of an oxygen mask.

WHAT has been the longest frame played in a world championship snooker final at The Crucible?

THE JUDGE: That was the epic final frame of the 1985 world championship final between Steve Davis and Dennis Taylor which lasted 69 minutes. Dennis won on the final black after Steve had missed an easy pocket. Amazingly, Taylor lost the first eight frames.

HOW much did Joe Davis win for his first world snooker championship victory?

THE JUDGE: Joe's prize money was £6 10 shilling (£6.50). He beat Noittingham publican Tom Dennis in the final that was staged in Camkins Billiard Hall in Birmingham in 1927. It was the first of 15 world titles, and Joe remained unbeaten until 1955. He notched up 687 century breaks.

WHO has been the youngest world snooker champion?

THE JUDGE: Stephen Hendry, who won the first of his seven titles in 1990 at the age of 21 years 106 days. He replaced Alex Higgins as the youngest champion. He became Scottish professional champion in 1986, and at 18, in 1987, became the then youngest ever winner of a ranking tournament when he beat Dennis Taylor 10-7 to capture the Rothmans Grand Prix.

THE '250' QUIZ CHALLENGE

195. Who did Stephen Hendry beat for his record 7th world title?
196. Who took over as youngest winner of a ranking tournament?

OTHER SPORTS

WHO has been the longest-odds winner of the world snooker championship?

THE JUDGE: Joe Johnson, who started the 1986 tournament as a 150-1 outsider. He made two century breaks in the last four frames to edge out Terry Griffiths in the quarter-final, and maintained this form to master scorching favourite Steve Davis 18-12 in the final.

WHAT was the biggest lead that Jimmy White had over Stephen Hendry in their classic 1994 world final?

THE JUDGE: Jimmy, trailing 5-1 at one stage, battled back to take a 10-9 lead but neither player could establish more than a two frame advantage and it went to 17-17, with everything resting on the final frame. Jimmy was looking on the way to a straightforward clearance that would have given him his first championship, but he missed a simple black and let Hendry in for his fourth of seven titles.

WHO was the 'Cheating Swordsman of Montreal'?

THE JUDGE: This was the label hung on Boris Onischenko, an army officer from the Ukraine, who entered the 1976 Olympics in Montreal as one of the favourites in the modern pentathlon. The silver medallist from Munich four years earlier exited the Games in disgrace after he had been caught cheating in the fencing stage of the five-discipline event. Onischenko's épée had been wired so that he could trigger the eletronic scoring system with his hand and register a hit at will. It was the British team who were the first to suspect that Onischenko was doing something illegal, and Jim Fox protested to the officials that his opponent was managing to score without hitting him. The Soviet athlete's sword was taken away and examined. Onischenko continued with a replacement weapon, but soon afterwards it was announced that he had been disqualified. The rules of the sport were changed, banning grips that could hide wires or switches. Jim Fox went on to lead the British team to the gold medal.

WHICH stadium was 'The House that Ruth Built'?

THE JUDGE: Yankee Stadium in New York City. Babe Ruth was such a crowd puller with the New York Yankees in the 1920s, that they had to build a larger stadium to accomodate the spectators who roared him on to a then record total of 714 home runs.

THE '250' QUIZ CHALLENGE

197. What was Joe Johnson's lucky omen as world champion?
198. What were the first names of baseball legend Babe Ruth?

195

IS it true that Jesse Owens once set six world records in a single day?

THE JUDGE: Not in just a single day, but inside a single hour! I can be precise about the time (3.15pm to 4.01pm), the place (Ann Arbor in the US) and the day (May 25 1935). It was the Big Ten inter-collegiate championships, and 21-year-old James Cleveland Owens (nicknamed Jesse because of his JC initials) was on the point of withdrawing because of a strained back. His coach persuaded him to try the first of the four events for which he had entered, the 100 yards. The rest is history. This was his record-rewriting timetable: 3.15pm – world record 100 yards dash of 9.4secs; 3.25pm – world record long lump of 26 feet 8.25 inches; 3.45pm – 220 yards in 20.3secs (also beating the 200 metres world record on the way); 4.00pm – 220 yards hurdles in 22.6secs (also a new record over the 200 metres course). It was the only time in athletics history than anybody had set world records both in the track and field on the same day, let alone in the same hour. Fourteen months later, Jesse became even more world renowned when he collected four gold medals at the Berlin Olympics. By the time he was 23, he had retired, and was having to do degrading things like run against racehorses and – a non-smoker – advertise cigarettes to make ends meet. Today, he would have been a multi-millionaire. What a way to treat a hero.

WAS it ever proved that the world records set by Florence Griffith-Joyner were not drug-assisted?

THE JUDGE: Flo-Jo went to her grave at the age of 38, the victim of a heart attack, and took her secrets with her. She had been a moderate sprinter until suddenly knocking big fractions off her times, culminating with an astonishing 10.49secs for 100 metres at the US Olympic trials in Indianapolis. In the Seoul Games, she won the individual 100m and 200m, anchored the gold medal winning relay team and took a silver in the 4 x 400m event. Spectacular in her space-age one-piece running suits and with six inch long fingernails, Flo-Jo made a lasting impression but many remain sceptical as to whether she was 'clean'.

DID Britain win any Olympic track golds in 1936?

THE JUDGE: Freddie Wolff, Godfrey Rampling, Bill Roberts and Arthur Godfrey Brown beat a crack US squad to take the 4 x 400m relay gold medal. Harold Whitlock, a 32-year-old car mechanic, won the 50k walk.

THE '250' QUIZ CHALLENGE

199. Who won an Olympic silver for Britain in the Berlin 400m?
200. In which event did Flo-Jo break the world record in Seoul?

WAS Sir Jack Brabham born in London?

THE JUDGE: No, but his grandfather was a Cockney from East London who emigrated to Australia. Jack, the son of a Sydney grocer, won three world motor racing championships – in 1959, 1960 and 1966, completing the hat-trick in a Brabham-Repco.

IS it true that Graham Hill did not start driving until he was 24?

THE JUDGE: It is true. Graham could not afford his own car until buying a wreck of a 1929 Austin in his mid-20s. He taught himself to rebuild it and the motoring bug bit so deep that over the next 22 years he drove in a then record 176 Grand Prix races and won 14 of them, including five at Monaco. He was world champion in 1962 and 1968, and became the only driver to also win the the Indy 500 (1966) and the Le Mans 24-hour race (1972).

IN which race did Nigel Mansell's tyre burst when he was within sight of the world title?

THE JUDGE: The 1986 Australian Grand Prix in Adelaide, which developed into one of the most dramatic of all time. It was the final race of the season, and Nigel was six points clear of Alain Prost and seven in front of Williams team-mate Nelson Piquet. A top-six finish was all he needed to clinch the championship. Entering the last third of the race, Mansell was second behind Keke Rosberg's McLaren, whose right rear tyre suddenly blew. Goodyear technicians tried desperately to inform the other Goodyear teams, including Williams, but as Mansell slipped into sixth gear and took off down the long Jack Brabham straight at close to 200mph, his own left rear tyre dramatically exploded. Prost, who had been back in third place, sped by to win the world title by two points. Nigel wrestled his car off into an escape road with a magnificent piece of driving control. He later discovered that had he crashed into the wall on the straight, the race would have been stopped and he would have been world champion. Nigel finally became champion in 1992.

HOW many times was James Hunt world champion?

THE JUDGE: James won just the one world motor racing title, in 1976. Shrugging off his 'Hunt the Shunt' reputation, he won six Grand Prix races in 1976 and clinched the title in the final race of the season.

THE '250' QUIZ CHALLENGE

201. Who did James Hunt pip by a point for the '76 F1 drivers title?
202. Who did Nigel Mansell succeed as F1 champion in 1992?

IN which position did Ayrton Senna finish in his first ever race in Great Britain, and can he be considered the greatest racing driver of all time?

THE JUDGE: Ayrton came to England from Brazil in 1981 to race Formula Ford 1600 for Ralph Firman and his Van Diemen team. Making his debut at Brands Hatch, he came home in eighth place. By the end of that first year in England he had won both of the series that he contested and his career was up and motoring. At the time of his tragic death during the 1994 San Marino Grand Prix at Imola, Senna was considered by many to have been the greatest motor racing driver of all time, with only Fangio fans able to give an argument (and now, of course, with Michael Schumacher coming into the reckoning). Ayrton had won the world motor racing championship three times (1988-90-91).

HOW many pole positions did Jim Clark gain in the first season that he won the world championship?

THE JUDGE: Jim Clark dominated the world championship in 1963, winning seven out of 10 races, and claiming seven pole positions. In the same year, he made his debut in the Indy 500 and finished second to Parnelli Jones. Clark, who along with fellow-Scot Jackie Stewart is among the few who can be mentioned in the same breath as Fangio, Senna and Schumacher, won a second championship in 1965, the same year that he won the Indy 500. The son of a Scottish sheep farmer, he won 25 of his 72 Grand Prix races before his death in an F2 race in Hockenheim in 1968.

WAS Stirling Moss the first British driver to win the world motor racing championship?

THE JUDGE: Stirling was never champion. He was runner-up for four successive years, first to the great Juan Manuel Fangio (1955-57) and then to the first ever British champion Mike Hawthorn, who beat Stirling for the title by just one point in 1958. Mike was killed the following year away from the track when driving his Jaguar in Surrey.

HOW old was Michael Schumacher when he first got behind the wheel of a car?

THE JUDGE: Michael's father, Rolf, built him a special kart and he competed in his first race at the age of five! The rest is history.

THE '250' QUIZ CHALLENGE

203. In which car did Michael Schumacher win his first world title?
204. Who was the first home-grown winner of a British Grand Prix?

WHO did Keith Deller beat in the Embassy World Darts final in 1983?

THE JUDGE: Keith Deller, a 23-year-old virtual unknown from Ipswich, beat Eric Bristow. With the match poised at five sets each, and Deller one leg from victory, the Crafty Cockney made a rare miscalculation. He passed up the chance to go for bullseye and take the leg, content to wait for his next visit to the oche. He was convinced the unseeded Deller would never make his 138 out-shot. But dead-eye Keith came up with a treble 20, treble 18 and double 12 to become world champion.

WHAT year was it when Don Fox missed a kick in front of the posts in the rugby league Challenge Cup final?

THE JUDGE: The 1968 final between Wakefield Trinity and Leeds was into its final minute, with Leeds leading 11-10. Don, one of the greatest kickers in the game, had already been named man of the match when he prepared to take a goal kick right in front of the posts. Now all Don Fox had to do was complete a triumphant afternoon for himself and Wakefield Trinity by converting. Amazingly, the Wakefield loose forward toe-poked it wide and sunk to his knees on the rain-sodden Wembley turf. He never played again, nor has he ever discussed the incident.

IN which year did the Oxford crew sink in the Boat Race?

THE JUDGE: There have been several instances, but the one that was captured by the TV cameras was in 1951. Oxford's decision to choose the Surrey bank proved disastrous, exposing the crew to the full force of a gale-force wind while Cambridge made quickly for the cover of the Middlesex bank. Water broke over the bows of the Oxford boat in the very first strokes and, after a minute, they were literally in deep trouble. The race was quickly abandoned while following boats picked up the soaked Oxford crewmen. The race was re-rowed the following Monday, this time on a still day, and Oxford were left high and dry as Cambridge pulled away to win by over 12 lengths.

HOW many world bowls titles did David Bryant win?

THE JUDGE: He had three singles victories in the world Outdoor championships, and in the Indoors events he won the world singles title the first three years it was staged from 1979. He also shared six more world indoor titles in the pairs.

THE '250' QUIZ CHALLENGE

205. Which Scot did Keith Deller succeed as world darts champion?
206. Who was David Bryant's regular indoor pairs partner?

THE JUDGE

WHO was the player who white-washed Stephen Hendry in the UK Championships in 1999?

THE JUDGE: His fellow-Scot Marcus Campbell, then ranked 73, beat Hendry 9-0. This was the lowest point in Stephen's year, but at the end of the season he won his record seventh world championship!

WHICH drivers have won the world motor racing championship most times?

THE JUDGE: Multiple winners: Juan-Manuel Fangio (5); Alain Prost and Michael Schumacher (4); Jack Brabham, Niki Lauda, Nelson Piquet, Ayrton Senna and Jackie Stewart (3); Alberto Ascari, Jim Clark, Emerson Fittipaldi, Mika Hakkinen and Graham Hill (2). The champions' table:-

1950	Guiseppe Farina (Italy, Alfa Romeo)
1951	Juan-Manuel Fangio (Argentina, Alfa Romeo)
1952	Alberto Ascari (Italy, Ferrari)
1953	Alberto Ascari (Italy, Ferrari)
1954	Juan-Manuel Fangio (Argentina, Maserati/Mercedes)
1955	Juan-Manuel Fangio (Argentina, Mercedes)
1956	Juan-Manuel Fangio (Argentina, Ferrari)
1957	Juan-Manuel Fangio (Argentina, Maserati)
1958	Mike Hawthorn (UK, Ferrari)
1959	Jack Brabham (Australia, Cooper-Climax)
1960	Jack Brabham (Australia, Cooper-Climax)
1961	Phil Hill (USA , Ferrari)
1962	Graham Hill (UK, BRM)
1963	Jim Clark (UK, Lotus-Climax)
1964	John Surtees (UK, Ferrari)
1965	Jim Clark (UK, Lotus-Climax)
1966	Jack Brabham (Australia, Brabham-Repco)
1967	Denny Hulme (New Zealand, Brabham-Repco)
1968	Graham Hill (UK, Lotus-Ford)
1969	Jackie Stewart (UK, Matra-Ford)
1970	Jochen Rindt (Austria, Lotus-Ford)

THE '250' QUIZ CHALLENGE

207. Who was awarded the F1 world title posthumously?
208. What is the name of the main Italian Grand Prix track?

OTHER SPORTS

1971	Jackie Stewart (UK, Tyrrell-Ford)
1972	Emerson Fittipaldi (Brazil, Lotus-Ford)
1973	Jackie Stewart (UK, Tyrrell-Ford)
1974	Emerson Fittipaldi (Brazil, McLaren-Ford)
1975	Niki Lauda (Austria, Ferrari)
1976	James Hunt (UK, McLaren-Ford)
1977	Niki Lauda (Austria, Ferrari)
1978	Mario Andretti (USA , Lotus-Ford)
1979	Jody Scheckter (South Africa, Ferrari)
1980	Alan Jones, (Australia, Williams-Ford)
1981	Nelson Piquet (Brazil, Brabham-Ford)
1982	Keke Rosberg (Finland, Williams-Ford)
1983	Nelson Piquet (Brazil, Brabham-BMW)
1984	Niki Lauda (Austria, McLaren-TAG Porsche)
1985	Alain Prost (France, McLaren-TAG Porsche)
1986	Alain Prost (France, McLaren-TAG Porsche)
1987	Nelson Piquet (Brazil, Williams-Honda)
1988	Ayrton Senna (Brazil, McLaren-Honda)
1989	Alain Prost (France, McLaren-Honda)
1990	Ayrton Senna (Brazil, McLaren-Honda)
1991	Ayrton Senna (Brazil, McLaren-Honda)
1992	Nigel Mansell (UK, Williams-Renault)
1993	Alain Prost (France, Williams-Renault)
1994	Michael Schumacher (Germany, Benetton-Ford)
1995	Michael Schumacher (Germany, Benetton-Renault)
1996	Damon Hill (UK, Williams-Renault)
1997	Jacques Villeneuve (Canada, Williams-Renault)
1998	Mika Hakkinen (Finland, McLaren-Mercedes)
1999	Mika Hakkinen (Finland, McLaren-Mercedes)
2000	Michael Schumacher (Germany, Ferrari)
2001	Michael Schumacher (Germany, Ferrari)

THE '250' QUIZ CHALLENGE

209. In which Grand Prix did James Hunt clinch his world title?
210. Who was runner-up to Michael Schumacher in 1994?

THE JUDGE

WHICH American football team has won the Super Bowl most times, and when did the competition start?

THE JUDGE: The first AFL-NFL World Championship Game, as it was originally called, was played seven months after the two major US leagues, the NFL and the AFL, agreed to merge in June 1966. It became the Super Bowl by the third game in 1969. The Super Bowl winner has been presented with the Vince Lombardi Trophy since 1971. The legendary Lombardi, whose Green Bay teams won the first two title games, died in 1970. Multiple winners: Dallas and San Francisco (5); Pittsburgh (4); Green Bay, Oakland-LA Raiders and Washington (3); Denver, Miami and New York Giants (2).

HAS any player in the Super Bowl won the Most Valuable Player award more than once?

THE JUDGE: Joe Montana, one of the all-time great quarterbacks, won it three times with San Francisco, and both Terry Bradshaw (Pittsburgh) and Bart Starr (Green Bay Packers) collected it twice. They were also quarterbacks. Starr won his awards in the the first two Super Bowls in 1967 and 1968. The award, the equivalent of the Man of the Match, is decided by the media and internet votes.

WHAT is the history of the Baseball World Series?

THE JUDGE: The World Series began in 1903 when Pittsburgh of the older National League (founded in 1876) invited Boston of the American League (founded in 1901) to play a best-of-9 game series to determine which of the two league champions was the best. Boston won by 5 games to 3. Since then the World Series has usually been a best-of-7 format.

WHICH teams have won the World Series most times?

THE JUDGE: New York Yankees are far and away the most successful team with 26 titles. Other winners: Philadelphia-Oakland A's and St Louis Cardinals (9); Brooklyn-Los Angeles Dodgers (6); Boston Red Sox, Cincinnati Reds, New York-San Francisco Giants and Pittsburgh Pirates (5); Detroit Tigers (4); Baltimore Orioles, Boston-Milwaukee-Atlanta Braves and Washington Senators-Minnesota Twins (3); Chicago Cubs, Chicago White Sox, Cleveland Indians, New York Mets and Toronto Blue Jays (2).

THE '250' QUIZ CHALLENGE

211. With which baseball team was Joe DiMaggio an all-time hero?
212. Who was the legendary coach of the Green Bay Packers?

OTHER SPORTS

WHAT is the Maurice Podoloff Trophy awarded each basketball season in the United States?

THE JUDGE: Named after the first commissioner (then president) of the NBA, the award goes each season to the basketball player voted the Most Valuable Player. The winners used to be selected by the NBA players (1956-80) before the job was taken over by a national panel of sportswriters and broadcasters. Kareem Abdul-Jabbar won the trophy six times. The other players who have won it more than once: Michael Jordan and Bill Russell (5); Wilt Chamberlain (4); Larry Bird, Magic Johnson and Moses Malone (3); Karl Malone and Bob Pettit (2).

DID the man after whom the Ferrari racing team is named ever drive competitively?

THE JUDGE: Enzo Ferrari drove for Alfa Romeo in the 1920s before ill health forced his retirement. He switched to car design with Scuderia Ferrari in 1929, working for Alfa Romeo. He first built and ran his own cars in 1940, calling them Auto Avio Costruzioni because his agreement with Alfa Romeo barred him from using his own name. The Ferrari name first appeared in 1947, and by the time he died at the age of 90 in 1988, Ferrari cars had won 93 Grand Prix races.

ON which horse did David Broome win the show jumping world championship?

THE JUDGE: David was riding Beethoven when he became champion in 1970, and eight years later led Britain to the team title. David was also three times the European champion – in 1961, and then on his finest horse, Mister Softee, in 1967 and 1968.

WHICH ice hockey star was nicknamed 'The Great One'?

THE JUDGE: Wayne Gretzky, the greatest scorer in the history of ice hockey. Born in Ontario in 1961, he was a child prodigy who was already scoring against seniors at the age of ten. Over the next three decades he scored more than one thousand goals. He had his most memorable moments with the Edmonton Oilers and then the Los Angeles Kings.

WAS David Wilkie born in Scotland?

THE JUDGE: David, 1976 Olympic 200 metres breaststroke champion, was born to Scottish parents in Colombo, Sri Lanka, in 1954.

THE '250' QUIZ CHALLENGE

213. In which event was Duncan Goodhew an Olympic champion?
214. On which horse did David Broome win his first European title?

THE JUDGE

HOW tall was basketball star Wilt Chamberlain?

THE JUDGE: Wilt the Stilt stood 7ft 2in and was a powerful force on the NBA courts throughout the 1960s and into the 1970s. He scored 31,419 points in 1,045 games, an average of 30.1 that has only been bettered by Michael Jordan. He played on two championship teams – the 1967 Philadelphia 76ers and the 1972 Los Angeles Lakers.

WHO were the Rowe twins, and what did they achieve?

THE JUDGE: Left-handed Diane and right-handed Rosalind won the world doubles table tennis championship in 1951 and 1954 and were runners-up three times during the 1950s. Born in Marylebone in 1933, the identical twins totally dominated women's table tennis in the first half of the 1950s before Rosalind retired following her marriage. Diane won six more English doubles titles with three different partners before marrying West German champion Eberhard Schöler in 1966.

HOW many world titles did Hugh Porter win?

THE JUDGE: Hugh, from Wolverhampton, was Britain's most successful pursuit cyclist, winning four world professional titles between 1968 and 1973. He attempted the Tour de France in 1968 but was forced to retire before the finish. Hugh married Olympic swimming champion Anita Lonsbrough in 1965.

WAS Britain's crack marksman Malcolm Cooper born in New Zealand?

THE JUDGE: Malcom, winner of two Olympic gold medals and six world championships, first took up shooting as a schoolboy in New Zealand where his father was stationed as a lieutenant in the Royal Navy. Born in Camberley, Surrey in 1947, Malcolm set an astonishing five world records in the 1986 world shooting championships.

HOW long did Bob Beamon's world long jump record stand?

THE JUDGE: Bob Beamon's famous 8.90m record set in the 1968 Olympics lasted 23 years and 316 days. Mike Powell took the record to new lengths when he reached 8.95m to beat Carl Lewis to the 1991 world championship. Beamon (and his rivals) could not believe it when he bounded to his record in Mexico, breaking both the 28ft and 29ft barriers for the first time.

THE '250' QUIZ CHALLENGE

215. In which Olympics did Malcolm Cooper win his 2nd gold medal?
216. Who did Bob Beamon succeed as Olympic champion?

SPORTS TRIVIA

WHY is a rude two-fingered salute in sport known as a Harvey Smith?

THE JUDGE: It all goes back to 1971 when that gritty Yorkshire competitor Harvey Smith was attempting to become the first rider to win successive Hickstead Derbys. He had forgotten to bring the trophy with him which he had won the previous year, and got a chewing off from Douglas Bunn, Hickstead's owner and vice-president of the British Show Jumping Association, a man with whom Smith had never seen eye to eye. Fired up at what he considered an unnecessary rollocking, Harvey duly rode Mattie Brown to victory. As he rode off at the end of a brilliant clear round, he clearly thrust two fingers in the direction of the judges. The controversial outcome was that Douglas Bunn informed Smith that he was being disqualified for his 'disgusting' gesture and that he would not receive either the trophy or his £2,000 prize money. Harvey claimed: 'It was a straightforward V for victory. Churchill used it throughout the war.' He won a war of words in front of the BSJA and was reinstated as the winner after showing the stewards dozens of photographs of Churchill giving the reverse V sign. The euphemism 'to give a Harvey Smith' was born.

WHY did both Graham Hill and his son Damon wear a rowing club's colours on their helmet?

THE JUDGE: Graham stroked the London Rowing Club's eight to victory in the Grand Challenge Cup at Henley in 1953 before he had a driving licence. He wore the club colours when starting his motor racing career and Damon did the same as a mark of respect to his Dad, who was killed in a plane crash in 1975.

WHAT is the middle name of Mike Tyson?

THE JUDGE: Several record books give the name as Gerald, but they are wrong. Mike's middle name is Gerard.

THE '250' QUIZ CHALLENGE

217. Which old-time manager groomed Mike Tyson as a fighter?
218. With which team did Damon Hill win his world championship?

THE JUDGE

WHEN was Abide With Me first adopted as the FA Cup final hymn?

THE JUDGE: Abide With Me was first introduced as part of the FA Cup community singing before the 1927 final between Cardiff and Arsenal. It was dropped in 1959, but there was such an uproar over its omission that it was brought back the following year.

IS it true that goalkeeper Gordon Banks used to work as a coalman?

THE JUDGE: I went to the great man himself for this answer: 'Yes, I worked as a coalbagger while waiting to get my big break with Chesterfield. It was only after I had done my National Service that things started to fall into place for me, and I was able to think of football as a long-term career. When I started the maximum wage was £20 a week.'

WHO was the first men's player at Wimbledon to wear a pair of shorts on court?

THE JUDGE: Britain's Bunny Austin, who caused a sensation by wearing shorts during the 1933 championships. The 1946 men's champion Yvon Petra, from France, was the last champion to win the title wearing long trousers. When 'Gorgeous Gussie' Moran wore a short, lace trimmed skirt at Wimbledon in 1949, she was accused of 'bringing vulgarity and sin into tennis'.

IS it a fact that the Hollywood cowboy Roy Rogers and his horse Trigger once appeared at Anfield?

THE JUDGE: It was Annfield, not Anfield! Roy Rogers and Trigger entertained spectators at half-time during a Scottish League match at Stirling Albion's old Annfield Park ground in 1954.

DID a Chinaman called Frank Soo play international football for England?

THE JUDGE: Frank Soo, who played 173 League games for Stoke either side of the war, had a Chinese father. He represented England only in unofficial wartime internationals. He was selected for England's first post-war Victory international, but was sidelined by an injury and his place was taken by Billy Wright to start one of the most productive and consistent international careers of all time.

THE '250' QUIZ CHALLENGE

219. Which England manager selected Billy Wright 105 times?
220. With which club did Gordon Banks start his League career?

IN which Olympics was a road cyclist held up by a train?

THE JUDGE: Organisers of the cycle road race in the 1920 Antwerp Olympics remembered to order passenger trains not to use the railway lines that criss-crossed the city during the event. But they forgot about freight trains. Second man home Harry Stenqvist protested that he had been held up for four minutes at a railway crossing, and he was eventually awarded the race.

IS it true that an Olympic marathon winner thumbed a lift during the race?

THE JUDGE: New Yorker Fred Lorz was first to cross the line in the 1904 Olympic marathon in St Louis. He had already been photographed with President's daughter Alice Roosevelt, and was about to be awarded the gold medal, when it was revealed that he had taken a lift for ten miles of the race. Lorz said it was a practical joke that had got out of hand, and was reinstated after first being banned from athletics for life. Thomas Hicks, Birmingham-born but an American citizen, was awarded the race, escaping disqualifcation himself after his trainer had given him strychnine and brandy to keep him going in scorching-hot conditions.

WHAT became known as Gary Sprake's signature tune at Liverpool?

THE JUDGE: This was Des O'Connor's version of Careless Hands. Unluckily for the Leeds and Welsh international goalkeeper, it was in the Top 10 in the charts in December 1967 when he managed to throw the ball into his own net while attempting to find a team-mate with a clearance. The Kop choir immediately broke into choruses of Careless Hands, and greeted Sprake with the song every time he came to Anfield.

WHO recorded the song 'Cricket Lovely Cricket'?

THE JUDGE: The full title was 'Victory Test Match Calypso' and was composed to commemorate the remarkable West Indies defeat of England at Lord's in 1950. It was recorded by Lord Beginner (alias Egbert Moore) accompanied by the Calypso Rhythm Kings. The main thrust of the song was the deeds of 'those little friends of mine, Ramadhin and Valentine'. They were the spin twins who bowled West Indies to a first ever victory in England by 326 runs. Ramadhin took 11 match wickets, and Valentine seven.

THE '250' QUIZ CHALLENGE

221. Which club did Gary Sprake join from Leeds United in 1972?
222. For which English county did Sonny Ramadhin play?

HAS there been a worse England tosser than Nasser Hussain?

THE JUDGE: An unfortunate but understandable description. It is difficult to believe that any captain has had worse luck with the coin than Nasser. In one sequence, he won the toss just once in 11 Tests, and he managed to go six successive games without the coin coming down in his favour.

HAS an Irishman ever been capped for the Republic at both soccer and rugby union?

THE JUDGE: Dr Kevin O'Flanagan, an amateur right winger with Arsenal in the immediate post-war years, played both football and rugby for Eire, on one occasion playing the two codes on successive weekends. His brother, Michael, also gained caps at both codes.

IS it true that tennis great Christine Truman could see out of only one eye?

THE JUDGE: Christine was ranked No 2 in the world in 1959 and in Britain's top three for 12 years despite the handicap of playing with a sightless left eye. She is now one of the excellent Radio 5 Live commentary team.

WHY is it that a derby match between two local teams is called a derby?

THE JUDGE: The original Epsom Derby, named after the 12th Earl of Derby and first run in 1780, was so popular that the name 'derby' was introduced to capture any sporting contest of equal importance. It was gradually accepted as representative of a match with red-hot local rivalry.

DID Barclays Bank once have an England international playing football for them?

THE JUDGE: This was David Jack, who after retiring from professional football joined a branch of Barclays and used to turn out for their mid-week team. He also tried his hand at management with Southend and Middlesbrough – football management that is, not banking.

WHAT does the 'S' stand for in F. S. Trueman?

THE JUDGE: It is Fred Sewards Trueman. Sewards was the maiden name of his grandmother, who was the mid-wife at his birth.

THE '250' QUIZ CHALLENGE

223. Who beat Christine Truman in the 1961 Wimbledon final?
224. Who succeeded Nasser Hussain as Essex captain?

SPORTS TRIVIA

WHO was the first man to run a mile in four minutes?

THE JUDGE: Yorkshireman Derek Ibbotson, when winning a mile in exactly four minutes in 1958 - the season after he had lowered the world record to 3min 57.2sec and four years after Roger Bannister's first sub-four minute mile.

WHY was the Saturday that Teal won the Grand National known as the Great Day of Sporting Conflict?

THE JUDGE: There were three other major events on the same Saturday of April 5 1952: England beat Scotland 2-1 at Hampden Park, England beat France 6-3 in the Five Nations rugby in Paris, and Oxford won the Boat Race.

WHEN did Chelsea Football Club record the song, Blue is the Colour?

THE JUDGE: Blue Is the Colour reached number five in the hit parade in 1972 and was recorded by the Chelsea squad that captured the FA Cup and European Cup Winners' Cup in 1970 and 1971.

FROM where does the term 'southpaw' derive?

THE JUDGE: The term originates from baseball. On most baseball grounds, the pitcher (ball thrower) pitches from east to west; therefore, his throwing arm is on the north side of the baseball ground. If he is a left-handed pitcher, his throwing arm is to the south – hence the name.

WHICH footballers appeared in the Sylvester Stallone film Escape to Victory, and was it a true story?

THE JUDGE: Pele, Bobby Moore, John Wark and Ossie Ardiles joined the Ipswich squad for the 1981 film shot by director John Huston. It was a re-make of a Hungarian film called The Last Goal, and it was alleged to be loosely based on fact.

IS it true that both Roger Bannister and Herb Elliott have lit the Olympic flame?

THE JUDGE: John Mark, an Achilles Club sprinter, lit the flame at Wembley Stadium in the 1948 Games during which student Roger Bannister worked as a voluntary steward. Herb Elliott was the torch bearer at the 1956 Melbourne Games.

THE '250' QUIZ CHALLENGE

225. Which British southpaw was called the Dartford Destroyer?
226. Who captained Chelsea's 1970 FA Cup winning team?

DID Stirling Moss start his career as a show jumper?

THE JUDGE; Yes, Stirling started with a different sort of horse power. He and his sister, Pat, were outstanding show jumpers. Pat stuck with it and became one of the world's leading horsewomen, while Stirling – who learned to drive at the age of nine – switched to motor racing. He became the greatest driver never to win the world championship, having to drive in the shadow of the magnificent Juan Manuel Fangio.

EXACTLY how far was Devon Loch from the finishing post when it collapsed in the 1956 Grand National?

THE JUDGE: Dick Francis, the thriller writer and Devon Loch's jockey, was my Fleet Street colleague for many years and tod me: 'I had just 55 yards to go to collect the biggest prize in the sport for both myself and Devon Loch's owner, the Queen Mother. It was the biggest shock of my life when he suddenly collapsed on his stomach with legs splayed front and back. By the time we gathered ourselves, ESB had galloped by to win.' The reason for the collapse remains a bigger mystery than has ever appeared in any of Dick's best-sellers.

WHAT happened to the football club called Clapton Orient, and why the name Orient?

THE JUDGE: Clapton Orient existed in East London in various forms from 1898 to 1946 before finally changing its name to Leyton Orient. Clapton and Leyton are adjoining boroughs. The Orient link evolved when employees of the Orient Shipping Line started backing the club.

HOW many shots did Jean Van der Velde take at the final hole at the 1999 Open?

THE JUDGE: Jean Van der Velde held a three-shot lead as he stood on the final tee at Carnoustie, with the Open title within his grasp. He put his drive on to the 17th fairway ... his second shot, having struck a stand and a rock, ended in heavy rough ... his third plopped into the Barry Burn, and the 33-year-old Frenchman removed his shoes and socks as he considered playing out of the water ... his fourth was a drop ... his fifth disappeared into a bunker ... his sixth rolled on to the green and his seventh, a putt from seven feet, went down the hole. Van der Velde then finished last in a three-way play-off for the title, with Paul Lawrie emerging as the winner.

THE '250' QUIZ CHALLENGE

227. Which rider won the 1956 Grand National on ESB?
228. Who was the third man in the 1999 Open golf play-off?

WHO was the first footballer sent off in a match at Wembley Stadium?

THE JUDGE: We have to go back to the 1948 Olympics when the captain of Yugoslavia, Boris Stankovic, was sent off while playing against Sweden. The first professional footballer ordered off at Wembley was Argentinian captain Antonio Rattin, who got his marching orders for disputing the referee's decisions during the 1966 World Cup quarter-final against England. The first player sent off in an FA Cup final at Wembley was Manchester United's Kevin Moran for a reckless tackle on Everton's Peter Reid in the 1985 final. The ten men of Man United won 1-0 thanks to a goal by Norman Whiteside.

IS it true that a batsman was once given out because he got lost on the London Underground?

THE JUDGE: True. This was Leicestershire wicket-keeper Tom Sidwell, who was one not out overnight against Surrey at The Oval in 1921. Making his way to the ground the next morning, he managed to get himself lost on the London Underground. He arrived too late to bat, and it went down in the scorebook as 'absent, lost on tube'.

HOW did 'hat-trick' come into the sports vocabulary?

THE JUDGE: The hat-trick has its origins in cricket. A 19th century hatter offered any bowler taking wickets with three consecutive balls a bowler hat. The original meaning of a hat-trick in football was three successive goals, and if a team-mate scored before all three were in the net it did not count. But now, any three goals in a single match is accepted as a hat-trick.

HAVE any footballers played in the Liverpool, Manchester and North London derbies

THE JUDGE: I can think of three – Brian Kidd (Man United, Man City, Everton and Arsenal), Paul Stewart (Man City, Tottenham and Liverpool), and Paul Walsh (Liverpool, Tottenham and Man City).

IS it right that Bob Wilson's middle name is Primrose?

THE JUDGE: It is, and poor Bob has taken a lot of leg pulling over it. Primrose is his mother's maiden name, and it is a Scottish tradition to use a family name as a second name.

THE '250' QUIZ CHALLENGE

229. Which England midfielder was sent off in World Cup 86?
230. Who completed a hat-trick against Australia in Sydney in 1999?

WAS there a goalkeeper who once got booked in the opponent's half?

THE JUDGE: This was Peru's eccentric goalkeeper Ramon Quiroga, who was booked in Poland's half for a foul on Grzegorz Lato during the 1978 World Cup finals in Argentina. Quiroga bowed twice to the referee as he raised a yellow card, and then retreated backwards to his goal 50 yards away.

WHICH of the Scottish international teams was nicknamed the Wee Wembley Wizards, and why?

THE JUDGE: This was the 1928 team that trounced England 5-1 at Wembley. Their tallest forward stood 5ft 7in tall. The teams: England: Hufton; Goodall, H. Jones; Edwards, Wilson, Healless; Hulme, Kelly, Dean, Bradford, W. Smith. Scotland: Harkness; Nelson, Law; Gibson, Bradshaw, McMullan; Jackson, Dunn, Gallacher, James, Morton. All but Dunn and Morton played in the English league. Jackson (3), Gibson and Alex James scored the Scottish goals. It was the only time this magnificent team of Wee Blue Devils played together. Bob Kelly scored England's only goal in the last minute.

HAVE two London-born boxers ever fought each other for the world heavyweight title?

THE JUDGE: Yes, when Lennox Lewis defended his WBC heavyweight title against Frank Bruno in Cardiff in 1993. Bruno was born in Hammersmith Hospital, West London, on November 16 1961. Lewis was born in Queen Mary's Hospital in West Ham's Stratford district on September 2 1965. Lennox won on a seventh round stoppage.

WHO was the first post-war British-born heavyweight to win a world championship belt?

THE JUDGE: Lennox Lewis was named WBC champion on the basis of his second round stoppage of Razor Ruddock in October 1992. London-born Michael Bentt took the WBO title from Tommy Morrison in October 1993, and lost it to Nigerian-born Herbie Hide in March 1994.

DID Geoff Hurst ever play cricket for Essex?

THE JUDGE: All-rounder Geoff played just one County match for Essex against Lancashire at Liverpool in 1962.

THE '250' QUIZ CHALLENGE

231. Which club did Geoff Hurst join from West Ham United?
232. In which round did Lennox Lewis stop Frank Bruno?

WHEN did Cassius Clay become Muhammad Ali?

THE JUDGE: Ali's last fight as Clay was when he took the world title with a sixth round stoppage against Sonny Liston on February 25 1964. He insisted on being referred to as Muhammad Ali for the return fight in Lewiston, Maine, on May 25 1965.

WHAT was the original name of Newcastle United?

THE JUDGE: They were formed as Stanley in 1881, and became Newcastle East End a year later before switching to Newcastle United in 1892.

DID both the BBC and ITV cover the 1966 World Cup final live?

THE JUDGE: Everybody recalls that it was Kenneth Wolstenholme who commentated on the match for BBC, but few seem to recall that ITV also screened the match, with Welshman Hugh Johns at the microphone. Brian Moore, later ITV's Voice of football, was the BBC radio commentator for the historic final.

IN which domestic football match have most penalties been awarded?

THE JUDGE: Referee Kelvin Morton set the Football League record on March 27 1989 when he awarded five penalties (including three in five minutes) as Crystal Palace beat Brighton 2-1 in a Second Division match at Selhurst Park. Brighton converted their one penalty, while Palace missed three of the four awarded to them. Portsmouth spotkick specialist Kevin Dillon scored a penalty hat-trick in a Full Members Cup tie against Millwall in 1986.

WHO was known as the Prince of goalkeepers?

THE JUDGE: John Edward Doig, a Scot who was a magnificent last line of defence for the 'team of all talents' that represented Sunderland in the 1890s.

WHICH football team is nicknamed The Biscuitmen?

THE JUDGE: This was the original nickname of Reading because biscuit-makers Huntley & Palmers had their headquarters near the Elm Park ground. They are now known as The Royals (Royal Berkshire).

THE '250' QUIZ CHALLENGE

233. Who was manager of 1988 FA Cup winners Wimbledon?
234. Who did Muhammad Ali beat in his second world title defence?

IS it true that Ireland once trounced West Indies in a one-day international cricket match?

THE JUDGE: Ireland beat West Indies by nine wickets at Londonderry in 1969. Skipper Douglas Goodwin (five wickets for six runs) and Alex O'Riordan (4-18) skittled the West Indians for 25 runs. The tourists included Clyde Walcott, Clive Lloyd and Basil Butcher.

HAS there ever been a 0-0 draw in an international game of rugby union?

THE JUDGE: It is not a common scoreline, but there have been several instances – most famously when Scotland held the All Blacks to a pointless draw at Murrayfield in 1964.

WHERE and when was the first Formula 1 race staged in the UK?

THE JUDGE: The first Formula One world championship race, called the British Grand Prix, took place at Silverstone in May 1950. Italy's Giuseppe Farina won in an Alfa Romeo from team-mate Luigi Fagioli.

WHEN did England play their first international football match overseas?

THE JUDGE: England beat Austria 6-1 in Vienna on June 6 1908. Two days later they met again, this time England winning 11-1.

WHO was the first world boxing champion?

THE JUDGE: James Figg, of Thane, Oxfordshire, who beat Ned Sutton in the first bare-knuckle boxing contest with a title at stake on June 6 1727. They had previously fought with cudgels.

WHAT was the name of the boat skippered by Tracy Edwards in the Whitbread race?

THE JUDGE: It was called Maiden, and had an all-girl crew. They completed the 1990 Whitbread Round-the-World Yacht race in 1990 in 18th place overall.

HOW did Alan Pettigrew get his name into the record books in 1984?

THE JUDGE: Alan set a world record by throwing a haggis 180ft 10in (55.1 metres) at Inchmurrin, Strathclyde.

THE '250' QUIZ CHALLENGE

235. Who was the third of the '3 Great Ws' with Walcott and Worrell?
236. Who was the last of the bare-knuckle heavyweight champions?

WHAT has been the highest-priced horse to finish in the frame in the Epsom Derby?

THE JUDGE: This was 500-1 shot Terimon, ridden into second place by Michael Roberts behind favourite Nashwan in the 1989 Derby. The only other horse to finish in the first three at odds of more than 100-1 was the 200-1 shot Black Tommy in 1857.

IS it right that the Derby might have been called the Bunbury?

THE JUDGE: When the Derby was first run at Epsom in 1780 the name of the race was decided by the toss of a coin between the 12th Earl of Derby and Sir Charles Bunbury. It was Bunbury, however, whose horse Diomed won the first ever Derby.

HAS a club ever won the European Cup and then had it taken away from them?

THE JUDGE: This happened to Olympique Marseille in 1993 after they had beaten AC Milan 1-0 in the final in Munich. Marseille subsequently had the cup taken away from them after they were discovered to have bribed opponents in French league games.

WHEN was the first TT race staged on the Isle of Man?

THE JUDGE: 1907, when just one race was held over 10 laps of the St John's Circuit. The single cylinder event was won by Charlie Collier on a Matchless travelling at an average speed of 38.2mph.

WHAT was unusual about the first ever Test match played at Edgbaston?

THE JUDGE: The 1902 first Test was abandoned as a draw after Australia had been dismissed for 36, their lowest ever Test score. Heavy rain made the pitch just about unplayable after England had scored 376 for nine declared. The Aussies were 46 for two in their follow-on when the match was called off. Wilfred Rhodes skittled them in their first innings with seven for 17.

WHICH was the first Test match to be televised?

THE JUDGE: The 1938 Lord's Test, when Walter Hammond scored 240 in England's first innings against Australia.

THE '250' QUIZ CHALLENGE

237. For which county did Walter Hammond score 33,664 runs?
238. Who rode odds-on Golden Fleece to victory in the 1982 Derby?

HAS a team scoring more than six goals had them all scored by different players?

THE JUDGE: There have been several cases. One that stands out is when Liverpool had nine different scorers in their 11-0 victory home to Stromsgodset (Norway) in the European Cup-Winners' Cup first round, first-leg in 1974. When Liverpool beat Crystal Palace 9-0 in a First Division match at Anfield on September 12 1990, they had eight players claiming goals. Steve Nicol (2), Steve McMahon, Ian Rush, Kevin Gillespie, Peter Beardsley, John Aldridge (pen.), John Barnes and Glen Hysen all got on the scoresheet.

WAS Wilt 'The Stilt' Chamberlain the first seven-foot player in the NBA?

THE JUDGE: The NBA's first 7-foot-tall player was Elmore Morgenthaler, who played for Providence in 1946.

HOW much money did Manchester United lose on the deal for goalkeeper Massimo Taibi?

THE JUDGE: United agreed to sell goalkeeper Massimo Taibi to Reggina for £2.5m - just 10 months after splashing out £4.5m to bring him to Old Trafford. The Italian, cruelly nicknamed the Blind Venetian, suffered a series of gaffes as he conceded 11 goals in his four nightmare games.

WHO has been the heaviest ever world heavyweight champion?

THE JUDGE: Primo Carnera scaled 19st 4lbs when he made his second championship defence against Tommy Loughran in Miami on March 1 1934. Loughran, former world light-heavyweight champion, weighed just 13st 2lbs. Carnera won on points over 15 rounds.

WHERE and when was the first speedway race?

THE JUDGE: The first speedway meeting was staged at Portman Road, Ipswich, in 1904.

HAS any rugby player ever scored more than five tries in a single match for the British Lions?

THE JUDGE: England wing David Duckham became the first player to score six tries in a tour match for the British Lions against West Coast-Buller at Greymouth in New Zealand in 1971.

THE '250' QUIZ CHALLENGE

239. For which club side was David Duckham a regular try scorer?
240. What was Primo Carnera's mountainous nickname?

WHY does Tony Jacklin have special reason to remember Brazil's 1970 World Cup final victory?

THE JUDGE: Because on the exact same day (June 21) that Brazil were beating Italy 4-1 to win the Jules Rimet Trophy outright, Tony Jacklin was becoming the first Briton since Ted Ray in 1920 to win the US Open.

WHEN and where was the first organised motor race?

THE JUDGE: The Paris-Bordeaux-Paris event on June 12 1895. It was won by a Panhard-Levassor driven by Emile Levassor at an average speed of 15mph.

HOW many players have shot sub-60 rounds on the highly competitive US tour?

THE JUDGE: There have been three – Chip Beck (1991), David Duval (1999) and – the first – Al Geiberger, who in 1977 shot a 59 in the Danny Thomas Golf Classic at the Colonial Golf Course in Memphis.

WHY was Micky Stewart known as 'Safe Hands'?

THE JUDGE: Alec Stewart's father was one of the finest fielders in first-class cricket. His peak achievement was at Northampton in 1957 when he held seven catches for Surrey in a single innings, a record for an outfielder.

IS the London Marathon the oldest annual event of its kind in the world?

THE JUDGE: That honour goes to the Boston Marathon, which was first run in 1897. It was won by John McDermott of New York. The race is traditionally run every April on Patriot's Day. The first London Marathon was not staged until 1981. Britain's Joyce Smith won the women's race, while American Dick Beardsley and Norwegian Inge Simonsen finished the men's race hand-in-hand for a sporting dead-heat.

WHICH footballer was known as the Galloping Major?

THE JUDGE: This was the nickname given to Ferenc Puskas when he was playing for the Hungarian army side Honved. His rank was major, even though he was rarely anywhere near a parade ground or military zone. All his battles were fought on the football field, where he used his magical left foot like a field-marshal's baton.

THE '250' QUIZ CHALLENGE

241. Which Olympic gold medallist founded the London Marathon?
242. On which course did Tony Jacklin win the British Open in 1969?

WHICH was the first 'all-ticket' football match?

THE JUDGE: The 1924 FA Cup final between Newcastle United and Aston Villa at Wembley. This followed the chaos at the first Wembley final in 1923 when more than 200,00 people got in to see the Bolton-West Ham match, when the official attendance was given as 126,047.

WHAT happened to Ian Woosnam in his first tournament after winning the US Masters?

THE JUDGE: Woosie won the famous US Masters green jacket at Augusta in 1991. The following week he missed the cut at the Benson and Hedges International at St Mellion, Cornwall, following two rounds of 82.

WHAT has been the biggest winning margin in an FA Cup final?

THE JUDGE: Bury 6, Derby County 0 in the 1903 final at Crystal Palace. Four of their goals came in a 20-minute burst in the second-half. Bury also completed another record by not conceding a single goal in the competition.

WHO is the youngest snooker player to score a maximum 147 in a recognised tournament?

THE JUDGE: Ronnie O'Sullivan, playing in the 1991 English Amateur Snooker Championship, compiled a maximum 147 break at the age of 15 years and 98 days.

HAS anybody scored more than ten tries in a major rugby league compeition?

THE JUDGE: George West ran in 11 tries for Hull Kingston Rovers against Brookland Rovers in 1905 in the Northern Cup, which later became the Challenge Cup.

HOW long was it between Brian Close's first and last Test caps for England?

THE JUDGE: Brian became England's youngest-ever Test cricketer when he played against New Zealand at the age of 18 years, 149 days in 1949. Twenty-eight years later, at the age of 45, he won his 22nd and final cap against the West Indies.

THE '250' QUIZ CHALLENGE

243. Which county did Brian Close captain after leaving Yorkshire?
244. Who did Ronnie O'Sullivan beat in the 2001 world final?

WHICH two teams featured in the first ever floodlit Football League match?

THE JUDGE: Portsmouth were beaten 2-0 by Newcastle United at Fratton Park on the evening of February 22 1956. There was a 30-minute delay during the game because the fuses failed

HAS a player ever kicked more than 20 goals in a single rugby league match?

THE JUDGE: There have been several instances, with dead-eye Jim Sullivan leading the way. He put the ball between the posts 22 times for Wigan when they beat the Cumberland amateur side Flimby and Fothergill 116-0 in a 1925 Northern Cup match.

WHAT has been the smallest recorded attendance at a Football League match, not counting those played behind closed doors?

THE JUDGE: Just 450 fans turned up at Spotland to watch the Fourth Division match between Rochdale and Cambridge in 1974.

WHICH US President first threw the ball to start the baseball season?

THE JUDGE: William Howard Taft, the 27th President of the United States, threw the first ball before the opening match of the season featuring Washington Senators in 1910. It started an annual tradition.

WHO has been the oldest cricketer to represent England in a Test match?

THE JUDGE: Wilfred Rhodes, who was 52 years and 165 days when he played his final Test for England against West Indies in Kingston, Jamaica, in April 1930. His Test career had lasted a record 31 years 315 days from his first cap against Australia at Trent Bridge in 1899 – in which W.G. Grace made his last England appearance at what was then the record senior age of 50 years and 320 days.

WHICH batsman was first to score a Test triple century?

THE JUDGE: This was England opener Andrew Sandham, who scored 325 in a total of 849 against the West Indies in the same 1930 Test in which Wilfred Rhodes made his final bow.

THE '250' QUIZ CHALLENGE

245. For which county was Andrew Sandham a prolific scorer?
246. What are the three opening words to the Pompey Chimes?

WHAT was the result of England's first international match at Wembley?

THE JUDGE: England and Scotland drew 1-1 in April 1924. Aston Villa inside-left Billy Walker scored the first goal in a Wembley international.

WHO was the first player to captain England while in goal?

THE JUDGE: A trick question, this. Most people would answer Frank Swift, who was appointed England captain in 1948. But England skipper Billy Walker switched from inside-left to goalkeeper after Fred Fox had been stretchered off in the 1925 international match against France.

WHAT record did Australia set in the qualifying rounds for the 2002 World Cup?

THE JUDGE: Australian striker Archie Thompson scored 13 goals as the Socceroos hammered Samoa a record 31-0 in their World Cup qualifier in 2001.

WHERE and when was the first Open golf championship staged, and over how many days?

THE JUDGE: The first Open championship was played at Prestwick over thirty-six holes on Wednesday, October 17 1860. Eight professionals were invited to take part by the Prestwick Golf Club with a championship belt as a prize for the winner. All the competitors were Scottish, with George Brown (Royal Blackheath Club) the one exile. Willie Park Snr. was the winner, beating his constant rival 'Old' Tom Morris by two shots with a score of 174 for three rounds of the twelve-hole course. One of the also-rans recorded 21 at one hole, a score that has never been topped on any subsequent Open card. For the record, the other five competitors were Robert Anderson, Alexander Smith, Willie Steel, Charles Hunter and Andrew Strath.

HAS the British Open golf championship ever been staged outside England or Scotland?

THE JUDGE: Yes, once – in 1951. This was the year that Max Faulkner interrupted the Bobby Locke monopoly on the Portrush course in Ireland. The colourful Faulkner collected £325 as his share of the new record total prize money of £1,700. He was to prove Britain's last victor for eighteen years.

THE '250' QUIZ CHALLENGE

247. Name the first British-born Open champion after Max Faulkner.
248. Which team won the first game played at Wembley Stadium?

DID Henry Cooper hold down a job while boxing professionally?

THE JUDGE: Sir Henry worked for most of his career, first as a plasterer and then as a greengrocer.

WHICH footballer was once listed in a club programme as Mister X?

THE JUDGE: Morton signed a new goalkeeper, and as the programme for the 1964 pre-season practice match went to press nobody was sure of his name. He went down in the line-up as Mr X. He was later identified as Danish goalkeeper Eric Sorensen, the first Scandinavian to make an impact in Scottish football.

IS it true that impressionist Mike Yarwood was on Manchester United's books?

THE JUDGE: Mike had a trial as a winger with Oldham but failed to make a good impression. He concentrated on his show business career, and later became President of his hometown club Stockport County.

DID Stanley Matthews consider taking up boxing rather than football?

THE JUDGE: Stanley was the son of a good-class professional featherweight, whose ring nickname was The Fighting Barber of Hanley. His father taught him to box from his early days, but then accepted that he was much more accomplished with his feet rather than his fists and encouraged him to concentrate on football.

WHERE is the Port Vale district that the club is named after?

THE JUDGE: There is no such place as Port Vale. The Potteries club is named after the house in Burslem where the founders first met to discuss establishing the club in 1876.

WHAT did Les Ferdinand mean when he said he was well blooded before his debut for Turkish club Besiktas?

THE JUDGE: Before his first game against local rivals Fenerbahce, fans of Les's new club sacrificed a lamb on the pitch and daubed its blood on his forehead and boots. He scored in a 3-1 victory.

THE '250' QUIZ CHALLENGE

249. Which League club did Stanley Matthews briefly manage?
250. With which club did Les Ferdinand start his League career?

QUIZ ANSWERS
PLUS YOUR SPORTS IQ
RATINGS TABLE

FOOTBALL

1. Lawrie Sanchez
2. Chelsea
3. Arsenal
4. Seven
5. FC Brugge
6. Germany
7. Oakwell
8. George Graham
9. Peter Taylor
10. Stoke City
11. Fulham
12. Billy McNeill
13. Wolves
14. Nat Lofthouse
15. Jimmy Dickinson
16. Bournemouth
17. Real Madrid
18. Dave Bowen
19. St Johnstone
20. Oxford United
21. Bolton Wanderers
22. Bill Nicholson
23. Trevor Francis
24. Ferenc Puskas
25. Manchester City
26. Manchester United
27. Everton
28. Liverpool
29. West Germany
30. Nottingham Forest
31. Partick Thistle
32. Don Revie
33. Ujpest Dozsa
34. Norwich City
35. Aberdeen
36. Harry Catterick
37. Billy Wright
38. Dave Sexton
39. Atletico Madrid
40. Bournemouth
41. Sir Alf Ramsey
42. Argentina
43. Japan

44. Peter McParland
45. Sweden
46. Kenny Dalglish
47. Burnley
48. West Bromwich Albion
49. Sheffield Wednesday
50. France
51. Allan Clarke
52. Ricky George
53. Billy Bonds
54. Ten
55. Bolton Wanderers
56. Italy
57. Aston Villa
58. Tottenham
59. PSV Eindhoven
60. Swindon Town
61. Scunthorpe United
62. Burnden Park
63. Jeff Astle
64. Real Madrid
65. Psycho
66. Romania
67. Tommy Docherty
68. Watford
69. Turkey
70. Ipswich Town
71. Huddersfield Town
72. Italy
73. Tottenham
74. Norwich City
75. Don Revie
76. Chelsea
77. West Bromwich Albion
78. Juventus
79. Benfica
80. Ron Greenwood
81. Selhurst Park
82. Swansea
83. Hull City
84. Nottingham Forest
85. Tottenham
86. Belgium

87. Vienna
88. Liverpool
89. Norwich City
90. Emlyn Hughes
91. Nine matches
92. Mexico 1986
93. San Marino
94. Chester City
95. Roker Park
96. Northampton Town
97. Juventus
98. Ray Crawford
99. Everton
100. Munich 1860
101. Southampton

BOXING

102. Yolande Pompey
103. Cardiff
104. Fifth round
105. Light-welterweight
106. Earls Court
107. Twelfth round
108. Brian Harper
109. Fifth round
110. Maurice Hope
111. Boston Tar Baby
112. James J. Jeffries
113. Eighth round
114. Brian Curvis
115. Jersey Joe Walcott
116. Felix Trinidad
117. 49 fights
118. Jose Urtain

CRICKET

119. 333
120. The Oval
121. Middlesex
122. Tony Lock
123. 334 runs
124. New Zealand
125. Sunil Gavaskar
126. Leicestershire
127. West Indies
128. Marcus Trescothick

HORSE RACING
129. Dancing Brave
130. 1994
131. Teenoso
132. Shahrastani
133. Pat Taaffe
134. Newmarket
135. Freddie Fox
136. Alleged
137. Tulyar
138. Crisp
139. Jenny Pitman

RUGBY
140. Australia
141. Fylde
142. Llanelli
143. Four tries
144. John Eales
145. Leicester
146. St Helens
147. Sheffield Eagles
148. Leeds

GOLF
149. Troon
150. Ben Hogan
151. Jack Nicklaus
152. 1976
153. Three times
154. Royal Birkdale
155. Samuel
156. Peter Oosterhuis
157. Muirfield
158. Sergio Garcia

TENNIS
159. Stefan Edberg
160. Pam Shriver
161. Ashley Cooper
162. Alex Olmedo
163. Ilie Nastase
164. Pat Cash
165. Goran Ivanisevic
166. Gabriela Sabatini
167. Table Tennis

OLYMPICS
168. Long Jump
169. Joaquim Cruz
170. Frankie Fredericks
171. Finnish
172. Long Jump
173. Dorothy Hyman
174. Brendan Foster
175. Andre Phillips
176. Bob Beamon
177. Norwegian
178. Cameroon
179. The beam
180. Nelli Kim
181. Rome 1960
182. Water Polo
183. Dentistry
184. John McCormack
185. Croatia
186. George Foreman

OTHER SPORTS
187. Leighton Rees
188. Doug Mountjoy
189. John Landy
190. Stephen Roche
191. Jim Clark
192. Dublin
193. Jamaica
194. Wide receivers
195. Mark Williams
196. Ronnie O'Sullivan
197. Lucky Shoes
198. George Herman
199. Godfrey Brown
200. 200 metres
201. Niki Lauda
202. Ayrton Senna
203. Benetton-Ford
204. Stirling Moss
205. Jocky Wilson
206. Tony Allcock
207. Jochen Rindt
208. Monza

209. Japanese Grand Prix
210. Damon Hill
211. New York Yankees
212. Vince Lombardi
213. 100m breaststroke
214. Sunsalve
215. 1988 Seoul Games
216. Lynn Davies

SPORTS TRIVIA
217. Cus D'Amato
218. Williams-Renault
219. Walter Winterbottom
220. Chesterfield
221. Birmingham City
222. Lancashire
223. Angela Mortimer
224. Ronnie Irani
225. Dave Charnley
226. Ron Harris
227. Dave Dick
228, Justin Leonard
229. Ray Wilkins
230. Darren Gough
231. Stoke City
232. Seventh round
233. Bobby Gould
234. Floyd Patterson
235. Everton Weekes
236. John L. Sullivan
237. Gloucestershire
238. Pat Eddery
239. Coventry
240. Ambling Alp
241. Chris Brasher
242. Royal Lytham
243. Somerset
244. John Higgins
245. Surrey
246. Play up Pompey
247. Tony Jacklin
248. Bolton Wanderers
249. Port Vale
250. QPR

FOOTBALL	Your IQ Ratings Table	ALL SPORTS
85-plus	Master class	201-plus
60 to 84	Excellent knowledge	150 to 200
45 to 59	Better than average	101 to 149
30 to 44	Average	70 to 100
Under 30	Read The Judge more often	Under 70

BILLY WRIGHT

A HERO FOR ALL SEASONS

Norman Giller has written the official authorised biography of Billy Wright, one of football's greatest of all heroes. It is not only the intimate tale of Billy's life and footballing times, but also the story of a football age that has disappeared from sight. The book includes a full summary and team for every single one of Billy's then record 105 games for England PLUS a statistical breakdown giving the line-up of every championship and FA Cup winning side of the 1940s and 1950s, the Golden Age when Billy Wright was a hero for all seasons with Wolves and England. The book will be on sale from September at £16.95, but you can get a special deal by visiting the official website at www.billywright.co.uk where you can also leave a tribute in the Billy Wright memorial book. Alternatively, you can order the book direct and post-free from Norman Giller at PO Box 3386, Ferndown, Dorset BH22 8XT, enclosing your name and address plus a crossed cheque or postal order for £15 made out to Norman Giller Enterprises.

THE GREATEST FOOTBALL QUIZ BOOK EVER!

This book is being prepared for publication by the same team that has brought you The Judge Book of Sports Answers. There is a challenge on every single page, and your knowledge will be tested as never before. This is an absolute must book for anybody who loves the beautiful game, and a source of endless information for quiz teams and quiz masters. You can order the book by going to The Judge website at www.thesportsjudge.co.uk or send your order to The Greatest Football Quiz Book Ever at PO Box 3386, Ferndown, Dorset BH22 8XT. Please send no money. We will be in touch with you when the book is ready. It will contain hundreds of quizzes and teasers that will keep you guessing and engrossed for hours.

The Judge is in session at www.thesportsjudge.co.uk